Labour Migration
The Internal Geographical Mobility of Labour
in the Developed World

Labour Migration
The Internal Geographical Mobility of Labour in the Developed World

Edited by
James H. Johnson and John Salt

David Fulton Publishers

David Fulton Publishers Ltd
2 Barbon Close, Great Ormond Street, London WC1N 3JX

First published in Great Britain by
David Fulton Publishers 1990

British Library Cataloguing in Publication Data

Labour migration: the internal geographical mobility of labour in the developed world.
1. Developed countries. Personnel. Internal migration
I. Johnson, James H. (James Henry), *1930–* II. Salt, John *1942–*
331.12'7'091722

ISBN 1-85346-120-2

Typeset by Chapterhouse, Formby L37 3PX
Printed in Great Britain by BPCC Wheatons Ltd, Exeter

Contents

Contributors vii

Preface viii

1 Labour Migration: the General Context 1

PART 1 – *INSTITUTIONAL FRAMEWORKS FOR LABOUR
       MIGRATION*

2 Migration and Job Transfers in the United States 17

3 Employee Movement in Large Japanese Organisations 32

4 Organisational Labour Migration: Theory and Practice in the
  United Kingdom 53

5 Regional Migration and its Inter-relationship with the Journey
  to Work in The Netherlands 71

6 Individual and Organisational Dimensions in the Migration of
  School Teachers 85

7 Labour Migration and Counter-Urbanisation in France 99

PART 2 - *DECISION-MAKING AND INFORMATION*

8 The Economics of Information in the Context of Migration 115

9 Migration and Job Vacancy Information 137

10 Migration and Dual Career Households 155

11 Migration Behaviour among the Unemployed and Low-Skilled .. 172

12 Moving Strategies among Home Owners 191

Index 210

Contributors to the book

PETER DOORN is a member of staff in the Faculty of Letters of the University of Leiden in the Netherlands.

RAY FORREST is a research fellow in the School for Advanced Urban Studies at the University of Bristol.

JAMES H. JOHNSON is Professor of Geography and Dean of Graduate Studies at the University of Lancaster.

BOB KITCHING is a research assistant and formerly a research student in the Department of Geography at University College London, working on labour migration problems.

GUNTHER MAIER is on the staff of the Interdisciplinary Institute for Urban and Regional Planning at the University of Economics, Vienna, Austria.

ALAN MURIE is senior lecturer in the School for Advanced Urban Studies at the University of Bristol.

ANTON VAN RIETBERGEN is a member of staff in the Department of Geography at the University of Utrecht in the Netherlands.

JOHN SALT is senior lecturer in the Department of Geography at University College London.

MARK SAUNDERS is a senior research officer with Hereford and Worcester County Council, who undertook his doctoral research at the University of Lancaster.

BRIAN SCHOFIELD teaches geography at a Sixth Form College in Blackpool, England and was formerly a research student at the University of Lancaster.

RALPH SELL is a demographic consultant in Rochester, New York, USA, and, until recently, associate professor of sociology at the University of Rochester.

JANINA SNAITH is human resource management consultant with Peat, Marwick, McClintock; her work on dual career families was part of her doctoral research at the University of Lancaster.

PAUL WHITE is a senior lecturer in the Department of Geography at the University of Sheffield.

RICHARD WILTSHIRE is a lecturer in the Department of Geography at the School of Oriental and African Studies, University of London.

Preface

This book attempts to illustrate some of the more important aspects of internal labour migration in the developed world. Labour migration consists of those moves of population in which a change of permanent residence is accompanied by a change of job; and the moves considered in this volume are 'internal' in the sense that they take place within a nation state. Such moves form only a fraction of the total amount of residential migration which takes place, but they are nevertheless important, quantitatively, economically and socially. In the mid 1980s, for example, nearly half-a-million heads of households in England and Wales moved home for job-related reasons in a single year; and the other members of their immediate families were also involved. As a result labour migration is a process which results in relatively long-distance relocation of skills of a variety of kinds and makes a considerable impact on the social life of the families and communities involved, both in the departure and arrival areas.

The method used by most of the contributors to this book is to present findings from their own research in order to reveal some of the dimensions of labour migration, although these individual chapters are also designed to provide a broader perspective on labour migration than this might suggest. Obviously a volume of this kind cannot pretend to cover all possible themes and contexts, but it does attempt to offer a more realistic version of what is involved in labour migration than is often the case. The book falls into two sections: the first looks at those aspects of labour migration which are strongly influenced by institutional factors; the second turns to a behavioural dimension and examines labour migration in the context of individual households.

In the preparation of this book we have been greatly assisted by our contributors who have prepared their texts to a fairly restricted timetable and have been generous in accepting editorial suggestions. We also owe a particular debt to our friend and colleague Robin Flowerdew who has been a welcome collaborator in research and an effective sounding-board for our ideas on labour migration for many years now. For assistance with some of the diagrams we are grateful to Claire Jarvis of the cartographic unit in the geography department, Lancaster University. We also would like to thank Jennifer Hogarth, who prepared the index.

1 September 1989

James H. Johnson
Lancaster University

John Salt
University College London

CHAPTER 1

Labour Migration: The General Context

James H. Johnson and John Salt

Movements of population may be classified in many ways, since population migration is a complex phenomenon, with many dimensions and causes. Even if attention is focused on those movements which involve a relatively permanent change of home there are different types of migration involved, depending on the reasons for moving. This book is concerned with one broad type of movement – internal labour migration.

Population movements which take place within a nation state may be described as 'internal'. Although in the developed countries of the world it is becoming increasingly difficult to separate internal moves of population from international moves because of the emergence of supra-national economic groupings of states and because of the freer movement of highly specialised workers, it still remains true that the great majority of migrants move within their own countries. In addition, an individual nation continues to provide a distinctive economic and political context for migration.

Labour migration consists of those moves of population where a change of residence is accompanied by a change of job. It might be assumed that labour migrants could be defined as those movers who are primarily motivated by job considerations and for many this would be certainly true; but other reasons for moving are also influential for those who are changing both home and job. Labour migration brings a change in the social environment of the people involved and in their housing conditions; it also has implications for the social and economic opportunities available to other members of a migrant's household. These other factors may dominate the decision of some households to migrate (Johnson, Salt and Wood, 1974). Although there is abundant evidence that the further a migrant moves home the more

1

likely it is that a change of job will also take place, it is better not to prejudge the deeper reasons for moving but simply to employ a definition which merely uses the coincidence of a parallel move of job and home as its basis.

The importance of labour migration

The scale of migration in a modernised country is immense. In England and Wales, for example, during the year before the 1981 census and in the middle of a period of severe economic recession, 9.6 per cent of the population moved home; and 10 years earlier, when the economy was booming, 11.8 per cent moved home. Many of these moves were over a short distance and probably did not involve a change of job, but 31 per cent of migrants in the year 1980–81 moved more than 10 km, and an estimate based on the Labour Force Survey for 1984 suggests that 450,000 heads of households moved for job-related reasons in the year before that survey (Owen and Green, 1989).

Some labour migrants form single-person households but many do not. As a result, other members of their households are drawn into the migration, so that the total movement of population involved is much greater than the number of jobs immediately filled by labour migrants. The person in the household for whose benefit the move is made is not necessarily the only employed person in the family; other members of the labour force as well as children and full-time housewives are involved, although perhaps with varying degrees of enthusiasm. Consequently labour migration results in relatively long-distance relocation of skills of a variety of kinds, not just those of the principal wage-earners. Since it involves a move from one community to another, it also makes a considerable impact on the social life of the families and communities involved, both in the departure and arrival regions. As a result, the act of moving often involves a household rather than an individual decision.

At a more general scale, in the countries of the modernised world labour migration forms the most important single force in the longer-distance relocation of population; and it is taking on much greater significance for two reasons. First, migration is becoming a more powerful demographic factor in producing changing regional population totals, partly because of declining rates of fertility and also because of related reductions in regional contrasts in natural increase. Second, migration may be developing a more direct role as a positive instrument in planning policy, since the redistribution of population to take advantage of available economic opportunities is of growing importance (Johnson and Salt, 1981).

Clearly labour migration appears to have policy attractions in a country like Britain, where skill shortages are becoming apparent in some parts of the country while unemployment levels are still unacceptably high elsewhere, although in fact numbers and types of vacancies do not always match up very convincingly with the pool of the unemployed (Green et al., 1986). The national importance of labour migration, however, is not restricted to its effects on general economic growth. The process also has a role in the development of settlement systems: for example, the planned growth of the

British new towns around London depended on the out-migration of an effective workforce from the conurbation. It also contributes an important, if still only partly understood, role in counter-urbanisation, the process found in many developed countries since the early 1970s in which smaller towns and rural areas have experienced greater rates of population growth than the largest cities (see Chapter 7 for a specific example).

At a more detailed scale labour migration has even more direct relevance for individual employers, although the structure of the firm and the occupational type of the workers it employs are important considerations in shaping the role of the process in a particular case. Finally, but not least, labour migration is of the greatest significance to individual labour migrants, not merely because of its importance for their economic well-being, but also because of the other opportunities that it may open up for the households involved. Again, however, movement does not necessarily bring benefits to all the households involved; and, as will be shown later, in some cases there are logical reasons for rejecting the possibility of moving.

Moves of jobs and moves of home

The majority of moves of home take place without any job change, since the possibility of undertaking a flexible journey to work gives increased independence to the employee who is choosing an attractive residential location. There are times, however, when a change of job imposes such an awkward or expensive journey to work that a move of home appears inevitable. In considering internal labour migration it is convenient to think of the national labour market as being divided into various local labour markets, each based on concentrations of jobs and characterised by local clusters of information about employment opportunities and the availability of suitable workers. Each of these local labour markets can be thought of as roughly coinciding with a local housing market; and, in turn, labour migrants are likely to be those workers who move from one local labour market to another.

In practice there are detailed problems with this concept, largely to do with difficulties in the actual delimitation of local labour markets. In large conurbations, for example, there are a number of sub-markets, like the inner city and different parts of the outer suburbs, which have a complex relationship with the wider labour and housing markets that embrace the whole urban area. In addition, the precise outer limits of a local labour market area are likely to be unclear partly because of the greater flexibility in their journeys to work possessed by those workers who have access to their own transport, but also because different types of workers are likely to have varying levels of tolerance to the journey to work.

For example, those who are well paid and have predictable journeys to fixed locations may find it acceptable to engage in longer journeys to work, if the residential environment that they are able to obtain as a result gives them sufficient personal satisfaction. An extreme case, but one becoming increasingly common in modern Britain, is provided by workers who choose to commute to distant destinations on a weekly rather than on a daily basis, as an alternative to moving their permanent residences. Many, but not all, of these workers are in occupational groups which employers have not thought it worthwhile to attract by providing assistance with the costs of permanently moving a family into the highly competitive housing markets of flourishing employment centres. As a result they may have been driven by lack of work in their home regions to seek employment further afield, although they do not find it possible or worthwhile to move their permanent homes. A different situation exists where finance is not a severe problem, but where other members of a potential labour migrant's household are unwilling to suffer the disruption to their lives and careers involved in moving home.

In considering the reaction of workers to their journeys to work probably the most important dimension is provided by the occupations involved. Those people employed in occupations without a fixed day-to-day location, like some building workers or various types of more mobile salespeople, are likely to be more tolerant of a longer daily journey simply because it is part of their normal expectations. At an individual level, too, some workers find themselves temperamentally more resilient to the rigours of long-distance commuting; and those women employees who are tied by their responsibilities for the running of their homes are often unwilling to accept a long journey to work, whatever their income.

This diversity of experience means that the limits of the labour markets in which individual workers operate may not coincide with the local labour markets which can be delimited using aggregate census information about commuting. As a result the outer limits of local labour markets are blurred and, especially in highly urbanised regions, show considerable areas of spatial overlap. It also follows that the likelihood of a move of home after a job change will be influenced not only by the distance between the old and new places of employment, but also by the personal circumstances of the individual household and the occupation of its principal wage-earner.

Occupations and labour migration

The classical economic approach to inter-regional migration stresses its role in the adjustment of the supply and the demand for labour. If supply of labour within a region exceeds demand either wages there will fall or unemployment will rise; but if demand exceeds supply a rise in wages will be produced. One result may be to encourage employers to relocate their enterprise in regions where labour is plentifully available and cheap. Another possibility is that migration will be encouraged, with unemployed workers moving to regions of labour demand and workers already in employment moving from areas of lower wages to areas where higher pay is available. There are obvious problems with such simple statements, since migration is induced by a mismatch in the supply and demand for particular occupations, not by the situation for the labour force as a whole. There are also various institutional arrangements, like trade union agreements and controls by professional organisations, which interfere with a free market in labour. In addition there are obvious non-financial social and behavioural dimensions which enter into decisions to move.

The economic argument can be taken further, however, by focusing on the characteristics of various types of occupation, which tend to react in different way to changing demands for labour. This is partly to do with the elasticity of supply of particular skills, since the occupational structure of the labour force contains barriers for a worker who may wish to change his or her occupational category. These barriers are largely based on the training and formal admission requirements needed for certain occupations and they are relatively fixed, in so far as formal education and training strongly determine the subsequent role of an individual in the labour force. As a result, if there are insufficient workers with specialised skills in a local labour market, it may well be easier to recruit workers from different areas than for local people to be put through the necessarily slow process of training. For relatively unskilled jobs, on the other hand, it may be simpler to employ local workers (possibly already in other types of employment if there is not a pool of unemployed) and give them the limited amount of training needed.

Hence labour migration would be expected to be less important for unskilled than for skilled and professional workers. Such considerations would also allow for one stream of migrants with a particular set of occupations to move into a region while another different occupational stream was moving in the opposite direction, thus providing an explanation for the apparently curious fact that labour migration both into and out of the same region often takes place simultaneously (Flowerdew and Salt, 1979).

There are also arguments to do with the functioning of society which would lead one to expect occupational differences in rates of labour migration. Migration produces a break in family and community ties, but the importance of these ties will vary among different social groups, thus influencing their attitudes to moving. Levels of resistance to migration may reflect differing values attributed to job advancement and community life. They may be a product of previous migration experience, with those who have moved before having less deep roots in local communities. They may be a reflection of educational experience, with highly trained workers having already abandoned the ties of home and local community by moving to a different location for further education. They may indicate varying levels of expectation that existing social ties can be maintained in the future despite increased physical distance. What these possibilities all have in common is that they are connected with social class and occupational type.

There are also relevant theories concerning individual human behaviour which stress the importance of the processes of search and decision-making. In some sense these provide a useful corrective to the cruder economic models by underlining the fact that no-one has perfect information about possibilities elsewhere. But they represent only a partial view of reality, when one recalls the variety of household circumstances (with the different mixes of considerations that must be involved in reaching a family decision to move) and the contrasting amounts of information available to different occupational groups. What they clearly indicate, however, is that the horizons of the more highly educated workers are likely to be broader, because of their access to sources of information which provide a national rather than a local perspective. Such ideas again offer a partial explanation of the higher levels of longer-distance labour migration found among professional and the more skilled technical workers.

This book provides a series of examples of some of the more important aspects of labour migration, chosen to highlight those dimensions of the process which have often received less attention than they may deserve in more general theoretical treatments. In most of these contributions research findings are emphasised in order to give specific empirical contexts for the ideas being advanced. The book falls into two broad sections.

- In the first part (Chapters 2–7) attention is given to those aspects of labour migration which are strongly influenced by institutional factors, with material being drawn from France, Japan, the United States and the Netherlands as well as the United Kingdom.
- The second part (Chapters 8–12) turns to behavioural dimensions of the process. After a theoretical discussion of personal search behaviour from an economic perspective, attention is given to specific examples of how different aspects of labour migration operate in the context of individual households.

What follows here is a survey of these two themes, designed to provide a framework for the later empirical chapters.

Institutions in the migration process

One theme which increasingly emerges in studies of why people migrate is the role of a range of institutions which influence the process (Flowerdew, 1982; Salt, 1987). Institutions, however, are easier to recognise than to define. Some of them are deliberately created to achieve set ends; other evolve as customary practice becomes institutionalised, with the gradual emergence of rules of operation which determine actions. Each institution should have certain characteristics: internal organisation; rules and regulations of operation; a hierarchical structure of decision-making; set goals; power to control its operations; and the ability to exert strong influence outside its own boundaries.

The importance of institutions is that they provide a framework within which individuals and households make decisions about whether to move or stay. They work according to their own sets of priorities which can easily constrain the actions of potential migrants. The institutions which bear upon migration include those which operate in the labour market, like employing firms and job agencies, and those effective in the housing market, like local authorities and finance providers.

Employers

Among the most important are employers. Many are nationally and even internationally organised and have geographically very extensive internal labour markets within their own firms (Doeringer and Piore, 1971), but employers fall into a considerable range of types. Some are highly complex organisations, especially the transnational corporations which sustain the global economy, with internal labour markets that may be fragmented or highly cohesive, reflecting their organisational structures. Their operations make an important contribution to labour migration, either through the redistribution of their existing labour force within their individual businesses or through their policies about their level of dependence on the external labour market for the recruitment of particular skills. At the other extreme are small employers, with few facilities for training or career development. Generally they have to recruit entirely from other companies and are highly localised in their operation.

The operation of the internal labour markets of companies is closely related to patterns and processes of labour migration. Mobility of staff between the separate parts of a multi-site operation is now a major element in the production process across the complete spectrum of the economy. Some of the factors involved are discussed in Chapters 2 to 4 – which present evidence to show that employer-related transfers of workers are now a major element in the total labour migration in the United States, the United Kingdom and Japan – and Chapter 7 provides similar evidence for France. Policies of attracting new recruits from other companies are related to how companies choose to organise their internal labour market. However, the analysis of individual employers shows a range of attitudes and policies towards labour migration (see Chapter 4); and it cannot be safely assumed that all will behave in the same way.

Corporate recruitment and staffing policies are not only made within the context of the individual organisation, since the organisation itself exists in an environment which is affected by the behaviour of other institutions. For example, Chapter 3 demonstrates how a Japanese employer – in this case a government department – operates in a highly structured employment system where continuity of employment is of paramount importance. Employees, too, can find that their recruitment and mobility aspirations are affected by the normal institutional arrangements associated with their particular occupational groups. These can include the need to acquire certain specific professional qualifications which reduce elasticity of supply, in medicine or engineering for example, or the manner in which the teaching profession has evolved in relation to staffing structures, as discussed in Chapter 6.

Finally, employers can change the location of the places of employment which they operate, frequently for reasons unconnected with members of the workforce but with major consequences for them. These consequences vary, depending upon the distance involved and whether existing staff were also invited to move. Of particular interest is the timing of subsequent moves;

and this feature is taken up in Chapter 5 where a case study shows that in a large urban labour market residential adjustment to a change in the location of a place of employment was gradual rather than instantaneous. Occupational selectivity took place, even where everyone had the opportunity to migrate, since part-time workers (especially if they were women) tended not to move.

Recruitment and relocation agencies

There are some institutions whose *raison d'être* is the organisation of migration. Significant among these are the recruitment and relocation agencies which provide information both to employers and to employees and can have the effect of channelling movement and giving shape to migration fields. Relocation agencies are often linked to chains of estate agents and have grown in importance in recent years. They offer a comprehensive service which will include selling a home, finding a new residence, and providing a financial package. They can influence the detailed geography of migration by directing movers to particular locations, helping to create enclaves of labour migrants. Packard (1972), in his *Nation of Strangers*, describes how certain suburbs in the United States have become largely populated by middle-class executives, most of whom stay just a few years before moving on (and up the career hierarchy) to be replaced by similar people, directed there by the relocation agencies.

Several chapters in this book call attention to the development of these types of institution. Their principal role is to make migration easier through the reduction of uncertainty for households. They provide information on a wide range of topics, including jobs, housing and schools in destination areas. They provide practical help too, figuring increasingly in the packages of relocation assistance developed by companies both for transfers within the firm and for their new recruits (Chapters 4 and 12). Relocation assistance is also becoming important for the dual-career household, as a response to the problems of the working wife discussed in Chapter 10. It is likely, however, that the existence of relocation assistance is helping to polarise the migration experience of different social groups. As pointed out in Chapter 11, a substantial number of potential movers among the low-skilled and unemployed generally receive little such help in planning and executing a move.

There are other institutions which play a role in the provision of information, and by so doing help to organise migration. They include the obvious and more mundane, like postal and telecommunication services, which are important in keeping friends and family in touch after separation by migration. Others are more directly concerned with specific aspects of information provision, like specialised journals or professional organisations. Employers are occupationally selective in how and where they advertise jobs. Workers also find job search a potentially costly exercise and hence seek to minimise the effort involved (Chapter 8). The consequence is that for those occupations for which vacancies are advertised widely because of low local elasticities of supply – generally the more skilled – migration over longer distances is likely to occur. For those for which the information field is local, migration is unlikely to occur. Consequently the selective nature of information provision and reception is an important factor in explaining the occupational selectivity of migration (Chapters 9 and 11).

Housing and migration

In all countries the provision of housing is institutionalised, and since, by definition, all labour migrants require to change their housing, the ability to cope with housing institutions is a major concern. It has long been acknowledged that housing can constitute a major barrier to migration for many people, although its exact influence remains elusive since the influence of housing in deterring a move varies with individual circumstances and in any case it is difficult to disentangle housing from the various other circumstances which surround migration (Johnson, Salt and Wood, 1974).

The importance of housing – selling, buying, finding, renting – is mentioned by all the contributors to this book. One of the key concepts to emerge is that of relative strengths in the housing market. Different groups have different levels of strength in different types of tenure. Generally the better-off are in a stronger position, especially in the owner-occupied market. Many of them are considerably helped by assistance from employers. However, as shown in Chapter 12, capital considerations are not necessarily important to owner-occupiers seeking to balance their strength in the housing market with strength in the labour market.

This theme is also taken up in Chapter 11. Here it is argued that for those renting housing from a local authority the factors which lead to weakness in the owner-occupied sector (such as poverty, the possession of a large family or alternatively being a single-parent family) are precisely those which give strength to applicants for public housing, because of the welfare points system of assessing allocation priorities. The possession of strength in the local authority housing market may be seen by the individuals involved as more than compensating for weakness in the labour market, including unemployment. Despite the seemingly economic rationality of undertaking migration to obtain work, immobility which preserves strength in the local public-rented sector of the housing market appears a sensible strategy to the people involved, for whom the maintenance of local social bonds and the provision of acceptable accommodation for their families may well be more important than access to relatively low-paid, unskilled jobs elsewhere.

Behavioural dimensions of migration

In all studies of the decision to migrate two questions stand out: who actually makes the decision and what information is used as a basis?

Decision-making

In a multi-person household the amount of weight given to each individual in decision-making is uncertain, but clearly some sort of acceptable joint decision has to be reached. As a result, criticism can be levelled at studies of the causes of labour migration which concentrate only on the circumstances and attitudes of the head of the household. Several members of a household may have an important input and all will have an interest. Even in a one-person household it is not easy to assess the order of priority actually allocated to different reasons for moving. Potential migrants of all kinds have problems enough in sorting out their own priorities and even more difficulty in expressing these frankly to a researcher; and those who have moved, frequently go through a period of *post facto* rationalisation. Discussions with households reported in Chapters 11 and 12 demonstrate that different individuals within a household have their own sets of priorities and that households develop strategies aimed at accommodating this range of interests. In some cases the end result is a move of job and home; in others it is a decision to stay in the same location.

It is also important not to assess the decision to move simply in terms of the household's position at any one moment of time. Chapter 12 emphasises the importance of this historical context for individual families. A household's present situation is strongly influenced by its past composition, its previous experience of moving home and, by implication, its planned expectations for the future. This same theme emerges in Chapter 11, which suggests that where periods of unemployment are commonplace for some types of workers it is wrong to regard those who happen to be unemployed at any one moment as somehow quite different from their peers who are currently working. What is important is the longer-term context within which a current state exists; and in making a decision about migration a household naturally draws on its experience of a range of situations.

The most severe problems in deciding whether to move or stay arise where different members of a household derive obvious benefits from opposite outcomes. This is well expressed in the case of dual-career couples whose circumstances are discussed in Chapter 10. Traditionally a wife's career has taken second place to that of her husband, a situation often leading to resentment where both are ambitious for advancement. Increasingly such households are developing geographical strategies to assist the career development of both partners: the larger urban labour markets are more likely to provide a full range of career opportunities for both, so dual-career households tend to move to such locations and then stay. Tensions may still arise when a logical promotion of one implies a relocation of home into another labour market. Some employers are now building into their relocation policies specific assistance for working spouses, knowing that without such facilities the strategically important workers they wish to relocate may not be prepared to move; but there are obvious limitations to what it is possible for an individual employer to do even if willing.

In contrast, in households where the notion of career development is not important, employment issues come much lower down the list of priorities. For many low-skilled workers satisfaction comes not from the job, but from the social relations found at the workplace and in the local community. In these cases employment prospects elsewhere are less likely to have a high priority. This point is developed in Chapter 11 where discussions with unemployed workers indicate the strength of ties to friends and locality.

Search and information

Decision-making is also influenced by the availability of appropriate information about opportunities elsewhere. Once the possibility of moving is considered the search process plays an important role in extending the information base of potential migrants, but access by householders to information varies, largely because of the cost of obtaining it (Chapter 8). All households will have incomplete information on some aspects of the migration process, but better-off households and those which employers wish to attract generally will have more information available to them. This is bound to affect the likelihood of a move and will certainly affect the process of search.

Employers wishing to recruit workers use a variety of advertising strategies. Some workers may get more privileged access to information about vacancies elsewhere than others. For example, some employers advertise all vacancies internally to their existing staffs, but others only advertise in this way below certain levels. A detailed example of the importance of the methods and scope of job advertising in encouraging the development of contrasting patterns of migration is discussed in Chapter 9. This demonstrates clearly that unskilled jobs were only advertised locally and that low-skilled workers used predominantly informal, spatially restricted sources of information. The opposite situation applies to the more skilled employees, especially professional and managerial workers. In consequence it is not surprising that the latter are much more likely to respond to job advertisements offering employment in more distant places, and that those with lesser skills will respond mainly to local advertisements.

Within the restrictions imposed by information availability and the framework set by institutional arrangements, individuals or households are often free to choose one of several locational strategies, each of which will convey some advantage. That choice is greatest for those types of employment which are evenly spread in relation to the general distribution of population. For example, Chapter 6 shows how school-teachers are able to trade the quality of residential location and educational environment against speed of career advancement in deciding whether to move and, if so, to what destination. It may be wrong, however, to regard migration decisions as resulting from long, careful deliberation. Most households decide on strategies which are predominantly short-term and responsive to immediate events, although decisions must still be arrived at, perhaps subconciously, in the light of whatever information is available and of past experience. Whatever the composition of the household, the amount and quality of information at its disposal, the nature of the employment of the principal wage-earner, and the time available for reflection and action, all migration decisions are based on a balance of factors, sometimes tipped towards immobility and sometimes pointing towards a move of home and job.

Themes for further enquiry

The issues which have been raised in this discussion form the substance of this book; but a volume of this kind, which brings attention to recent research findings and provides a context for them, can never be comprehensive. What it does serve to demonstrate are the many dimensions surrounding internal labour migration in developed countries and it calls attention to some of the important issues involved in explaining why people move (or stay) and with what consequences for the individual, the region and the nation. It is traditional for studies reporting current work to call for more research and here there is no exception. Individual authors indicate detailed problems for research in their chapters, but there are four general themes for further enquiry which it is appropriate to mention here.

● First there is an obvious need to test the wider generality of some of the specific examples discussed in this book, since these require replication in other areas and contexts.
● Second, it is necessary to examine the degree to which labour migration is a dynamic process – that is, how it changes through time and responds to the evolving economic, social and political environments in which it occurs. We cannot assume, for example, that the patterns of labour migration associated with one period of economic boom (or recession) will necessarily be repeated in the next.
● Third, and following from this, the nature and significance of the links between internal and international labour migration need elaboration, both at theoretical and practical levels, in the light of the growing economic integration among states at the global level.
● Finally, the role of labour migration in settlement planning policies and in the economic development of local labour markets needs detailed evaluation, since the fit between housing policies, labour migration and the location of economic growth is far from clear, not only in Britain but in many other Western countries.

References

Doeringer, P. B. and Piore, M. J. (1971) *Internal Labour Markets and Manpower Analysis*. Lexington: D.C. Heath.

Flowerdew, R. (1982) 'Institutional effects on internal migration' in Flowerdew, R. (ed.) *Institutions and Geographical Patterns*. London: Croom Helm. pp. 209–27.

Flowerdew, R. and Salt, J. (1979) 'Migration between labour market areas in Great Britain'. *Regional Studies*. **13**: 211–31.

Green, A. E., Owen, D. W., Champion, A. G., Goddard, J. and Coombes, M. G. (1986) 'What contribution can labour migration make to reducing unemployment?' in Hart, P. E. (ed.) *Unemployment and Labour Market Policies*. Aldershot: Gower.

Johnson, J. H., Salt, J. and Wood, P. (1974) *Housing and the Migration of Labour in England and Wales*. Farnborough: Saxon House.

Johnson, J. H. and Salt, J. (1981) 'Population redistribution policies in Great Britain' in Webb, J., Naukkarinen, A. and Kosinski, L. A. (eds.) *Policies of Population Redistribution*. Oulu: IGU Commission on Population Geography. pp. 77–92.

Owen, D. W. and Green, A. E. (1989) 'Spatial aspects of labour mobility in the 1980s'. *Geoforum* **20**: 107–26.

Packard, V. (1972) *A Nation of Strangers*. New York: McKay.

Salt, J. (1987) 'Contemporary trends in international migration study'. *International Migration* **25**: 241–51.

PART I
Institutional Frameworks for Labour Migration

CHAPTER 2

Migration and Job Transfers in the United States

Ralph R. Sell

Migration within the United States

Each year about one American in five changes residence – almost twice the rate of Britain and France (Long, 1988: pp. 260, 280). Most moves take place within the same community without disrupting social networks. At 1983 rates newborn Americans could expect on the average 10.5 moves in a lifetime: 6.4 within-county moves, 3.8 intercounty migrations and 0.3 residence changes across an international boundary (Long, 1988: 304).

One approach to the acknowledged variation in causes and consequences emphasises stated reasons for moving. Their use as psychological motivations originated in studies of the 'pushes and pulls' in migration decisions, those factors inducing dissatisfaction with the current residence and encouraging selection of a particular destination. Less frequently, reasons for moving are treated as contextual markers delineating the degrees of freedom in actual or potential migration decisions (Sell, 1983a). This latter application showed the important and widespread use of employer initiated and directed job transfers in migration processes. Consequently a major explanation for the high levels of migration in the US implied just the opposite of the inference of a generalised rootlessness, since transferred employees by their nature have strong attachments, rooted in employment and industry rather than local community.

This chapter will document the important role of job transfers in the United States migration process and emphasise the use of transfers by private sector corporations. The role of transfers in organisational, occupational and population structures and processes will be discussed, and

17

associated corporate policies will be outlined using results from a study of transfers by three corporations and a review of relocation industry materials. The United States Census Bureau on several occasions collected representative statistics on reasons for moving. A 1963 survey found that out of a male labour force of 43 million, 296,000 were transferred during the preceding year. Reasons surveys became regular with the 1973 Annual/American Housing Survey (AHS).* By the mid-1970s, the male labour-force-aged population increased to 52 million, but transfers increased more rapidly. Frequencies for this period were: 1973: 761,000; 1974: 832,000; 1975: 726,000; 1976: 797,000; 1977: 915,000 (Sell, 1982: p. 861). These data confirm the rapid increase in job transfers from the 1960s to the 1970s and show the magnitude of year to year variation in transfer activity.

Of course, other household members also were transferred and in this sense 2.2 and 2.7 million persons were transferred annually during the mid 1970s – about one per cent of the US population (Sell, 1982: p. 861). This is a higher proportion than the equivalent for the UK (0.7 per cent) in the 1980s (Chapter 4).

Comparable detailed analyses of more recent AHSs have not been accomplished. Long (1988: p. 235) tabulated the 1979 to 1981 AHS, limited to long distance interstate migrants, and found that 'job transfer' was the most frequently stated reason (22.2%) with about 460,000 households transferred annually. The 1983 AHS is the last year in which transfers have the potential to be treated separately because in subsequent surveys the basic questionnaire combines transfers with other employment reasons. Based on unpublished tabulations of the 1983 AHS, 744,000 householders reported that a job transfer was the main reason for leaving their previous residence, a figure in the lower range of variation in the late 1970s (Hartnet, 1987). It should be noted that for 1983, rates for all changes of residence, residential mobility, and interstate migration were the lowest on record over the 1948 to 1984 period (Long, 1988: p. 51).

In sum, job transfers are the most important source of employment-related migration in the United States and the numerical importance of transfers in migration processes cannot be ignored. A more theoretical point is that the stereotypical microeconomic employment-related migration decision model only applies to a minority of US migrants, in spite of its dominance in migration analyses. In particular this model assumes substantial choice in destination selection, whereas for transferees such choices are severely circumscribed if not dictated outright.

Corporate transfers in migration processes

The AHS shows the importance of job transfers, but provides little information about the organisational and occupational context. To fill in the

*The annual housing survey's major deficiency for analyses of job transfers is that it contains no information on occupation or industry of employment.

picture, richer but less comprehensive sources of information about specifically corporate transfers are now considered. In changing to a corporate focus, it is important to keep in mind that the AHS covered the total non-institutionalised US population in its sampling frame, thereby including migrations induced by all geographically extensive organisations, such as the non-barracks-housed military, a variety of federal and state government units, many religious institutions and national and state non-profit organisations. Although transfer-inducing processes within these organisations may well be similar to profit-making corporations, parallels remain unexamined.

Frequency of corporate transfers

There are no comprehensive and reliable estimates for the United States of the number of *corporate* transfers or of their community impact. A less than perfect source is the Employee Relocation Council, a non-profit agency formed in 1971 and supported both by corporations and real estate firms.* The ERC publishes *Mobility*, billed as 'the communication vehicle for the relocation industry', and periodically surveys members about transfer activity and policies. Unfortunately the ERC considers the basic data as proprietary, provides limited methodological details and there is no straightforward way to generalise to the many non-member corporations. The ERC estimated about 300,000 corporate transfers per year during the 1970s. Since most transfers include family members, the demographic impact in any case is several times greater than suggested by these household estimates. Other sources at about the same time indicated decreasing corporate transfers because of high cost (*Personnel Administrator*, 1978; *Business Week*, 1981). A mid-1988 press release from the ERC stated that the 400 corporations responding to an ERC questionnaire 'transfer about 280,000 employees each year, a number that has steadily increased since the early 1980s'. Clearly those 400 do not cover all US corporations and they are more likely to consist of the larger corporations which transfer more frequently. Nonetheless, taking this pronouncement literally, it actually agrees with the 1983 AHS figures showing a dip in transfer activity during the early 1980s and a subsequent rebound.

One thing certain from a review of *Mobility* articles is the substantial variation across corporations in the numbers of annual transfers. A General Electric Corporation executive reported that GE alone transferred between 8,000 and 10,000 employees annually during the 1980s (Roberts, 1987). Firms in the household-moving industry also survey corporate clients and provide additional evidence of substantial variation in transfer activity. Based on a 1986 telephone survey of 604 large firms listed in *Fortune* magazine, eight per cent of the firms transferred over 500 employees each

*The ERC helped establish a comparable British agency in 1986 (*Mobility* November/December 1986: 32), see Chapter 4.

during 1985; at the same time 20 per cent transferred fewer than 20 (Merrill Lynch, 1986).

In sum, neither precise corporate transfer rates nor data on changes in activity are available. Using the AHS as an upper boundary and the limited ERC surveys as a lower one, I would estimate that between 300,000 and 500,000 transfers occur per year on average. Including family members, well over one million people are involved in normal years. No overwhelming increasing or decreasing trend is apparent since the large increase of the 1960–70s.

Organisational structure and job transfers

The first distinction about transfers from an organisational viewpoint concerns whether the transfer is of individuals or the complete firm. It is not known which is numerically more important, although the transfer and/or closure of whole facilities receives more public notice because of its presumed community impact (Zipp and Lane, 1984). From the relative coverage given to issues in *Mobility*, routine individual transfers appear to dominate.

Two related trends account for the expanded use of individual job transfers:

● the growth of existing centralised organisations into geographically extensive ones; and
● the formation of new entities which are from the start geographically extensive.

Such organisations rely on internal labour supplies to accommodate changing personnel needs. Historically these were predominantly government bureaucracies and/or military forces and in fact the Prussian version of such organisations provided, through Max Weber's intellectual stereotypes, our classic bureaucratic image, along with the idea that entry is at the bottom and advancement occurs by well-defined rules. As this organisational form expanded and was applied to non-governmental sectors, so did the internally managed and geographically extensive mobility.

Corporate job transfers and employment structure

Paralleling organisational development, labour force changes have occurred as well. Although any two-fold typology is likely to be simplistic, at least heuristically employment consists of two sectors:

(1)   a **primary sector** with relatively high pay, employment stability, opportunity structures related to individual effort and abilities, liberal benefits such as pension plans and employer-subsidised health insurance, and implicit norms against capricious employment termination;
(2)   a **secondary sector** of jobs lacking such amenities.

Occupants of primary sector jobs develop firm-specific dependencies because of accumulated seniority, vested pension rights, personally useful communication networks, relatively stable co-worker interaction patterns and employer-specific occupational knowledge (Berg, 1981; Hodson and Kaufman, 1982; Kalleberg and Sorenson, 1979; Mann, 1973). These dependencies inhibit inter-firm movement of personnel. However, within any firm labour and personnel requirements vary over time. Occupational transfers become an allocation technique because the same firm-specific dependencies which inhibit inter-firm market allocation induce employees to relocate (Sell, 1983b).

Research supports the above distinction in the use of transfers. Brett's (1986: p. 23) comparison of transferred and non-mobile employees found that employees who identified with their companies were more likely to accept a job transfer than those who did not. She suggested that in order better to control employees, more efforts should be directed at establishing and maintaining an 'organisational culture with which employees can identify'. Looking at the same concept from a different vantage point, within-company transfers were shown to be a way to lower unwanted turnover of employees by transferring those who were either frustrated or bored in their present positions and who would probably leave if not transferred (Dalton and Todor, 1987). Data from the AHS discussed above showed that incomes were higher for transferred men than for migrants who moved for other employment-related reasons. In addition, cross-sectional income 'returns' for age and education were significantly greater for transferred migrants (Sell, 1983c). These items suggest that transfers disproportionately occurred among primary labour force jobs with their characteristically steeper age-income gradients (Kalleberg and Sorensen, 1979). One analysis claimed that frequent transfers were economically rational organisational responses to avoid low productivity in jobs for which it is inherently difficult for management to evaluate productivity, presumably a key characteristic of primary sector jobs (Ickes and Samuelson, 1987). The above evidence is far from definitive and both the occupations and the particular labour force niche of transferred employees need elaboration.

Relocations and social mobility

Presumably corporate entities have more power in transfer processes than potential transferees, but nonetheless employees are not powerless and many attempt to use transfers to further their personal goals. Corporate employees, especially those with upward mobility aspirations, are keenly aware that mobility is structured and they pay considerable attention to the relationship between geographical and occupational change (Kanter, 1977; Margolis, 1979). Although clear both to employees and scholars that not all transfers are promotions (Veiga, 1981), the structure of this relationship between occupational and transfer-induced geographic mobility remains to be described. In this regard, a corporate informant suggested an important 'headquarters-boonies' dimension, 'boonies' here referring primarily to the corporate structure and only secondarily to geographic location. He believed that the upwardly mobile would exhibit a back and forth pattern early in their careers. However, their location when moves stopped would indicate the final evaluation, with successful 'stars' in headquarters and the less successful in branch facilities. This parallels Rosenbaum's (1983) notion of 'tournament mobility', whereby one loss or pause in the normative mobility trajectory signifies the end of upward mobility.

One use of human capital theory in the migration literature suggested a contrasting pattern under at least some circumstances. It was predicted that, in repeat migration sequences, 'failures' would tend to return to their places of origin. Failure here means that the benefits of an initial move were not as great as expected. Similarly, 'successful' migrants would tend either to stay at their first destination or, if they migrated again, to move to yet another place because of the positive reinforcement obtained at the first-move location. Empirical results confirmed this logic only for less-educated and initially unemployed persons. The more-educated return migrants did not behave as 'failures' (DaVanzo and Morrison, 1983). These findings may have resulted from the inclusion of many transfers by the more-educated occupants of primary sector jobs, since return transfers to headquarters might be examples of successful migrants. To the extent that a 'headquarters-boonies' pattern occurs among transfers, it would lend support to this interpretation.

Corporate relocations and population dynamics

A well-known demographic fact is that for each instance of a redistributive net-migration, a far greater number of circulatory moves occurs (DaVanzo and Morrison, 1983). Corporate activity could partly explain this finding. Relocations may result from 'vacancy chain' mobility processes (White, 1970), and if links are coincident with geographically separate facilities, circulation results. In addition to mobility processes, Edstrom and Galbraith (1977) found that potential managers were often rotated without occupational advancement through many sub-units to gain extensive personal contacts and first-hand knowledge of the whole corporation. An origin-destination matrix in one 'market-dependent' Australian corporation showed that transfers were in fact largely circulatory (McKay and Whitelaw, 1977: p. 109).

Other arguments imply that a distinctive redistributive component could be present as well. If internal labour markets are corporate wide, expansion and/or transfer of facilities might produce non-circulatory transfers. Furthermore, Veiga (1981) found that individual transfer-created vacancies were sometimes not filled. At least a part of corporate activity results in a net redistribution of employees and their families with concurrent effects upon population distribution.

Corporate sources of job transfer information

Job transfers from personnel records

To examine these issues, information about 1,757 company-paid transfers was collected from the personnel records of three geographically extensive corporations in one North East US metropolitan area (1,134 for Corp 1, 467 for Corp 2 and 156 for Corp 3). Of the total, 9.4 per cent (N = 166) transferred at the start of employment, often from locations lacking a corporate facility and about one per cent (N = 18) had either their origin or destination outside the US. These 184, plus 37 cases without complete location data, were not analysed further (Sell, 1989). The data vary somewhat across corporations in time period and completeness, and in estimating transfer rates the different years were treated separately; otherwise data were combined. Occupations were coded into the 1980 Standard Occupation Codes (US Census 1983) and employed full-time socio-economic status scores, separately for men and women, were assigned to occupational codes (100 = high, 0 = low status; Ford and Gehert, 1984; Nam and Power, 1983).

Two separate techniques were used to examine occupational mobility. The first compared origin and destination socio-economic status scores. This admittedly crude measure matches neither the perceptions of the persons transferred nor their superiors in all cases, particularly since such perceptions are quite different (Veiga, 1981). The ambiguity centres around the perceived degree to which the new job has enhanced subsequent mobility or made it more difficult. For example, a new job with somewhat lower status may well be considered a promotion if the new job's structural location is more central in the corporate hierarchy or in a unit growing rather than declining in size and/or influence. Because of these deficiencies a second measure was also used. As will be shown, the occupations of transferees were concentrated in only four categories: managers, professionals, technical sales and 'other'. As a second promotion/demotion measure, these categories were considered as being ranked from high to low and occupational mobility measured as a move up or down this fourfold ranking.

Characteristics of corporate transferees

For the period around 1980, the three corporations annually transferred about 0.5 per cent of their employees (Sell, 1989). Based on the AHS, there was an overall transfer rate of about 10 per 1000. Given the differences in methodology and population covered, these rates may be regarded as comparable, and by implication suggestive that transfer activity by these three corporations was not exceptional.

The table in Figure 2.1 presents characteristics describing transferred corporate employees. Compared to migrants interviewed on the AHS, these corporate transferees were on average a few years older and had received a few years more education (Sell, 1983a). Fewer than 10 per cent were women and over 80 per cent were married and relocated with their spouses. These

Figure 2.1 Characteristics of transferees in three US corporations, circa 1980

N	1536
Average age	35.7
Average education	15.2
Percent home owners (origin)	76.9
Percent home owners (destination)	85.7
Percent relocating with spouse	83.1
Percent women	8.8
Average number of children	1.5
Average origin occupational status	80.6
Average destination occupational status	81.9
Percent relocated with job promotion*	17.3
Percent relocated without job change*	75.4
Percent relocated with job demotion*	7.3

*Based on changes in fourfold major occupational categories

figures are similar to those available for transferees of the General Electric corporation: 97 per cent male, 91 per cent married, with a mean age of 39 (Roberts, 1987), again allowing the inference that the three corporations were not atypical. These low transfer rates for women clearly identify some differential organisational processes relating to women and transfers, but they are uninformative by themselves as it remains unknown if fewer women are offered relocation (perhaps because of an under-representation in affected jobs) or whether women more often refuse offers. That 77 per cent of these migrants were homeowners before they moved is most unusual because renters are almost always over-represented in migrant populations in the US (Speare *et al.*, 1975). This illustrates the pronounced effects of corporate relocation policies which subsidise home purchase and continued ownership.

Regarding the issue of transfers and occupational mobility, Figure 2.1 shows that the average socio-economic status scores were above 80 for both origin and destination occupations. Origin occupations in terms of the four-fold major categories were: 33.1 per cent managers, 11.0 per cent professional, 51.5 per cent technical and sales, and *only 4.4 per cent for all other occupations.* Even within these categories, jobs were heavily concentrated: 50.4 per cent had sales occupations. These jobs usually required a degree of technical expertise and the best summary description would be technical sales representative. Traditional 'blue collar' occupations were quite rare.

Comparing the origin (80.6) and destination (81.9) status scores shows that little if any advancement occurred, suggesting that transfers were not a source of upward mobility. The last three lines in Figure 2.1 show the percentages of job transfers in which the destination fourfold job category was higher, the same as, or lower than the origin. Although 75 per cent retained the same major occupational category, when changes did occur, changes up the scale were more frequent (17.3%) than changes downward (7.3%). Reviewing the occupations themselves, upward mobility which occurred with occupational transfers was generally via entry into the lower level management positions which, in spite of occupational statuses similar to the origin technical sales positions, have presumably better future prospects.

Headquarters effect

For a variety of reasons, transfers involving a headquarters facility are likely to be different and Figure 2.2 presents characteristics of employees on this basis. One outstanding effect upon the headquarters community must occur through local housing markets since 93 per cent of those transferred into the headquarters region became homeowners; and these are not just any homeowners but homeowners who have their purchases almost completely subsidised by their employers.

Figure 2.2 Characteristics of relocated persons by relationship of corporate headquarters to the transfer

Characteristic	Headquarters location		
	Destination	Origin	Neither
N	572	404	560
Average age	35.9	36.3	35.1
Average education	15.6	15.3	14.8
Percent women	10.0	10.9	5.9
Percent homeowners (origin)	87.4	68.5	77.6
Percent homeowners (destination)	93.0	81.6	84.3
Occupational status (origin)	82.4	80.1	79.6
Occupational status (destination)	83.3	81.0	81.3
Percent relocated with promotion*	22.9	22.4	11.1
Percent relocated with same job*	61.4	70.3	86.8
Percent relocated with demotion*	15.7	7.3	2.2

* Based on changes in fourfold major occupational categories

Persons transferred either to or from the headquarters on average were one year older and had about half a year more schooling. Although these differences are not large, they are in line with an occupational status differential. As would be expected of a headquarters facility, all transfer activity with the headquarters involved persons with higher occupational statuses.

In terms of the promotion/demotion measure, both transfers into and away from the headquarters facility were twice as likely to be accompanied by a promotion than were transfers among non-headquarters units (about 22% versus 11%). Demotions were most likely (15.7%) to occur in transfers *into* the headquarters facilities, a pattern not expected on the basis of the comments concerning a 'headquarters-boonies' mobility pattern. A detailed examination of the before and after occupations of these 'transfers to headquarters with a demotion' moves (data not shown) presents some clarification. Stereotypically, these moves included a job change from a manager of some sort to a non-managerial technical marketing position. One possibility is that these units classified as headquarters include employment which, although geographically part of headquarters, was not functionally a part. A second possibility relates to the rather crude measurement of 'demotion'. It may be that even though the socio-economic status comparisons suggest demotions, the mere fact of headquarters location may not lead transferred employees to perceive a demotion. Qualitative knowledge of these three corporations provides examples of both circumstances, but does not lead to a suspicion of which was quantitatively more likely. It must be emphasised that in spite of these hints, the majority transferred without a change in major occupational category. Transfers were most likely to be lateral moves both in terms of occupational status and major occupational category.

Transfers among non-headquarters units involved slightly younger and less educated persons, even fewer women, and were concentrated among somewhat lower occupational statuses: 86.8 per cent moved without a major occupational category change.

Relocation policies

For the three corporations

Information about transfer policies was collected from these corporations. For all three, reimbursement of the direct financial costs of a transfer was a stated corporate goal but the interpretation of 'direct' and the degree of policy formalisation varied. One corporation had no written policies, a second had written but rather general policies, and a third used a quasi-legal analogue in that a file of specific costs to be covered or not covered had accumulated over the years. These precedents guided both transfer managers and employees in specific instances. For example, would the company pay to move:

(1) Firewood? (No)
(2) Swimming pools? (above ground, Yes; in-ground, No)
(3) Other household members? (spouses, Yes; elderly parents, Yes; 'partners', No).

By the time of survey the issue of 'partners' had become problematic and I was told informally that the 'No' was routinely ignored in those cases where partners played the social role of spouse (see below).

The greatest difficulty in applying the 'no financial loss' standard occurred over how to temper the impact of inter-regional variations in housing costs. During the period covered, the largest part of the transfer costs were associated with preventing financial burden resulting from home purchases at the new location. To accommodate this, the three corporations provided salary supplements for a period of years to lessen the impact of housing costs differentials. But in a perhaps never ending cycle of policy frustration, supplement expiration has been noted as a source of employee complaints (Hall, 1981).

From the employee relocation council

The ERC estimates suggest that on average each transfer costs corporations around $35,000; not surprisingly transfer departments are under pressure to prevent increases in this figure. This conflicts with the general goal of preventing the financial burden falling on employees and, needless to say, employers and employees frequently diverge about what is and is not a burden. As one way of diffusing this conflict, corporations hire outside firms to manage the transfer. Since many such firms are divisions of large real estate agencies, whose employees earn commissions based on a percentage of housing costs, another conflict of interest appears. Many corporations utilise more than one firm and simply alternate usage, playing one firm against the other, to keep costs in line (Collie, 1986).

In 1984, 73 per cent of companies provided home-finding services to transferred employees (Collie, 1986). Househunting trips are routinely paid for employees and their spouses, with a significant minority willing to include children. Most companies have purchase plans for homes at the origin location and this has induced them to pay attention to the values of homes. Since transferred employees are likely to be transferred again, corporations do not wish employees to 'overbuy', as corporations may ultimately suffer the losses. This has led to strong encouragement to use appraisal firms to determine market values.

A 1988 ERC announcement showed that the practice, if not the policy, of moving employees' partners had been formalised and partners were now routinely transferred to 'avoid disrupting the family lifestyle' of employees (ERC, 1988). Another family issue surrounds special problems presented by dual-earner households, and the ERC has been sensitive to this for some time. The 1984 survey stated that, 'the dual-income issue has not proved to be a major deterrent to employee transfer' (Collie, 1986: p. 54), even though Brett (1986: p. 20) reported that dual-earner families were significantly less likely to accept transfers. About a third of the ERC corporations report either formal or informal assistance in finding employment for spouses (Gregory and Crosby, 1988), but even this assistance was most often not particularly extensive. Among those assisting, while 58 per cent reported that they helped by referring spouses to an employment agency, only 12 per cent paid agency fees (Merrill Lynch, 1986). One suggestion as to why dual-earner households have not become a bigger problem is that the types of transferred jobs select males who select or are selected by females who are not career oriented. Certainly, the exceptional dual-career, as opposed to dual-earner, household creates problems and is likely to be particularly visible. But generally this occurs to a small minority of transferred employees. Consequently this issue has not significantly interfered with the use of transfers as an allocation technique. While this explanation for the lack of special problems associated with dual-earner households is speculative, one point is certain. There is little evidence that corporations have advanced inventive solutions to a significant change in the employment structure of households.

Some policy exceptions

The picture just provided is a rather rosy one of corporate America mustering resources to ensure that employees remain satisfied and productive throughout the transfer process. It should be clear from details of these policies that they are not applied to all workers who are transferred, but are limited to certain relatively pampered sectors of the corporate work force – the primary sector discussed above. There is a second type of transfer, the relocation of whole facilities, which presumably would include traditionally working-class employees. Information on such transfers is more scattered and space does not allow proper coverage here (Zipp and Lane, 1984). However, of 606 corporations surveyed, 18 per cent reported group moves in 1985 and 39 per cent reported that their group move policies were different from their regular transfer policy (Merrill Lynch, 1986). This is not to suggest that group move policies are stingier. I would imagine that in group moves, an employer goal would be to move favoured employees and leave others behind. That this is not always the case comes from one report of a group move of 150 employees, deemed successful because nearly all (88%) transferred from Long Island, New York to Boca Raton, Florida (Loth, 1988). Plant relocations ought to be treated differently from routine organisational processes as they surely include different occupational sectors, corporate policies and effects upon the lives of employees and their families.

Conclusions

Large scale geographically extensive government-type bureaucratic organisations have always relied on external markets for a restricted portion of their personnel needs. The spread of this organisational form and associated personnel allocation processes to other spheres is well-advanced in corporate America. Furthermore the image of the workforce as composed of a primary and secondary sector of good and not-so-good jobs maps well to corporations, and the hypothesis that transfers occur mainly among pampered primary jobs was largely confirmed. However, transfers were not limited to upwardly mobile corporate managers. Technical sales occupations figured prominently in the corporations studied, with transfers and promotions only indirectly connected. If transfer and mobility are connected, as much of the organisational literature suggests, the connection is far more subtle and complex than a one-to-one correspondence. One remaining issue related to occupational structure and processes is the degree to which the financial and organisational support provided for individual transferees is equitably offered to employees in group transfers, which of necessity include a significantly wider range of occupations.

Although much speculation and concern has been directed at the impact of the increasing number of dual-earner households, no strong evidence emerged that transfer processes have changed as a result. Women were significantly under-represented in transfers 20 years ago and remain under-represented. The occupants of the technical sales occupations transferred by the three corporations studied were predominantly college trained engineers, and because women continue to be generally under-represented in this occupational area, it could explain the lack of more widespread difficulties with the transferred employees themselves. With respect to the wives of the employees transferred, the results were clear only to the extent that the reporting of widespread difficulties had not occurred, even though the relocation industry has been sensitive to potential problems for at least a decade. Other social changes, most notably the treatment of employees' 'partners', have been accommodated.

Classic theories of labour migration generally emphasise geographic wage and price differentials as the underlying force in migration processes. For migration exchanges and population redistribution flowing from job transfers, such generalised income differentials play a rather small part. Potential transferees are not responding to geographic salary differentials, but to institutionalised organisational forces. Furthermore, the expenditure side of geographically based wage and price differentials, housing costs – the largest component in contemporary America – are systematically subsidised by corporate employers with policies specifically intended to remove this important factor from the migration decision. Much more needs to be learned about these corporate and organisational processes and how they impact upon migration and population dynamics.

References

Berg, Ivar (ed.) (1981) *Sociological Perspectives on the Labor Market*. New York: Academic Press.
Brett, Jeanne M. (1986) 'Why Employees Relocate'. *Mobility*, May/June: 17–23.
Collie, H. Chris (1986) 'ERC: Focusing on Relocation Trends'. *Mobility*, March/April: 53–55.
Dalton, Dan R. and Todor, William D. (1987) 'The Attenuating Effects of Internal Mobility on Employee Turnover: Multiple Field Assessments'. *Journal of Management* 13 (4): 705–711.
DaVanzo, Julie and Morrison, Peter (1983) 'Repeat Migration in the US: Who Moves Back and Who Moves On?' *The Review of Economics and Statistics* May: 119–138.
Edstrom, A. and Galbraith, J.R. (1977) 'Transfer of Managers as a Coordination and Control Strategy in Multinational Organizations'. *Administrative Science Quarterly* 22: 248–63.
Employee Relocation Council (1988) Press release dated 21 June, 1988. 1720 N Street NW, Washington, DC 20036.
Ford, Kathleen and Gehert, Judith (1984) 'Occupational Status Scores from the 1980 Census Public Use Samples'. Unpublished paper, Department of Population Dynamics, The John Hopkins University.
Gregory, Jewell and Crosby, Marlene (1988) 'Spouse Relocation Assistance Comes of Age'. *Mobility* 9 (1) January/February.

30

Hall, Walter R. (1981) 'The Relocation Differential Challenge'. *Mobility* 2 (5): 19–22.

Hartnet, Bill (1987) Personal communciaton from unpublished tables U-1-10 and U-1-12.

Hodson, Randy and Kaufman, Robert L. (1982) 'Economic Dualism: A Critical Review'. *American Sociological Review* 47 (6): 727–739.

Ickes, Barry W. and Samuelson, Larry (1987) 'Job Transfers and Incentives in Complex Organizations: Thwarting the Ratchet Effect'. *Rand Journal of Economics* 18 (2): 275–286.

Kalleberg, Arne L. and Sorensen, Aage B. (1979) 'The Sociology of Labor Markets', *Annual Review of Sociology* 5: 351–379.

Kanter, Rosabeth Moss. (1977) *Men and Women of the Corporation*. New York: Basic Books.

Long, Larry. (1988) *Migration and Residential Mobility in the United States*. New York, Russell Sage Foundation.

Long, Larry H. and Hansen, Kristen A. (1979) *Current, Population Reports* P-23, No. 81. Reasons for Interstate Migration. Washington, D.C.: US Government Printing Office.

Loth, Betty M. (1988) 'Group Move Well Done'. *Mobility* May/June.

Mann, Michael. (1973) *Workers on the Move: the Sociology of Relocation*. Cambridge: Cambridge University Press.

McKay, John and Whitelaw, James S. (1977) 'The Role of Large Private and Government Organizations in Generating Flows of Inter-regional Migrants; The Case of Australia'. *Economic Geography* 53 (3): 28–44.

Margolis, Diane R. (1979) *The Managers: Corporate Life in America*. New York: William Morrow and Company Inc.

Merrill Lynch (1986) *A Study of Employee Relocation Policies Among Major US Corporations*. White Plains, NY: Merrill Lynch Relocation Management Inc.

Nam, Charles B. and Power Mary G. (1983) *The Socioeconomic Approach to Status Measurement*. Houston: gap and Gown Press.

Packard, Vance (1972) *A Nation of Strangers*. New York: McKay.

Roberts, Bruce (1987) 'An Interview'. *Mobility*, 8 (8): Fall.

Rosenbaum, James E. (1983) *Careers in a Corporation: The Internal Stratification of an Organization*. New York: Academic press.

Sell, Ralph R. (1989) 'Individual and Corporate Migration Decisions: Residential Preferences and Occupational Relocations in the United States' in Patrick C. Jobes and John M. Wardwell (eds) *Noneconomic Migration*. (Forthcoming).

Sell, Ralph R. (1983a) 'Analyzing Migration Decisions: The First Step–Whose Decisions?' *Sociological Quarterly* 24 (Winter): 93–105.

Sell, Ralph R. (1983b) 'Market and Direct Allocation of Labor Through Migration'. *Sociological Quarterly* 24 (Winter): 93–105.

Sell, Ralph R. (1983c) 'Transferred Jobs: A Neglected Aspect of Migration and Occupational Change'. *Work and Occupations* 10 (2): 179–205.

Sell, Ralph R. (1982) 'A Research Note on the Demography of Occupational Relocations'. *Social Forces* 60 (3): 859–865.

31

Speare, Alden, Goldstein, S. and Frey, W. H. (1975) *Residential Mobility, Migration, and Metropolitan Change*. Cambridge, Ma.: Ballinger Publishing Co.

US Bureau of the Census (1983) *Census of Population and Housing, 1980*. Public-Use Microdate Samples Technical Documentation. Washington, DC: US Department of Commerce.

US Bureau of the Census (1981) *Statistical Abstract of the United States: 1981*. (102nd edition) Washington, DC: US Government Printing Office.

Veiga, John F. (1981) 'Do Managers on the Move Get Anywhere?' *Harvard Business Review* **59** (2): 20–38.

White, Harrison C. (1970) *Chains of Opportunity*. Cambridge, Ma.: Harvard University Press.

Zipp, John F. and Lane, Katherine E. (1984) 'Plant Closings and Control over the Workplace: A Case Study'. Unpublished paper, Department of Sociology, Washington University.

CHAPTER 3

Employee Movement in Large Japanese Organisations

Richard Wiltshire

Patterns of inter-regional labour migration in Japan are heavily influenced by the existence of numerous large multi-locational organisations, public and private, and by the adherence of these organisations to a particular set of personnel management practices which, in addition to stimulating the development of strong internal labour markets, also generate high levels of mobility within those markets. Some of these practices can be identified as explicit 'migration policies' (Johnson and Salt, 1980), while others have migrational consequences that are important but coincidental. Their combined effect, however, has been to make personnel transfers within internal markets the leading cause not just of labour migration, but of inter-regional migration in general. This is confirmed, for example, by the results of a 1980–81 survey by the National Land Agency, which showed that almost 30 per cent of residential migration between the three metropolitan regions (centred on Tōkyō, Ōsaka and Nagoya) and the rest of the country was primarily attributable to this one cause, as compared with less than 12 per cent generated by workers entering employment for the first time and under nine per cent resulting from workers switching employers (Kokudochō, 1982).

Transfers and the lifetime employment system

The importance of the lifetime employment system

The most important of these practices, in as much as it determines the fundamental conditions of employment and hence the terms under which other measures can be implemented, is the so-called 'lifetime employment system', the essence of which lies in the granting of tenure of employment within the organisation (though *not* in a specific occupation) through to the age of retirement. This elite status is held only by a minority of the labour force (Levine, 1983: p. 31); Abegglen and Stalk (1985: p. 201) quote a figure of 30 per cent, but also suggest that an accurate estimate of the true percentage is not possible. The system, moreover, is under increasing (though as yet far from terminal) stress in the face of technological change, industrial adjustment and the ageing of the workforce (Abegglen and Stalk, *op. cit.*: p. 209; Inagami, 1986). Nevertheless, the crucial point in the present context is that this tenured minority, which consists in particular of managerial and professional staffs in both the public and private sectors, as well as skilled blue-collar workers in large manufacturing and commercial enterprises (Koike, 1983), is highly mobile, both vertically and spatially. The composition of this elite is clearly replicated in the occupational and sectoral structure of the migration streams generated by personnel transfers. Thus the same National Land Agency survey revealed, for example, that 22 per cent of transferee migrants were managers or administrators, and another 19 per cent were professional and technical workers, despite the fact that these two groups constituted only 4 per cent and 8 per cent of the labour force respectively. Similarly, almost 30 per cent of transferees were in government service, and nearly 12 per cent were employed in the finance, insurance and real estate sector, although neither sector employed more than 4 per cent of the labour force. It can be readily appreciated then that an analysis of the mechanisms underlying the mobility of this predominantly white-collar elite is an essential component of research into labour migration in contemporary Japan.

Advantages and disadvantages of the lifetime employment system

Within the private sector, the continuing adherence to the lifetime employment system and the tenure associated with it stems from the perceived advantages of the system to the employer; these include

- the ability to reap the benefits of investments in human capital (in the form of on-the job training);
- the consequences for staff morale and loyalty (including the identification of the individual's interests with those of the organisation);
- economics in labour costs (when remuneration is linked closely to age and seniority as in the commonly-practiced *nenkō joretsu* system, and
- acceptance of technological change (Hanami, 1982).

These advantages must be weighed against certain obvious disadvantages, particularly the difficulties of trimming the labour force during recession and the risk of granting tenure to staff who prove to be incompetent. The first can be partially overcome by segmenting the labour force between an elite of 'permanent' employees who are included within the lifetime employment system, and who thus cannot be fired, and a large residual of untenured 'temporary' employees who can be. The costs of recession can also be passed on through the networks of subsidiaries, small suppliers and subcontractors that surround each large firm, whose workers also lie outside the lifetime employment system. As for the risk of hiring incompetents, this is reduced by combining rigorous initial entry criteria, based in particular upon formal academic qualifications, with comprehensive programmes of on-the-job training that may last throughout the employee's working life.

The precise interpretation of tenure in the private sector can be varied to some extent at the discretion of the organisation concerned. This can best be observed in industries suffering from the effects of structural recession, such as iron and steel. Both managerial and skilled production personnel within the big steelmakers have been transferred 'voluntarily' to newly-created subsidiaries which are involved in a bewildering array of activities, from mushroom farming to body-warmer assembly, and which enjoy very uncertain life expectancies (Sargent and Wiltshire, 1988). In the public sector, however, where the lifetime employment system persists in response to the same calculus of advantages and demerits, the status of permanent employees is reinforced by laws covering the rights and responsibilities of public servants which apply throughout the bureaucracy (Yamaguchi, 1983; Tsuji, 1984: Chapter 5). These laws can be changed by the Diet, but not by the bureaucracy itself.

Career mobility under the lifetime employment system

Organisational stability and spatial instability

As for the tenured employee, there is a price that he must pay in return for his protected status. He is forced to accept that the organisation that has employed him enjoys the freedom to move staff from one job to another, either entirely at its discretion or with the agreement of its normally compliant company union (Inagami, 1983). Indeed, the employer may be obliged to make the greatest possible use of this freedom, in order to maximise the flexibility of personnel management within the constraints imposed by the lifetime employment system (Ono, 1973). From the employee's standpoint this represents a sacrifice of occupational and, by implication, spatial stability in return for a secure position within the organisation concerned.

The former may be less of a burden in Japan than in other economically advanced nations, since there is in general a low level of job-identification within the labour force (Suzuki, 1981: Chapter 3). Cole (1979: p. 101) notes the low level of 'occupational and job consciousness' in Japan, and concludes that ' . . . the large Japanese firm is characterised by strong internal labour markets, but the criteria for distinguishing rights and obligations are not those of explicit job classifications with standard wage rates'. The sacrifice of spatial stability is a more serious matter, however, particularly for the senior employee with domestic responsibilities, who faces a difficult trade-off between moving his family from place to place, thereby disrupting his children's education (a serious concern in a society in which formal academic qualifications are the major determinant of employment prospects), and alternatives such as long distance commuting or even living apart from the family, for days, months, even years on end. This is an important topic, since the outcome of this trade-off will determine the extent to which personnel transfers are translated into actual migrations; I will return to it in due course.

The tenured employee is likely to be the subject of a transfer at any stage during his working life through the effects of a variety of detailed personnel management practices, some of them explicitly linked to mobility, others only implicitly, which impact upon him at various points in his career. These practices may be seen in turn as logical consequences of, or rational adjustments to, the organisation's overriding commitment to the lifetime employment system itself. University graduates are particularly prone to be transferred as part of their career development; Inagami (1983) reports that over 62 per cent of manufacturing companies with 5,000 or more employees have a declared policy of transferring employees to facilitate career development in some way.

Mobility in early career

During the early years of employment, the critical determinant of geographical mobility is the organisation's training policy. It is common practice for large employers to hire new staff, and especially trainee managers straight from school or university, on the basis of general academic performance rather than specific skills (Abegglen and Stalk, 1985: p. 199). New entrants then undergo years of on-the-job training (rather than formal management training, which remains unusual: see Suzuki, 1981), that exposes them to as many facets of the organisation's operations as possible. The explicit purpose of this practice is to develop a capable and flexible cadre of potential senior managers in-house; one obvious consequence, however, is a high level of intra-organisational mobility, both vertical and spatial, during the course of this training period. Extended training periods combined with frequent transfers on and between shopfloors are also the norm for blue-collar workers in large enterprises (Shimada, 1983).

No selection procedure is perfect, of course, and changing times bring new challenges to which some staff cannot respond. It is vital for the wellbeing of the organisation as a whole, therefore, that some mechanisms exist to steer 'tenured incompetents' away from the mainstream of management to make room for the able. Clearly this problem is by no means unique to Japanese employers; it is particularly important in the Japanese context, however, that surgery of this type be undertaken with the minimum possible loss of face. Again, personnel transfers play an important role as one such mechanism. For example, in a study of one of Japan's leading banks, Rohlen (1974: p. 149) notes:

> Smaller branches are generally situated in more rural areas, and reassignment to such isolated and unimportant places is a kind of exile

worse than a simple reduction of command. In a similar fashion, less competent men in the ranks below section chief also tend to be given positions in the less important offices, some of them spending almost their entire careers moving from small branch to small branch and never experiencing the more glamorous and more challenging work of the main office. In these ways people judged incompetent or undesirable are shuffled about in the system without being dismissed or demoted.

Mobility in late career

There are other personnel management practices, too, which stem from the peculiarities of the Japanese context and which particularly affect staff later on in their careers. Most notably, there is the necessity, noted by Craig (1975) and Yamaguchi (1979) amongst others, of preventing former colleagues being placed in a superior-subordinate relationship to each other, implying a loss of face for one of them. Where this is unavoidable, as for example when one senior civil servant is chosen to head the administration of a ministry, it is customary for his contemporaries to mark the event by resigning (Skinner, 1983: p. 59). This need not be as drastic a step as it sounds; it is also common practice for senior bureaucrats, and particularly those in the economic ministries, to resume their careers at lucrative salaries in the private sector after they have resigned, a practice popularly known as *amakudari* – 'descent from heaven' (Curtis, 1975; Johnson, 1978: Chapter 5; Johnson, 1982: Chapter 2). At less exalted levels, a compromise can often be achieved more easily simply by moving the affected staff to different offices – and different places. A second local peculiarity of note again arises in the public sector, as a consequence of the delegation of administrative functions from central government ministries to prefectural authorities (Samuels, 1983: Chapter 2). It is common under these circumstances for central government officials to be posted on rotation to positions within the prefectural bureaucracies, as a means of ensuring that central government directives are observed and obeyed (Tsuji, 1984: Chapter 1).

The standard career pattern of the managerial employee, once he has become familiar with the various facets of the organisation's operations, and assuming he has not already been diverted into a career cul-de-sac, involves spending the remaining years within the organisation rising through a succession of increasingly senior posts – sometimes in new places, sometimes not – until retirement, which in this context can occur at a very early age. The Japanese bureaucrat typically retires during his fifties, for example, and then finds employment in the private sector, or perhaps in the secretariat of one of the country's numerous quangos (Ojimi, 1975; Dore, 1985: p. 21). For the employee retiring from a large manufacturing concern, subsequent employment is likely to be in an executive post in a subsidiary or subcontracting company within the same economic grouping or *keiretsu* (Noda, 1975). In most cases these new jobs lie outside the orbit of the lifetime employment system; in this sense, then, 'lifetime employment' is a rather misleading term.

In the years leading up to retirement, most employees find that the tapering of the organisation's staff complement at progressively higher levels works to their disadvantage, for only a few can reach the very top. At this stage, the standardised personnel practices that had propelled the tenured employee through a succession of posts and locations give way to politics, power and patronage as the key career determinants (Craig, 1975: pp. 11–12). Those who are not destined for the highest levels may find themselves posted to branch offices, joint ventures, or satellite companies, to make room for the next generation of leaders (Glazer, 1969).

Mobility and organisational structure

Order and the scale of observation

Seen in close focus then, the tenured employee's career consists of a succession of vertical and spatial movements within the organisation, movements necessitated by a succession of personnel management practices that impact upon him. Through the employee's eyes, and particularly for an employee who is not destined to reach the top, his career may appear to be 'a planless tangle of reassignments and delays' (Plath, 1983: p. 9). It follows that an interpretation of a particular individual's career requires a careful analysis of each of these practices in the context of that individual's own characteristics and abilities. Several detailed studies of this kind have been made, notably in the anthropological literature (e.g. Long, 1983; Noguchi, 1983; Skinner, 1983).

Viewed from a greater distance, however, there are some clear geographical regularities that emerge from the aggregate pattern of mobility within an organisation, patterns that appear to depend very little upon the characteristics of the individuals concerned, or indeed upon the fine details of management practices. In the long term, the survival of an organisation depends upon its ability to rejuvenate its staff at all levels, and particularly those who lead it: this, after all, is the *purpose* of extensive training policies leading to higher management positions. This rejuvenation, which is necessitated by the natural ageing process of any workforce if by nothing else, can occur through hiring new staff to senior levels from external labour markets, or by upgrading staff from within internal ones – by far the preferred option in the context of large Japanese organisations. When internal labour markets prevail at all levels in the managerial hierarchy, then the replacement of retiring senior staff will create 'vacancy chains' or 'movement chains' reaching deep into the heart of the organisation concerned, as described in a more general context by Hägerstrand (1969: p. 102), even to the point where the hiring of a fresh young university graduate can be explicitly linked to the departure to retirement of a specific senior manager.

White (1970: p. 8) identifies several types of system linking employees to jobs, in which the duration of vacancies (posts without holders) and limbos (employees without posts) displays characteristic features. Japan's tight internal labour markets have a strong tendency to act as 'coordinated systems', in which both vacancies and limbos are negligible in length; indeed, given the frequency with which transfers are undertaken, it is hard to imagine how else personnel changes could be managed without creating chaos in the organisation's operations. The result is that personnel transfers in Japan, and those of managerial staff in particular, tend to form distinct 'simultaneous chains' in White's terminology, chains of ostensibly simultaneous moves which thread their way down through the entire organisation, vertically and spatially. A detailed example will be given later; at this point though it is worth noting a further Japanese twist. Retirement can in theory take place at any time; recruitment however must be timed to the rhythm of the Japanese academic year, which begins in April. As a result, recruitments, transfers, and indeed retirements, the three main elements in each chain, display a strong seasonality (see also Suzuki, 1981: Chapter 3), further reinforced by the transition between financial years (Skinner, 1983: p. 63). This is obvious to anyone visiting a Japanese railway station in the spring; it is also reflected objectively in surveys that record temporal patterns of migration. Thus, for example, the National Land Agency survey records that in 1981 more than two thirds of all migration caused by personnel transfers occurred during just two months – March and April.

Organisational structure as a constraint

Where transfers take place within coordinated systems, the precise details of who joins a particular chain can only be understood with reference to the way in which the managers within the organisation who arrange these chains interpret specific personnel policies and evaluate the career prospects of each individual. In aggregate, however, the various chains make sense not as discrete events with their own peculiar explanations, fascinating though those explanations might be. Rather, they present a picture of an organisation reproducing itself, in response to the natural ageing of its workforce. For the aggregate pattern of moves, a more fundamental constraint than the details of personnel management practices is likely to assume importance, namely the hierarchical structure of the organisation itself, within whose limits those practices are implemented. The more clearly defined and rigid the hierarchial structure, and the greater the strength of organisational tenure, so the narrower will be the limits within which personnel policies can discriminate between individual employees, and the greater will be the power of the structure itself as an explanation of migration patterns. The focus of interest is thereby shifted from the details of personnel policies (and personalities) to the intricacies of organisational structure.

At this point a familiar problem arises, that of constructing generalisations about organisational structures that are valid beyond the level of the individual case study (see Flowerdew, 1981: pp. 222-3). The distinction drawn by McKay and Whitelaw (1977, 1981) between scale/contact, resource, urban hierarchy, and market dependent organisations is an obvious starting point, based as it is upon the functions an organisation actually performs. Nevertheless, even in the case of market dependent organisations there is scope for considerable variation, both in the number and location of markets a particular organisation may choose to enter, and in the level at which those markets are defined. For example, two local offices serving small market areas can always be combined by administrative fiat to form a regional office serving a larger area, and enjoying much higher status within the organisation than either of its predecessors. It may be more helpful to think in terms of a continuum in the level of sustainable diversity in organisational structure, marked at one extreme by dynamic private manufacturing concerns in footloose industries, free to manage their affairs as they see fit, and at the other by established government bureaucracies tied firmly by law or convention to the operation of a particular vertical structure and the obligation to extend a service to all parts of the country. At the former extreme, detailed mobility policies are the key to understanding transfer patterns, but the prospects for constructing widely applicable generalisations with wide applicability are limited by the diversity of policies and organisational structures. At the latter extreme, personnel transfers are likely to be mechanistic and systematised, of the 'simultaneous chain' variety, and largely explicable in terms of a narrow range of common organisational forms.

Stable and unstable organisations

There is scope for work at both extremes of this continuum within the Japanese context. Transfers of blue-collar workers during recessions, for example, cannot be understood without specific reference to the particular sectors and firms concerned and the mix of personnel reduction policies adopted, some of which will be mobility-related, others not. Rohlen (1979), for example, has examined the response of leading Japanese companies to the recession of the 1970s, when a mixture of layoffs, bans on new recruitment, wage cuts, and transfers to sales departments, to subsidiaries, and even to unrelated firms, was adopted in varying proportions, depending on the particular circumstances of the company concerned. As regards the current structural recession in the steel industry, Sargent and Wiltshire (1988) give details of various adjustment policies, affecting both blue- and white-collar workers, in the specific context of the Nippon Steel Corporation.

For the majority of personnel transfers in Japan, however, the normal range of practices that flow from the logic of the lifetime employment system are the main consideration, applied within fairly stable organisations that are characterised, on the management side in particular, by a rather limited range of vertical and spatial structures. The archetype of such organisations is the government bureaucracy, and it is in the bureaucracy that the best illustrations can be found of the critical role of organisational structure in understanding the spatial characteristics of personnel transfers. There are many examples to choose from, since most Japanese ministries have large networks of field offices located throughout the country (Kubota, 1969: Chapter 5; Samuels, 1983: Chapter 2; Johnson, 1982: Chapter 2; Yamaguchi, 1979; Wiltshire, 1983). The one selected here is the case of personnel transfers within the Employment Security Bureau of the Japanese Ministry of Labour.

Case study: mobility in a Japanese bureaucracy

The Employment Security Bureau

The Employment Security Bureau of the Japanese Ministry of Labour is responsible for the provision of a number of public services, including unemployment insurance payments and employment counselling and placement, for which purpose it controls a network of 481 Public Employment Security Offices (hereafter PESOs) located in cities and town throughout Japan. It is, in other words, a classic example of a market dependent organisation. The vertical structure of the Bureau is divided into two discrete segments – an upper level, staffed by elite central government bureaucrats recruited from the nation's leading universities, and a lower level, for which staff are recruited from within the forty-seven individual prefectures, also on the basis of competitive civil service examinations. The upper level bureaucrats spend most of their working lives in Tōkyō, but can be posted to the provinces at various points during their careers, in particular as the head or 'section chief' (*kachō*) of one of the Employment Security Sections (hereafter ESS) that are located within each prefectural government. The spatial characteristics of these postings have been examined elsewhere (Wiltshire, 1983); suffice it to note here that they generally follow a simple rotational pattern, in which each transferee is called back to Tōkyō after a year or two, to be replaced by another official from Tōkyō on a reciprocal basis.

At the lower level, managerial staff spend their careers in transit between the ESS located within a particular prefectural government's headquarters and the various PESOs located within the same prefecture. Promotions to the upper level are extremely rare, and it is most unusual for a bureaucrat at the lower level to be posted anywhere outside his own prefecture.

To illustrate the characteristics of structural controls on mobility at this lower level, data have been extracted from the Employment Security Bureau's in-house journal, *Shokugyō Antei Kōhō*, for the period 1975–87. This journal regularly contains reports on personnel transfers at the level of PESO deputy manager and above, which include the name of the official, the post he has vacated and the post he now occupies. The differences between prefectures in the designation of posts within either the prefectural headquarters or individual PESOs are very slight; all share a formal management hierarchy similar to that which has been widely adopted amongst large Japanese organisations, public and private, including common ranks such as section chief, deputy section chief (*kachō hosa*) and chief clerk (*kakarichō*).

Seasonality and chaining

It is clear from the data that transfers at this level conform very closely to the generalisation made above about seasonality in Japanese internal labour market activity. For the 1975–87 period as a whole information was obtained on a total of 7,586 transfers, of which all but 76 officially took place on 1 April of the year concerned, a level of seasonal peaking even higher than that noted earlier for all personnel transfers in Japan. There is also clear evidence to demonstrate the importance of coordinated transfers and simultaneous chains. For example, each of the 535 transfers recorded for 1 April 1987 belonged to one of 216 distinct chains, of which no fewer than 185 (85.7%) could be traced to the retirement of specific individuals. The mean number of participants recorded in these retirement-led chains (including the retiree himself) was 3.6, as compared with only 2.0 participants for other chains; most of the latter were simple reciprocal transfers between posts at a similar level in the management hierarchy.

Some of the simultaneous chains traceable in the data are very long indeed. That shown in Figure 3.1, for example, includes a total of ten moves (including the retirement at its head), and illustrates the full range of moves that can take place – within the prefectural headquarters, between the headquarters and local PESOs, and from one PESO to another. These moves are constrained in turn by a strict vertical management hierarchy with a distinct geographical component, within which each post, and by implication each place, is carefully differentiated from every other.

Figure 3.1 Example of a simultaneous chain. Hiroshima Prefecture, 1 April 1987

	Old rank	Section/Office	Location	New rank	Section/Office	Location
1	Section Chief	EIS	Hiroshima (HQ)	Retired	–	–
2	Chief Manager	ESS	Hiroshima (HQ)	Section Chief	EIS	Hiroshima (HQ)
3	Manager	PESO	Mihara	Chief Manager	ESS	Hiroshima (HQ)
4	Manager	PESO	Takehara	Manager	PESO	Mihara
5	Deputy Section Chief	ESS	Hiroshima (HQ)	Manager	PESO	Takehara
6	Inspector	ESS	Hiroshima (HQ)	Deputy Section Chief	ESS	Hiroshima (HQ)
7	Manager	PESO	Miyoshi	Inspector	ESS	Hiroshima (HQ)
8	Deputy Manager	PESO	Hiroshima	Manager	PESO	Miyoshi
9	Manager	PESO	Hiroshima Saijo	Deputy Manager	PESO	Hiroshima
10	Chief Clerk	ESS	Hiroshima (HQ)	Manager	PESO	Hiroshima Saijo

Key
ESS = Employment Security Section
EIS = Employment Insurance Section
HQ = Prefectural Headquarters
PESO = Public Employment Security Office.

Source: Extracted from lists published in *Shokugyō Antei Kōhō*, 1 April 1987.

Mobility and hierarchy

This differentiation and its geographical expression can be detected most easily when the rank of the employee is held constant; in transfers, for example, involving a direct move from the position of PESO manager in one city or town to the same position in a PESO somewhere else. Over the entire 1975–87 period there were a total of 869 such transfers. To identify the hierarchial relationships between places, data on these transfers were converted into interaction matrices for each prefecture, matrices which were then rearranged in such a way as to maximise the total value of the elements below the diagonals. In theory, if there is perfect hierarchial differentiation of every post, then all transfers should appear below the diagonals of the interaction matrices, and all elements above the diagonals should be zero.

When this procedure was applied to the 869 transfers of PESO managers it was found that all but 24 (2.8%) lay below the diagonal of the appropriate optimised matrix, and of these 24 exceptions all but one arose because of reciprocal exchanges of personnel between two or more PESOs. It appears, therefore, that there is a strong, indeed almost perfect hierarchical relationship between PESOs within each prefecture which constrains the direction of transfers between any two locations.

But what determines the precise position of a particular PESO relative to others in the hierarchy? In an organisation dedicated to providing a service to the general public, the obvious criterion to look at first is the number of people actually served. Unfortunately data are not available on how many people use each PESO; it is possible, however, to calculate as a surrogate the base populations from which these users are drawn, since each PESO has a defined service area (Rōdōsho, 1987a).

The 1980 populations of 445 of the 481 service areas were calculated from the results of the national census of that year. (Of the remaining 36 PESOs, 28 have service areas which include subdivisions of municipalities for which no data are recorded in the census, and 8 are specialised institutions serving mariners and port workers, whose service areas overlap those of several conventional ones.) Over the 1975–87 period there were a total of 738 direct transfers of managers between these 445 PESOs, of which no fewer than 598 (81%) were transfers to PESOs with larger service area (in population terms), and only 140 (19%) to PESOs with smaller service areas. Moreover, when transfers were to PESOs with smaller service areas the differences in population were generally marginal, the main exceptions being in heavily urbanised prefectures such as Tōkyō and Ōsaka. In such prefectures population may well be a poor surrogate for the PESO's actual clientele, which will tend to be inflated in areas where universities are concentrated or where there are large numbers of small factories.

The high correlation between the direction of postings and the workload of each PESO reinforces the point made earlier concerning the importance of administrative decisions in defining service areas in market dependent organisations; not only are such decisions arbitrary, but they are continually rendered obsolete by changes in population distribution, particularly in areas undergoing rapid suburbanisation. As a result, the pattern of transfers can easily reflect the distribution of the population whenever the service areas were last adjusted, not as it is at present.

In Figure 3.1 there is one example of a transfer involving not only a direct move between two PESOs, Hiroshima and Miyoshi, but also a simultaneous upgrading, from deputy manager to manager. It is significant that this formal increase in rank is associated with a move to a *smaller* place (Hiroshima City's population in 1980 was 900,000; that of Miyoshi City only 38,000). Analysis of the data for the entire 1975–87 period reveals that this is very much the norm; of 390 recorded transfers involving promotion from deputy manager to manager, only 13 (3.4%) were to places further up the hierarchy of PESOs (as defined by the optimised interaction matrices for transfers of managers); the remaining 377 transfers (96.6%) were all downwards. In summary then, when rank remains constant, the individual moves up the hierarchy of PESOs; when rank increases, he moves down again – but for only one move, after which the geographical ascent is resumed. Further-more, in a limited number of cases this rule even applies in reverse. Sixty-two transfers were recorded involving an apparent demotion in rank, from PESO manager to deputy manager (there is an example in Figure 3.1); in every single case, the transfer was to a PESO much further *up* the hierarchy.

Geographical mobility and vertical mobility

So far the only moves examined have been between PESOs, for which there is very clear evidence of structural constraints on the direction of movement. What about transfers within the prefectural headquarters, and between the headquarters and the PESOs? In both cases the data are somewhat harder to analyse, due to ambiguities surrounding the interpretation of various head-quarters posts. While there are several posts common to all prefectures, others are unique to one or two places (especially specialist posts found only in the big cities), while others can be held by more than one official simul-taneously (or are 'pooled' in White's terminology). To simplify the analysis of transfers within the various headquarters buildings, the data were aggregated across prefectures, and the less common posts (arbitrarily defined as those occurring with a frequency of below twenty) were excluded. The interaction matrix for the 670 transfers remaining was again optimised to maximise the values below the diagonal; despite the complications and ambiguities, only 77 transfers (11.5%) remained above the diagonal. Within the headquarters too, then, there is a strict vertical hierarchy of positions complementing that found amongst the PESOs.

As for transfers *between* a prefectural headquarters and the various PESOs within its jurisdiction, analytical difficulties are compounded not just by the presence of both 'pool jobs' and low frequency positions within the headquarters, but also by the intricate interlacing of field and headquarters posts within each prefecture's managerial hierarchy, the fine details of which depend in part upon the size distribution of service areas at the intra-prefectural scale.

For an illustration of these points, consider Figure 3.2. This shows transfers between what are normally the three most senior posts open to pre-fectural officials; the manager (*jochō*) of the PESO in the prefectural capital, the section chief (*kachō*) of the Employment Insurance Section (hereafter, EIS) within the prefectural headquarters, and the chief manager (*shūkan*) of the ESS, again within the prefectural headquarters. Data for Ōsaka and Tōkyō are excluded from the table, because the headquarters of these, the two largest prefectures, are organised along rather different lines from the other 45 prefectures.

From the data in Figure 3.2 it is clear that there is a strong match between the pattern of transfers and the vertical relationship of the three posts – of the 845 transfers (including moves into retirement) shown in the table, only 94 (11.4%) fail to take place in the expected direction. Equally interesting, however, is the nature of the exceptions. The highest position, that of manager of the PESO in the prefectural capital, is normally a terminal point

Figure 3.2 Transfers from the three most senior posts open to prefectural officials, 1975–87*

From:	Manager, PESO, Prefectural Capital	Section Chief, EIS, Prefectural Capital (HQ)	Chief Manager, ESS, Prefectural Capital (HQ)
To:			
Retirement	276	154	7
Manager, PESO, Prefectural Capital	–	114	55
Section Chief, EIS, Prefectural Capital (HQ)	3	–	143
Chief Manager, ESS, Prefectural Capital (HQ)	0	0	–
Manager, #2 PESO† [of which: #2 PESO larger than Prefectural Capital]	6 [5]	11 [10]	32 [5]
Manager, other PESO [of which: #3 PESO††]	2 [1]	4 [1]	19 [10]
Other HQ post, Prefectural Capital	4	4	11
TOTAL	291	287	267
Of which, moves in expected order	276	268	205
(%)	(94.8)	(93.4)	(76.8)

Key
ESS = Employment Security Section
EIS = Employment Insurance Section
HQ = Prefectural Headquarters
PESO = Public Employment Security Office.

Notes
* excluding Tōkyō and Osaka Prefectures
† PESO with the largest population in its service area, excluding the PESO located in the prefectural capital
†† PESO with the second largest population in its service area, excluding the PESO located in the prefectural capital – in nearly all cases, this is the PESO with the third largest service area population in the prefecture concerned. For further details see text.

Source: Extracted from lists published in *Shokugyō Antei Kōhō*, various issues.

in a bureaucratic career. Of the tiny number of exceptions to this rule, the largest group (5) consists of transfers to other PESOs with one distinguishing characteristic: their service areas have larger populations than those served by the PESO in the prefectural capital. The absolute number of cases is small, in part because there are only seven prefectures in which the population of the prefectural capital's service area is not the largest. The point to be made, however, is that the fate of a person holding this post is clearly determined in part by the particular size distribution of service areas in the prefecture within which he is employed.

The conclusion is reinforced by the fact that a similar pattern emerges for holders of the second highest position, that of section chief in the EIS within the prefectural headquarters. A much small proportion of employees in this position pass directly into retirement (54 per cent, as against 98 per cent for the highest position), since there is at least one higher post available to them. Otherwise, we again have very few cases in which transfers are not self-evidently upwards, and the largest single group of exceptions (10) consists of transfers to PESOs with service areas that have larger populations than those served by the PESO in the prefectural capital.

For occupants of what is normally the third highest position, chief manager of the ESS, there are rather more cases that appear to be exceptions to the rule of upward mobility. A very small proportion indeed heads straight for retirement (3%), in part because there are now at least two other possibilities for career advancement. Conversely, a substantial minority of transfers (51, or 19%) are to PESOs other than those located in prefectural capitals. Of these 51, only a small number are to PESOs with service areas larger than that served by the PESO in the prefectural capital. Instead, the largest single group of transfers (27, or 10% of all transfers) consists of moves to the most important PESO in a prefecture other than that located in the prefectural capital, where the population served is *less* than that served by the prefectural capital. In addition, of the remaining transfers to PESOs which fall outside this category, the majority are to PESOs that rank third in their prefectures on the basis of population served. We may infer then that the fate of a person holding the post of chief manager in an employment security section is similarly determined in part by the particular size distribution of service areas in the prefecture within which he is employed. If there are one or more PESOs, other than that located in the prefectural capital, that are of sufficient importance (in terms of population served), then he is liable to be posted away from the prefectural capital one more time before achieving either of the two highest posts (or retiring). If the prefecture happens not to contain any large alternatives, he is more likely to remain in the prefecture capital until retirement. The situation is analogous to that facing more senior staff, except that the range of alternatives is greater; or to put it another way, the threshold population required of a PESO's service area before it can be considered a potential destination for a transferee at this level is lower. It is not possible, however, to infer an absolute figure for this threshold that applies throughout the country; it is clearly much lower in more rural prefectures, where the population even of the second largest service area is often no larger than that of the smallest service areas in Japan's great cities.

Variations in organisational structure

Thus far, we have looked at the pattern of transfers on a disaggregated basis – moves between PESOs, moves within the prefectural headquarters, and moves between headquarters and PESOs – and found evidence for structural constraints on the direction of movement in each case. Nothing has been said, however, about the *relative importance* of these three types in different prefectures. There are two important variables here – the absolute numbers of posts to be filled, and the manner in which posts in the headquarters and in the PESOs are interlaced in the vertical structure of each prefectural organisation. Superficially at least, simple numbers of posts are powerful determinants of the numbers of transfers between PESOs and within each prefectural headquarters – the Pearson's correlation coefficients for these two types of transfers (between absolute numbers of moves and posts) are 0.94 and 0.79 respectively, both highly significant in statistical terms. Nevertheless, there is evidence to suggest that the relative contributions of the three types of transfers are *not* in proportion simply to the number of posts on offer. If the balance between headquarters and PESO posts were the sole determinant of the composition of transfers by direction, then a binomial expansion based upon the proportions of these two posts should yield a reasonable prediction of the shares of the total number of transfers accounted for by moves between PESOs, within headquarters, and between PESOs and headquarters.

It does not. For example, the binomial expansion underpredicts the proportion of transfers that take place between PESOs and headquarters, by an average of eight percentage points, and for 43 out of 47 prefectures. Conversely, direct transfers between PESOs are overpredicted for 39 out of 47 prefectures. One implication of this is that PESO staff face a higher probability of being transfered back to headquarters, and a lower probability of being moved instead to another PESO, than would otherwise be the case. This suggests that there is some tendency to rotate staff between PESOs and headquarters on a reciprocal basis, much as described earlier for the ministry bureaucrats who are rotated in from Tōkyō to head each prefectural employment security section. The headquarters, in other words, can be seen to perform a 'switching point' role, along the lines hypothesised by McKay and Whitelaw (1981: p. 110). (We may note here also that Yamaguchi (1979) reports a similar pattern of oscillation between head-quarters and field posts in another section of the bureaucracy, the Ministry of Construction.) The question of whether this tendency is a matter of deliberate policy (to keep PESO staff up to date with ideas at the centre, for example), or a logical consequence of the way PESO and headquarters posts structurally interact (as already described for the three leading posts), remains to be determined. The fact, however, that the binomial predictions consistently underestimate transfers within the headquarters at low predicted levels, and that the underpredictions of transfers between PESOs are also confined to prefectures with low predicted levels, suggests that there are structural constraints at work, linked in particular to the sizes of the PESO network and the headquarters complement, both of which are in turn related to the overall population of each prefecture.

To summarise the results of this brief case study, there are definite vertical and spatial structures that constrain the direction of personnel transfers in this particular section of the Japanese bureaucracy, structures necessitated at root by the adoption of the lifetime employment system and internal labour markets, but which vary in detail between the various branches of the organisation on the basis of factors such as the magnitude of the populations being served.

Discussion

As was explained at the outset, transfers within the bureaucracy represent an extreme case in which the role of structural factors in determining patterns of transfers is maximised. Nevertheless, it has also been shown that bureaucrats form a substantial component of the overall transferee migrant population, and it is also true that a majority of Japan's major private companies share a rather similar vertical organisational structure; indeed, many of their senior employees enjoy careers very much like those of government bureaucrats (Mannari, 1974: p. 127; Togura, 1979). These are reasons to believe, therefore, that the points raised in the case study may be of broader relevance to the study of personnel transfers in Japan. They also show a much more formally structured system of transfers than that found in the UK and US.

In conclusion, however, it is appropriate to ask three broader questions. First, to what extent are personnel transfers in Japan translated into actual residential migrations? Most of what has been said, after all, concerns the place of work, *not* the place of residence. Second, what (if any) are the implications of the Japanese experience for the development of a general theory (or theories) of geographical labour mobility? And third, what (if any) are the practical benefits to be gained from analysing the mechanisms inherent in Japan's internal labour markets?

Transfers and migration

It has already been noted that senior employees with domestic responsibilities face a different trade-off between moving their families from place to place, with serious consequences for the education of their children in particular, and various inconvenient alternatives such as long distance commuting or living apart from the family. Over the past few years much media attention has been focused on the last of these alternatives, living apart from the family on a weekly, monthly or even longer-term basis. A survey covering over 300 of Japan's largest private companies suggests that around one transfer in three results in an employee temporarily forsaking his family (*tanshin funin*), a proportion that rises to one in two for employees in their forties (Rōmu Gyōsei Kenkyūjo, 1986). Another survey with a somewhat broader base suggests that a total of around 175,000 families may be affected in this way at any one time within the private sector alone (Rōdōsho, 1987b). It is, in other words, a widespread phenomenon, and one which results in personnel transfers stimulating rather less geographical mobility that might otherwise be the case.

Nearly every large employer now provides some sort of assistance to staff who find it necessary to live apart from their families, even though, as Honda (1988) points out, around 80 per cent of employers would prefer that staff migrated with their families rather than without. This assistance can take many forms – almost 90 per cent of firms provide accommodation in company dormitories or housing (similar provision is made for those migrating *with* their families); over half (and substantially over half in very large firms) pay a special 'separation allowance' to affected staff, which averaged ¥ 30,000 (£135) per month in 1986; and nearly half pay allowances to cover the cost of occasional trips home. A small percentage of companies grant their employees special leave for this purpose, and some are even willing to finance trips by families to visit their missing breadwinners. At the same time, many employers have adopted measures to encourage the migration of the entire family, such as coordinating the timing of personnel transfers with the rhythm of the school year (for which, as we have seen, there are other sound reasons), paying any additional costs associated with switching schools, and taking responsibility for the care and management of the family's home while they are away. Some employers have even introduced a system of 'regional employment', in which employees can opt to remain within a specified geographical area, though at the expense of the more rapid promotion possible within the company's broader organisation; in effect, sacrificing vertical mobility for spatial stability (Anon., 1985). In short then, there are a whole range of specific mobility policies tied to this one phenomenon.

The theoretical significance of the Japanese experience

Two points should be made. First, while Japanese labour management practices obviously have some unique aspects, it would be a mistake to believe that Japan has little in common with other places. The career of the Japanese manager in particular has many parallels with that of senior staff in major European or American corporations. This implies that analyses of Japanese data may have broader implications for the study of personnel transfers at a more abstract level, despite the difficulties of international comparison (see Flowerdew, 1981: p. 222). Thus, for example, the observations made here on the direction of transfers between PESOs serving populations of different sizes, and the broader comments on *tanshin funin*, closely reflect points raised by Flowerdew (*ibid.*, p. 217) in his general review of organisational constraints on migration. The tightness of Japan's internal labour markets, however, particularly in very large organisations, does suggest that it is in the elaboration of the geographical aspects of White's 'coordinated systems' of matching jobs to people that empirical work on Japan is most likely to make a contribution to the wider study of geographical labour mobility. Second, it should be clear from the discussion of *tanshin funin* above that theoretical work linking personnel transfers to migration must take into account not only the range of mobility policies that companies can deploy, but also the range of possible responses on the employee's side, including separation from the family and, in a country like Japan with excellent ground and air transportation networks, long-distance commuting. Indeed, given the spectrum of possibilities lying between daily commuting and full family separation for a year or more, it is unclear at what point 'labour migration' proper may be said to have occurred.

The practical significance of the Japanese experience

Finally, there is the question of the practical significance of understanding the geography of Japanese labour mobility. A decade ago, this topic could reasonably have been considered a matter of marginal interest to anyone except the Japanese and Japanologists; but no longer. With the emergence of Tōkyō as one of the three global financial centres, of Japanese banks and securities houses as major players in the world's financial markets, and of Japanese manufacturers as major investors in overseas plants, Japanese personnel transfer systems are now impinging upon a wide range of countries, in two ways. First, they are bringing in Japanese staff, and boosting international migration figures in the process. Second, and of much greater practical concern, as a manifestation of the lifetime employment system they represent a significant barrier to the career prospects of 'local' employees of Japan's powerful multinational companies. At present it is rare for foreign employees to be promoted on the main career track within a Japanese company's headquarters (Kuwahara, 1987). Without opening up internal labour markets to foreigners, however, it is difficult to see how able staff can be adequately motivated, while it remains unclear whether foreign staff would be willing to accept the degree of spatial and occupational instability that the Japanese manager accepts as an inevitable part of his job. This is obviously a matter of both theoretical and practical interest, and at a truly global scale. Here the difficulties associated with national peculiarities, as cited by Flowerdew (1981: p. 222), become a central focus of concern, to be measured against the common yardstick provided by the internal structure and personnel practices of the multinational corporation.

References

Abegglen, J. C. and Stalk, G. Jr. (1985) *Kaisha: The Japanese Corporation.* New York: Basic Books.

Anon. (1985) 'More Businesses taking a Second Look at Employee Relocation'. *Japan Economic Journal.* 28 December **28**, 8.

Cole, R. E. (1979) *Work, Mobility, and Participation: A Comparative Study of American and Japanese Industry*. Berkeley: University of California Press.

Craig, A. M. (1975) 'Functional and Dsyfunctional Aspects of Government Bureaucracy' in Vogel E. F. (ed) *Modern Japanese Organization and Decision-Making*. Berkeley: University of California Press. pp. 3–32.

Curtis, G. L. (1975) 'Big Business and Political Influence' in Vogel E. F. (ed) *Modern Japanese Organization and Decision-Making*. Berkeley: University of California Press. pp. 33–70.

Dore, R. P. (1985) *Flexible Rigidities*. London: The Athlone Press.

Flowerdew, R. (1982) 'Institutional Effects on Internal Migration' in Flowerdew R. (ed) *Institutions and Geographical Patterns*. London: Croom Helm. pp. 209–27.

Glazer, H. (1969) 'The Japanese Executive' in Ballon R. J. (ed) *The Japanese Employee*. Tōkyō: Tuttle.

Hägerstrand, T. (1969) 'On the Definition of Migration'. *Scandinavian Population Studies*, 1: 63–72.

Hanami, T. (1982) 'Worker Motivation in Japan (II)'. *Japan Labour Bulletin*, 21 (3): 5–8.

Honda, S. (1988) 'Tanshin Funin no Genkyō to Mondai'. *Shokugyō Antei Kōhō*, 39 (8): 4–5.

Inagami, T. (1983) *Labour-Management Communications at the Workshop Level*. Tōkyō: Japan Institute of Labour.

Inagami, T. (1986) 'Changing Japanese-Style Employment Practices'. *Japan Labour Bulletin*, 25 (10): 4–8.

Johnson, C. (1978) *Japan's Public Policy Companies*. Washington DC: American Enterprise Institute for Public Policy Research.

Johnson, C. (1982) *MITI and the Japanese Miracle: The Growth of Industrial Policy, 1925–1975*. Stanford: Stanford University Press.

Johnson, J. H. and Salt, J. (1980) 'Labour Migration within Organizations: An Introductory Study'. *Tijdschrift voor Economische en Sociale Geografie*, 71 (5): 277–84.

Koike, K. (1983) 'Internal Labour Markets: Workers in Large Firms' in Shirai T. (ed) *Contemporary Industrial Relations in Japan*. Madison: University of Wisconsin Press. pp. 29–61.

Kokudochō Keikaku Chōseikyoku (1982) *Wagakuni no Jinkō Idō no Jittai*. Tōkyō, Government of Japan, National Land Agency.

Kubota, A. (1969) *Higher Civil Servants in Japan*. Princeton: Princeton University Press.

Kuwahara, Y. (1987) 'Labour Problems in Japanese Companies Overseas'. *Japan Labour Bulletin*, 26 (5): 5–8.

Levine, S. B. (1983) 'Careers and Mobility in Japan's Labour Markets' in Plath D. W. (ed) *Work and Lifecourse in Japan*. Albany: State University of New York Press. pp. 18–33.

Long, S. O. (1983) 'Intertwined Careers in Medical Practice' in Plath D. W. (ed) *Work and Lifecourse in Japan*. Albany: State University of New York Press. pp. 110–15.

Mannari, H. (1974) *The Japanese Business Leaders*. Tōkyō: University of Tōkyō Press.

McKay, J., and Whitelaw, J. S. (1977) 'The Role of Large Private and Government Organizations in Generating Flows of Inter-Regional Migrants: The Case of Australia'. *Economic Geography*, **53** (1): 28–44.

McKay, J., and Whitelaw, J. S. (1981) 'Organizations, Management and Structural Change: The Role of Executive Mobility' in Linge G. J. R. and McKay J. (eds) *Structural Change in Australia: Some Spatial and Organizational Responses*. Canberra: Australian National University. pp. 87–118.

Noda, K. (1975) 'Big Business Organization' in Vogel E. F. (ed) *Modern Japanese Organization and Decision-Making*. Berkeley: University of California Press. pp. 115–45.

Noguchi, P. H. (1983) 'Shiranai Station: Not a Destination but a Journey' in Plath D. W. (ed) *Work and Lifecourse in Japan*. Albany: State University of New York Press: pp. 74–95.

Ojimi, Y. (1975) 'A Government Ministry: The Case of the Ministry of International Trade and Industry' in Vogel E. F. (ed) *Modern Japanese Organization and Decision-Making*. Berkeley: University of California Press. pp. 101–12.

Ono, T. (1973) 'Intra-Firm Labour Markets: Personnel Practices and Mechanisms for Adjustment'. *Japan Labour Bulletin*, **12** (4): 4–16.

Plath, D. W. 'Life is Just a Job Résumé?' in Plath D. W. (ed) *Work and Lifecourse in Japan*. Albany: State University of New York Press. pp. 1–13.

Rōdōsho (1987a) *Shōwa 62-nendo Shokugyō Antei Gyōsei Soshiki Shokugyō Noryoku Kaihatsu Gyōsei Soshiki oyobi Shisetsu Ichiran*. Tōkyō: Government of Japan, Ministry of Labour.

Rōdōsho (1987b) *Shōwa 61-nen Chingin Rōdō Jikan Seido Chōsa*. Tōkyō: Government of Japan, Ministry of Labour.

Rohlen, T. P. (1974) *For Harmony and Strength*. Los Angeles: University of California Press.

Rohlen, T. P. (1979) ' "Permanent Employment" Faces Recession, Slow Growth, and an Ageing Workforce'. *Journal of Japanese Studies*. **5** (2): 235–72.

Rōmu Gyōsei Kenkyūjo (1986) *Tenkin o meguru Kakushu Toriatsukai no Jittai*. Tōkyō: Labour Management Research Institute.

Samuels, R. J. (1983) *The Politics of Regional Policy in Japan: Localities Incorporated*? Princeton: Princeton University Press.

Sargent, J. and Wiltshire R. (1988) 'Kamaishi: A Japanese Steel Town in Crisis'. *Geography* **74** (4): 354–57.

Shimada, H. (1983) 'New Challenges for Japanese Labour-Management Relations in the Era of Global Structural Change'. *Japan Labour Bulletin*. **22** (7): 5–8.

Skinner, K. A. (1983) 'Aborted Careers in a Public Corporation' in Plath D. W. (ed) *Work and Lifecourse in Japan*. Albany: State University of New York Press. pp. 50–73.

Suzuki, N. (1981) *Management and Industrial Structure in Japan.* Oxford: Pergamon Press.

Togura, N. (1979) 'Daikigyō Kanrishoku no Chiiki Idō' in Itō, T., Naitō, H. and Yamaguchi F. (eds) *Jinkō Ryūdō no Chiiki Kōzō.* Tōkyō: Taimeidō. pp. 183–86.

Tsuji, K. (ed) (1984) *Public Administration in Japan.* Tōkyō: University of Tōkyō Press, 1984.

White, H. C. (1970) *Chains of Opportunity: Systems Models of Mobility in Organizations.* Cambridge: Harvard University Press.

Wiltshire, R. (1983) 'Personnel Transfers and Spatial Mobility: A Case Study of the Employment Security Bureau'. *Science Reports of Tōhoku University, Seventh Series (Geography).* 33 (2): 65–78.

Yamaguchi, F. (1979) 'Kanchō Kanrishoku no Chiiki Idō, in Itō, T., Naitō H. and Yamaguchi, F. (eds) *Jinkō Ryūdō no Chiiki Kōzō.* Tōkyō: Taimeidō. pp. 186–93.

Yamaguchi, K. (1983) 'The Public Sector: Civil Servants' in Shirai T. (ed) *Contemporary Industrial Relations in Japan.* Madison: University of Wisconsin Press. pp. 295–311.

CHAPTER 4

Organisational Labour Migration: Theory and Practice in the United Kingdom

John Salt

Introduction

Theories to explain internal migration in advanced industrial countries have largely failed to get to grips with two fundamental and interrelated phenomena: the organisation of employment and the development of internal labour markets (ILMs) by employers. Most explanations either rely on models based on broad economic forces or on the behaviour of migrants using supply side information from social surveys. Largely missing has been the incorporation of demand side variables, reflecting the way in which migration is related to employment structures. This chapter explores some of the more important demand side issues, particularly those relating to the internal labour market policies of large employing organisations in Britain.

The concept of the ILM is crucial in understanding much of modern labour migration. All employers have an ILM within which the tasks to be performed in production (manufacturing and services) are allocated. Large employers have complex ILMs which are organised on a multi-location basis; hence the process of allocation of tasks and personnel can involve the geographical relocation of individuals between locations. Sometimes this geographical movement of employment is short distance, at others a simultaneous move of home is also necessary because a longer distance relocation is involved. To ease the latter, employers endeavour to provide a magic carpet consisting of a relocation package that pays the costs of moving, often with an additional allowance as well.

The existence of ILMs also has an impact on movement between firms via the external labour market (ELM). A person changing employer will, in effect, be moving between ILMs. How these markets are organised may be a major element in the decision to leave (such as a redundancy or lack of promotion prospects); it will certainly affect recruitment into the new employer, most obviously through the degree of openness of ports of entry into the various occupations and levels that characterise the ILM.

The aim of this chapter is to indicate the importance in labour migration of the internal labour markets of large employing organisations. Using survey evidence, it begins by reviewing the scale and characteristics of this form of migration in the UK and then presents a theoretical framework for explanation which emphasises the importance of the internal structure of the ILM. Using selected case examples it demonstrates how that structure can determine geographical patterns of movement. Finally, it shows how complex patterns of assistance have been developed to smooth the paths of those who relocate, thus giving them considerable advantage over those less blessed.

Migration within internal labour markets

Scale

It is only comparatively recently that the scale of this form of migration has been realised in the United Kingdom (Johnson, Salt and Wood, 1974; Johnson and Salt, 1980) and in the USA (see Chapter 2). Its existence in Australia was pointed out by McKay and Whitelaw (1977a, 1977b) though few data are available on its scale there. The situation for Japan is discussed in Chapter 3. So far, information from the rest of Europe is negligible but Chapter 7 provides some data from France.

Figure 4.1 indicates that in 1981 over half of inter-regional migrants in the UK (defined as those employed both one year before and at the time of the Labour Force Survey) did not change employer. The figures for 1975 and 1979 were similar. The Organisational Labour Migration Study* carried out by the author and surveying nearly 100 UK corporate employers in 1982–3, indicated 150,000–180,000 transferees per annum in the early 1980s. This was the first time an attempt had been made to calculate the numbers. The figure was arrived at by calculating the relocation rates of sectors of the economy from the employer sample, and multiplying them by the proportion of total employment in the economy as a whole accounted for by each sector.

Data were also collected on the size of relocated households, which averaged 2.3 people. This gives a total movement figure in the UK, due to ILM transfers, of 345,000–400,000 each year. This represents less than one per cent of all residential moves, but about a third of those over 20 kilometres. These proportions are lower than similar ones recorded for the US (Chapter 2) but are significant none the less. A more recent suggestion has

*Funded by the Economic and Social Research Council

Figure 4.1 Inter-regional migration 1980–81

Destination region	(a) All inter-regional movers	(b) Total employed both dates	(c) Worked for same organisation	(d) b/a %	(e) c/b %	(f) c/a %
Northern	20228	6087	3001	30.1	49.3	14.8
Yorkshire and Humberside	37792	14093	9467	37.3	67.2	25.1
East Midlands	44508	13737	8034	30.9	58.5	18.1
East Anglia	40243	17555	7278	43.6	41.5	18.1
Greater London	95325	42131	25515	44.2	60.6	26.8
Rest of South East	159094	76726	46068	48.2	60.0	29.0
South West	63037	27946	16069	44.3	57.5	25.5
West Midlands	33034	14152	7366	42.8	52.0	22.3
North West	36800	14784	7805	40.2	52.8	31.2
Scotland	34833	15382	11275	44.2	73.3	32.4
Wales	17219	5681	3052	33.0	53.7	17.7
Great Britain	582113	248274	144930	42.7	58.4	24.9

Source: Labour Force Survey, 1981.

put the number of relocations in the UK at around 250,000 per year (Atkinson, 1987). Unfortunately there is no indication of how that figure was arrived at, and particularly whether it includes moves to join companies as well as relocations within their ILM; but there can be no doubt that corporate labour market operation has a substantial role in British internal labour migration.

Its role in international movement is also greater than has been appreciated. About two-thirds of long-term work permits issued by the British Department of Employment in 1987 were to corporate transferees. Unpublished data from the Labour Force Survey for 1987 suggest that about half of all Britons going to work abroad are corporate transferees. At the same date the equivalent figure for Australia was 51 per cent (Appleyard, 1987). Increasingly these executive nomads form a major element in the global division of labour. What is especially relevant about such internationalisation is that it indicates the increasing integration of national and international ILMs in many companies. For some managers and professionals transference can just as easily be overseas as to another location in the UK. Mobility in these circumstances can be a response to global and not just national imperatives. One consequence is that for many people ILM migration within a country may be a response to a process also involving the international relocation of labour. Some of the housing consequences of this relationship are explored in Chapter 12.

Characteristics of ILM migrants in Britain

Data on the characteristics of those relocating are few. Only two major studies exist, the Organisational Labour Migration Study (OLMS) (Salt,

1984) and the more recent study carried out by the Institute of Manpower Studies (Atkinson, 1987). The nature of these studies varied. The first adopted an organisational perspective, focusing on over 90 large employers; the second concentrated on only six employing organisations, but surveyed 6,000 managers within them by means of a postal questionnaire.

The picture they produce is remarkably consistent. Most transferees are in professional, managerial and senior technical grades, and this group can be recognised in most employing organisations as a potentially mobile one. In contrast, manual workers do not move, except in some nationalised industries or in response to special circumstances. Indeed, when offered a relocation most manual workers refuse (Salt, 1987).

The OLMS found that rates of transfer are highest in retail organisations, followed by financial institutions, government departments, manufacturing firms, transport and communications undertakings and public utilities (Salt, 1986). Rates of movement vary considerably by employer. In many organisations there is a mass of low-skilled workers who are never likely to be transferred. However, for those staff whose occupations put them at some risk of relocation annual mobility rates can be quite high: eight out of 76 organisations had rates of 10 per cent or more, the highest being 24 per cent.

Individually, 40 per cent of managers and professional staff had relocated in the previous ten years, three with the present employer, one to join it (Atkinson, 1987). Both studies agree that mobility is particularly associated with early career phases, but not necessarily associated with promotion (see below). Patterns vary considerably between companies, moves and promotions occurring at different ages. Most movers are male, but there is evidence that females are becoming increasingly likely to relocate: Atkinson found that a third of the women in his sample had relocated in the previous decade. Career advancement is the most common reason given for willingness to relocate, two-thirds saying that was the prime motive, compared with a third who were attracted by a higher salary in the new post (Atkinson, 1987). This finding is consistent with the association of relocation and promotion found in the OLMS and discussed below.

The number of women who are relocated is relatively small. Less than 10% per cent of transferees in the organisational labour migration study were women; a later study came up with a figure of 21 per cent (Merrill Lynch, 1986). Women who are relocated seem to be relatively young and unencumbered: in one study in 1986 half were married but only one in six had children, and 75 per cent were aged between 26 and 35, the main child-bearing period (PHH Homequity, 1987).

Types of intra-organisational mobility

Corporate transfer is a response to a range of situations. All large organisations transfer staff on a recurrent basis as part of career development. Other important causes are rationalisation, consequent upon changed trading conditions and the need to move staff from closing or declining locations; and expansion, where developments in new locations require inputs of experienced employees. Training programmes often involve the planned movement around the company of young recruits, who gain experience in several aspects of the business. Frequently, organisations engage in a wholesale shift of activities from one site to another, especially from London. For example, in 1986 STC Plc decided to relocate 44 professional engineering staff from north London to Harlow: all but one went, although only four had to move home (CBI, 1987, 13-15). Other causes of relocation include change of control, usually involving the movement of small numbers of senior staff into new acquisitions; and migration, usually of limited duration and associated with specific projects in construction and heavy engineering. In any organisation it would not be uncommon to find several of these types of relocation at the same time.

Explaining migration within corporate labour markets

Demand and supply

Explaining relocation of staff within corporate labour markets requires an approach different from that adopted in most studies of migration. Neither classical nor neoclassical economic models are of much use because the migrants are not a homogeneous group responding to labour market conditions, but instead consist of a series of specialist non-competing groups. Behavioural approaches are equally flawed because they focus on the decision-making process of the potential migrant and fail to take account of the fact that he or she is constrained in choice by what is on offer from the employer, and may, in any case, be virtually required to move if a career within the firm is to be developed successfully. An approach is necessary that focuses first on how employers allocate tasks to their workforce, and then on how the friction of distance and disturbance in any consequent migration is smoothed.

Of critical importance is the structure and operation of the ILM. On the demand side the structure reflects the spatial division of labour in the organisation, which may involve the migration of various types of employee moving between employment nodes. Movement is a response to an allocation system which reflects three things: degree of openness to the ELM, geographical size and occupational distribution, and rules which govern the priorities for distributing workers among jobs. On the supply side the concept of career is crucial. A career consists of a sequence of jobs held by an individual and related to each other by the acquisition, perhaps through geographical mobility, of skill and experience. Careers have stages which are related to mobility propensity. The early career phase is associated with a high degree of mobility as knowledge and expertise are being acquired, often in different locations. Mid-career can be a period of consolidation, with less movement than previously. In later career phases mobility may pick up again, with promotion to senior positions.

Figure 4.2 British Telecom: principal intergrade movements and promotion channels

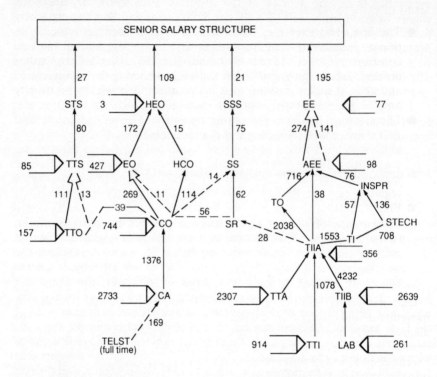

Key to grades

STS	Senior Telecoms Superintendent
TTS	Telecoms Traffic Superintendent
TTO	Telecoms Traffic Officer
HEO	Higher Executive Officer
EO	Executive Officer
HCO	Higher Clerical Officer
CO	Clerical Officer
CA	Clerical Assistant
TESLT	Telephonist
SSS	Senior Sales Superintendent
SS	Sales Superintendent

SR	Sales Respresentative
EE	Executive Engineer
AEE	Assistant Executive Engineer
INSPR	Inspector
TO	Technical Officer
STECH	Senior Technician
TI	Technician 1
TIIA	Technician 2A
TIIB	Technician 2B
TTA	Trainee Technician Apprentice
TTI	Trainee Technician Improver
LAB	Labourer

Key to movements

▷ Open entry

——▶ Advancement/in-line promotion

– – ▶ Promotion/change of grade by special selection

Organisational career

We can put demand and supply together and see the geography of the ILM in terms of three principal theoretical constructs.

● The first consists of the *spatial dynamics* of the organisation. Functional specialisation leads to interaction and interdependence between constituent locations (Pred, 1973; Dicken, 1986). Being able to work in different parts of an organisation allows the accumulation of experience and skill, qualities the employer may exploit by a further transfer to another job on site or to another location.
● The second is the idea of *organisation man* (Whyte, 1957; Jennings, 1971). This is related to the concept that the individual has career hopes and aspirations which can best be achieved by progress through the corporation. When progress seems thwarted, a move to another firm may occur via the ELM. Mobility within the organisation may be regarded as a tangible sign of career development (Jennings, 1971).
● Finally, putting these two constructs together, we arrive at the concept of an *organisational career*. This is a relatively standardised set of roles to be performed by an employee which interact with a relatively patterned flow of individuals through these roles. Organisational careers have a patterned sequence of positions related to work content and an ordered movement of individuals among these positions.

One example of such a sequence is Figure 4.2, which illustrates intergrade movements and promotion channels in British Telecom in 1980/1. The diagram demonstrates how different functions within an organisation develop their own career lines which may or may not interact with each other. Promotion occurs in a series of vertical steps. At each level new recruits come into the company from the ELM via ports of entry ('open entry'), others are promoted internally. At each level the number of internal promotions exceeds the open entry, but both diminish as the paths move towards the common senior salary structure. What is especially noticeable is the lack of movement between the career lines.

The organisational career may encompass a variety of work locations in a firm. A natural progression for an employee may therefore involve a sequence of geographical moves within the network of locations which comprise the firm's occupational space. It is clearly important to understand how ILMs work, and how organisational careers within them may lead to geographical relocation. The next section reviews some of the main characteristics of ILMs that bring about migration, and the processes which produce them.

Internal labour markets

Characteristics of internal labour markets

One of the consequences of the growth of the modern large corporation has been the evolution of the internal labour market of the firm. In their classic work, Doeringer and Piore (1971) argued that the ILM had its origins in the allocation of manual workers within a company. The major factors involved are threefold.

- The first is skill specificity, arising from the fact that companies may engage in types of production requiring either specific skills, perhaps relating to particular technologies, or specific tasks to be performed. It makes sense for a company with a labour force having these skills to seek to maintain them through an allocation and promotion system rather than risk losing them in the ELM and being forced to recruit and train new people.
- Secondly, and related to the need for specific skills, is the ability to train. It is sensible for companies to provide appropriate on-the-job training so that staff can learn the exact skills required.
- The third element is the evolution of customary procedures for allocating labour to tasks within the company and the provision of appropriate rewards, done through an unwritten set of rules largely based on past practice and precedent. The consequence of going to work for another company is that the worker loses his place in a hierarchy run largely on the grounds of seniority.

There are cost savings to the company in developing an ILM. Turnover costs are reduced, giving benefit to the company. The labour force gains through greater security. The rules of operation provide security and advancement, with workers accepting employment on the assumption that the rules will continue to operate in the future, thus helping to engender a mutual loyalty. There are also technical efficiencies in the recruitment, screening and training of labour.

Doeringer and Piore point to significant differences between manual and managerial ILMs. The latter tend to span more than one establishment, frequently including all plants in the corporation. Other contrasts with the ILM for manual workers include the stress placed upon ability in the rules determining promotions, often to the exclusion of seniority, and the provision of an implicit employment guarantee in many middle level managerial jobs. The last makes it easier to accept a geographical transfer since continuity of employment in the longer term is more readily assured, because doubts about moving to a new area and then being out of work are assuaged. The internal labour markets for clerical and technical workers also tend to be vertically structured with regard to entry jobs and vertical promotion, but mobility is much less likely to involve geographical transfer.

Operation of the ILM

It was possible in the OLMS to identify several key aspects of organisational structure which determine how an ILM works, and hence the extent to which it generates migration among the locations at which it operates. Of particular importance is its internal structure. Typically such an organisation consists of a group of partially independent companies or divisions, which may themselves be multi-locational. As will be seen below, the corporate ILM may not therefore function as an integrated whole, except at the highest management levels. These key aspects include the method and responsibility for vacancy filling, the organisation of the personnel function, the role of employee appraisal, the existence of a management development system (MDS), the relationship of the personnel function and the MDS to overall organisational control, the influence of powerful individual executives ('medieval barons'), and finally the degree of employee choice (Salt and Flowerdew, 1989).

The role and significance of each of these varies from company to company, determining the direction, volume and character of movement within the corporate ILM as a whole. In some organisations a unified structure exists. The consequence is that mobility may occur between any pair of sites, depending on vacancies or on the process of career development. The map of its ILM migration thus reflects the relationship between all the locations of the company. Single product employers, such as vehicle or computer manufacturers, normally come into this category. This is not to say that important channels of mobility do not evolve in such cases: head offices and research laboratories, for example, often become foci of movement.

In other organisations the ILM of the group as a whole may be sharply subdivided. Extreme cases occur where acquisition in conglomerate groups has created an organisation whose constituent parts are loosely linked. In these cases the ILM as a whole is likely to function only at the level of a common pensions system – and often not even then – or is restricted to the most senior management, which forms a group resource. In such circumstances little mobility occurs across constituent company boundaries within the group. From this extreme to the point at which the divisional organisation forms a totally integrated ILM network, an increasing amount of cross division movement may occur, though its detailed geographical pattern will reflect the working of the key variables described above. This will now be demonstrated from a series of case examples.

Migration and the internal structure of the organisation

The complex relationships between the internal structure of an employing organisation and migration within its ILM can be illustrated by studying specific cases, taken from a broad spectrum of the economy. In what follows, seven organisations are considered: an electronics manufacturer; a traditional 'metal bashing' engineering company; a food/chemicals producer; a brewery; two retail chains; and a bank. They are used to illustrate two points in particular: the varying degrees of self-containment, related to the internal structure of the organisation, and the association of self-containment with promotion. The role of management career development will be seen to be crucial.

Case studies

In the electronics group, with a total employment of 12,000, of whom 2,300 were in occupations regarded by the organisation as potentially mobile (mostly management, professional and senior technical grades), there was a strong degree of decentralisation into eighteen constituent manufacturing companies. The philosophy of the group was to develop the autonomy of these companies, promoting staff from within them wherever possible, since company morale and ethos were thought to require the involvement and commitment of employees with their particular company. However, two-thirds of the 41 relocations in an 18-month period during 1981-2 occurred between the companies. This resulted from a career development system closely tied in with the development of the group and the constant spawning and expansion of new companies. The pattern was for a new product to be developed in a laboratory and a tiny nucleus of people then to be established in a different location further to develop, produce and market it. The nucleus may have included people from a number of existing locations and companies within the group.

The more traditional engineering group had 20,000 employees, 1,300 of whom were potentially mobile, in 60 companies divided into eleven product divisions. Of 89 moves in two years, 47 were within the same company, 28 between companies, and the rest were moves from the head office. Only top management and graduates in their first year of employment were centrally administered, responsibility for filling other vacancies being in the hands of the individual company managing directors. The normal pattern was to look first at candidates within the constituent company, and only if there was no-one suitable was the group personnel department consulted about possible candidates from elsewhere in the group. The result was a preponderance of mobility within rather than across company boundaries.

The food and chemicals organisation had 70,000 employees in 34 companies administered in thirteen product divisions. Of 380 moves in 1981-2, 80 per cent were within the divisions, although the degree of divisional self-containment ranged from 42 to 100 per cent. Although each company had its own personnel department, there was a very strong management development system at group level, which co-ordinated all managerial and professional staff moves. The high degree of self-containment in mobility stemmed from product specialisation within the divisions rather than from company autonomy.

The brewery combined production and distribution. The 26,000 employees, 1,500 in potentially mobile occupations, were divided into 16 divisions and 244 moves occurred over two years. For the most part there was not particular product specialisation that required specific skills, so mobility across the group as a whole was feasible. In fact most posts were advertised throughout the group, so information on vacancies elsewhere was relatively freely available. Group personnel tended to act in an advisory rather than an executive capacity so there was no central direction. In these circumstances it is not surprising that a majority of the moves – 57 per cent – involved a divisional change. This process was aided by a slimming down in the group which led to the transference of staff surplus in some divisions to vacancies in others.

The bank employed 45,000 people in over 2,000 branches, and in 1980 had 1,073 transfers of over 20 miles between work locations. There was a strong element of decentralisation into 19 regions, and this was reflected in the organisation of staffing. With the exception of a small group of managerial high fliers, career development was largely in the hands of regional staff managers. In consequence, mobility for managerial employees in the early career stages tended to be intra-regional. Unlike most other organisations banks tend to have some geographical mobility at sub-managerial levels. Part of this is to allow staff to gain experience in different aspects of retail banking. Again the consequence was fairly local movement within the region. A substantial element, however, consisted of female employees who used the widespread branch network to change their employment location in association with the relocations being experienced by husbands or (in the case of young female staff) parents. In these cases inter-regional movement ensued, since it was the bank's policy to accommodate such moves when possible. The overall result was a complex map of migration in which about two-thirds of all moves crossed a regional boundary.

The two retail organisations had contrasting divisional structures. One was a chain of newsagents with a regional structure; the other, a clothing chain, divided into five brand-name divisions. The first employed 4,000 people and had 193 relocations in two years. The annual rate of mobility among those potentially mobile was very high, about 25 per cent. This resulted from rapid expansion which meant that many trainee managers were on the move and also more experienced staff were being relocated to open up new branches. As a result, 89 per cent of transferees were aged under 30. The group was divided into 17 regional divisions, but only 23 per cent of moves occurred within the regions so there was a low degree of divisional self-containment. The career development system in operation emphasised the virtues of mobility for managers, particularly to avoid staleness (and thus enhance shop profitability) but also to encourage employees who saw better career prospects through mobility from shop into divisional management. The vacancy filling process brought in the central personnel department at an early phase. Appraisal records of managers were held at group level, so the information on all possible candidates across divisions could be drawn on. Hence, although it was policy to look first at other people in the division where the vacancy occurred, it was easy to widen the search to potential candidates from the rest of the group.

The clothing chain had 6,000 employees, 1,000 of whom were in the potentially mobile category, in five brand divisions. In one year 98 relocations occurred, but there were no moves across divisional boundaries. Hence the system was completely self-contained at divisional brand level. Furthermore, annual rates of mobility varied enormously between divisions, ranging from 2.4 to 44.5 per cent. This situation arose mainly because the company went through a period of major restructuring during the 1970s. This involved losing some of the original core business while at the same time expanding in new areas and making acquisitions. Hence, although there were elements of common policy making, including recruitment and management training, strong divisional identity was maintained.

Smoothing the path

In addition to having a controlling interest in corporate relocation, employers have adopted a range of policies designed to smooth the paths of those they wish to move. Whether these provide a complete magic carpet is debatable; what is certain is that transferees have a tremendous advantage over those whose migration has to be funded entirely from their own resources. Of critical importance are the level and range of relocation allowances.

Relocation allowances

The detailed package provided for a relocating employee varies with the company. In some the scale and nature of assistance is related to seniority, on a 'to them that hath' basis. In others the package is broadly the same for all employees, although where allowances are a percentage of salary this naturally favours the better-paid. Housing assistance normally helps owner occupiers more than renters. Often a fillip to greater equality in the package results from the need to move the whole staff of an office or unit of production. In these cases staff association or trade union involvement often ensures the same conditions for all who are asked to relocate.

One consequence of the more formal role of relocation in career development has been a tendency in recent years for a convergence in the scale and nature of aid available when different corporate packages are compared. This process has been aided by the greater amount of information becoming available through management consultancy firms and relocation agencies. Companies are increasingly finding the need to be aware of the going market rate in assistance packages. The establishment by the Confederation of British Industry of an Employee Relocation Council in 1986 was a response to this need, and its quarterly journal, *Relocation News*, provides much information on current levels of assistance.

In the typical relocation package today the actual expenses of agents' fees, legal costs, and survey fees would be reimbursed. Full removal costs are usually paid plus, in many cases, the expense of storing and insuring furniture. Two or three days leave at the time of removal would not be exceptional, while travel and subsistence costs at time of removal would also be paid. Housing assistance is a major element in today's package. Bridging loans are common, usually with time limits set at three or six months. The costs of providing temporary accommodation in the new location would be covered. This might take the form of hotel or rented accommodation, either for the transferee alone while waiting for the old home to be sold and the family to move to the new house and location, or for the whole family during any hiatus. House-hunting costs for accompanying spouses and children are now commonly paid. To bridge the gap between low and high cost housing areas some form of excess rent allowance is usual. Finally, an increasing number of companies pay a disturbance allowance, in the form of a lump sum compensation for the upheaval of moving and to pay for such costs as new carpets, curtains and school uniforms.

Such a scheme of housing assistance is designed to help the owner occupier rather than the renter. The rationale behind this is that it is the former who is most likely to be required to move, since most managers and professionals own their own houses. For those who rent, not only is the scale of assistance lower (and they cannot pocket the capital gain released when moving from a higher to a lower cost area), but there is less practical help in finding new accommodation. This system clearly militates against the recruitment by southern employers of those skilled workers from the north who rent their accommodation. In order to counter this arthritic effect the CBI began a pilot project in East Anglia in 1988 to help put companies relocating employees, especially skilled ones from the north, in touch with housing associations. In return for nomination rights in housing association properties, the employer is expected to provide funds or land which could be developed for housing. At the time of writing the results of this project are not available, but it represents another element in the relocation package, as well as extending assistance into a new area.

Given the wide range of costs covered, and the variation geographically and in terms of seniority, it is not surprising that the cost of moving one individual can differ greatly from that of moving another. One survey estimated that the annual cost of relocation to British industry was around £250 million per annum, at an average cost of £10,000 per move, but that the cost of each relocation ranged from £1,000 to £23,000, depending on grade, marital status and geographical location (CBI, 1986: pp. 2–4). These figures broadly concur with those reported in the early 1980s, when an average of £10,000 and a median of £7,000 were recorded (Salt, 1986). This coincidence may be explained in part by the absence of any trend in the cost of moving house between 1983 and 1987 which, on a £100,000 house, remained static at £2,750, the result of rises in survey and removal costs being counteracted by falls in agents' and solicitors' fees (Woolwich Building Society, 1988).

The main variable element in the relocation package is the disturbance allowance. In 1988 lump sum examples included a straight five weeks salary, £700 plus 10 per cent of salary, £2,770 plus a £1,810 removal allowance, and £2,000 or 6 per cent of the new house price, whichever was the less. A typical excess rent allowance payment would be £585 per annum for 5 years, reducing each year for the next four years (Incomes Data Services, 1987). In most cases a person subsequently relocating away from a high cost to a low cost housing area would be able to pocket the fruits of capital gain made possible by the earlier assistance when moving up the house price gradient.

Despite these large sums of money and the frequency of relocation, one company in five does not know the real cost of relocating staff. Indeed, there seems to be a tendency to underestimate, only one company in three accepting the cost as over £6,000 (Merrill Lynch, 1986). In contrast, when Rank Xerox engaged in a group move in 1985 they found the costs ranged from £11,700 to £15,000, the sums including expenses, house price guarantee, disturbance allowance and bridging loan (CBI, 1986: pp. 2–3).

Relocation agencies

A characteristic of corporate transfer in recent years has been the increasing use of relocation agencies and the growing comprehensiveness of the service they offer. Successive annual surveys by one major agency confirm the former point: 17 per cent of 300 firms interviewed used relocation agencies according to a survey in 1986 (Merrill Lynch, 1986). The same survey found that the main reason why companies used these agencies was to reduce stress for those transferred and increase their productive time at work.

Recently relocation agencies have broadened the scope of their services. Black Horse Relocation introduced an education counselling service in 1988; for a fee of £500 lists of schools and their prospectuses in destination areas can be provided, interviews with potential head teachers arranged and counselling of individual children through structured interviews organised (CBI, 1988). The most recent extension of relocation services is the 'consortium service'. One such scheme involves twenty companies, each of which specialises in some aspect of relocation. The aim is to provide a service from a single source which addresses all questions and provides all answers to relocation-related problems. The service includes strategic analysis, location and site search, facility management, personnel policies, communications programmes, and education, redundancy, severance and resettlement counselling.

Sources of friction

Resistance to location

Despite the upheaval caused to family life, resistance to relocation is still relatively low. Basically, a manager knows that his career progression may depend upon taking advantage of whatever opportunities are presented, especially if the invitation to go is accompanied by a look at the management succession plan. There is some evidence, though, that resistance is increasing – 14 per cent of employers experienced this trend according to one survey (Merrill Lynch, 1986). The main reasons quoted were disruption to family life and the different costs of living across the country. In order to maintain the motivation of staff who are confronted with a move, some employers are now paying much more attention to social issues, including the integration of staff into the local community and the solution of educational problems.

It is in the best interests of firms to counter resistance to relocation. It has been estimated that the cost to the employer of a refusal to move is of the order of £3,000–£4,000, incurred in executive time searching for a replacement, recruitment and advertising, not having the right person in the job at the right time and extra administration (PHH Homequity, 1987).

It is important for companies to foster a corporate culture in which mobility is taken as a usual and expected requirement of progression within the career structure. When the workers involved are in their late twenties acceptance of mobility is highest and resistance least; and the organisations likely to have least problems in moving employees around the country are those which get them mobile early in their careers. Conversely, those organisations which have difficulty in persuading staff to go are those which allow managers to develop their early careers *in situ*, without ever warning them of the possibility of movement in the future (Atkinson, 1987).

The working wife

Because the vast majority of those relocated are men, the problem of the spouse's career becomes, by definition, that of the working wife. As the role of married women in the workforce has grown, along with the move towards equal opportunities, the corporate wife has ceased to play the passive role so much assumed of her in the past. Increasingly, the working wife wants recognition as a dual-career partner, and expects support in maintaining the continuity of her career. Some American organisations have responded by offering 'spouse employment assistance', which means helping the wife find employment in the new location as part of standard corporate policy (Greenbury, 1988). This help takes a number of forms, including the provision of appropriate training programmes where new skills are required, career counselling and skills analysis. The aim is to develop a 'portable career' for spouses. However, it seems the first problem is for many employers to recognise that a problem exists. The majority of employers still do not provide help for a relocating spouse (Merrill Lynch, 1986).

Taxation

One persistent irritation for companies wishing to compensate employees for relocation is that the Inland Revenue insists that financial aid above a certain figure is taxable. The situation is made more complex in that a degree of independence has been given to local tax officers in agreeing tax-free levels. In effect, however, most local tax inspectors follow civil service relocation guidelines, and tax excesses beyond them. This rule has hit disturbance allowances, most of which are as much sweeteners as payments for actual costs incurred. Changes announced in 1987 raised the general amount that was tax free to £17,000, depending on circumstances, the aim being to take account of the costs of moving someone to higher cost housing areas.

Conclusion

There is no doubt that geographical mobility within corporate ILMs is a major element in the migration exchanges that occur between local labour markets in the UK and elsewhere. However, our knowledge of how ILMs work geographically is weak and will only be strengthened by detailed studies of large employers.

Geographical patterns of labour mobility that may only be partly explained by traditional formulations, such as gravity or area differentials models, can often be seen as a response to the location of employment nodes in large corporations. It follows that explanation of the patterns necessitates

68

an understanding of the processes by which employers allocate their labour force. The case examples discussed above demonstrate the effectiveness of such an approach.

Movers in ILMs may not completely escape the traumas involved in labour migration. The psychological costs of leaving a home, environment and friends can never be compensated for easily. Nevertheless, the path is smoothed for many, and the smoothing process has become institutionalised. Corporate movers have clear advantages over those who receive less assistance, particularly the low-skilled and unemployed discussed in Chapter 11.

It follows too that any government labour migration policy must take into account the growing dichotomy between a highly mobile elite, for whom geographical relocation is a normal part of career development, and others, whose mobility is less sought after by employers and is not financed by them. Migrants continue to move from positions of strength, the sources of which are increasingly located in corporate manpower planning.

References

Appleyard, R. T. (1987) 'Australia 1986' *Annual Report of the SOPEMI Correspondent*. Paris: Organisation for Economic Cooperation and Development.

Atkinson, J. (1987) 'Relocating managers and professional staff'. *IMS Report N. 39*. Institute of Manpower Studies, University of Sussex.

Confederation of British Industry (1986) 'Group moves within Britain'. Report in *Relocation News*, 1, 2-3.

Confederation of British Industry (1988) 'Helping to overcome the house price divide'. *Relocation News*, 5, 7-8.

Confederation of British Industry (1987) 'Relocation and tax - recent developments'. *Relocation News*, 4, 1.

Dicken, P. (1986) *Global Shift*. London: Harper and Row.

Doeringer, P. B. and Piore, M. J. (1971) *Internal Labour Markets and Manpower Analysis*. Lexington: D.C. Heath.

Greenbury, L. (1988) 'Relocating the working wife'. *Relocation News*, 5, 3-5.

Incomes Data Services (1987) 'Relocation' *Study 399*. London: Incomes Data Services Ltd.

Jennings, E. E. (1967) *The Mobile Manager*. Ann Arbor: University of Michigan.

Johnson, J. H., Salt, J. and Wood, P. A. (1974) *Housing and the Migration of Labour in England and Wales*. Farnborough: Saxon House.

Johnson, J. H. and Salt, J. (1980) 'Employment transfer policies in Great Britain'. *The Three Banks Review*, 126, 18-39.

McKay, J. and Whitelaw, J. S. (1977a) 'The role of large private and government organisations in generating flows of inter-regional migrants: the case of Australia'. *Economic Geography*, 53, 28-44.

McKay, J. and Whitelaw, J. S. (1977b) 'The structure of job-providing organisations, and the patterns of linkages in the Australian urban system'.

Paper presented to the Institute of Australian Geographers, Annual Conference, Townsville.

Merrill Lynch Ltd. (1986) *Fourth Annual Study of Employee Relocation Policies among UK Companies*. London: Merrill Lynch Relocation Management International.

PHH Homequity Ltd. (1987) *Report on a Study on Employee Mobility*. Swindon: PHH Homequity Ltd.

Pred, A. R. (1973) 'The growth and development of cities in advanced economies'. *Systems of Cities and Information Flows*, Lund Studies in Geography, Series B, No. 38, 9–82.

Salt, J. and Flowerdew, R. (1989) 'Socio-economic selectivity in labour migration' in Stillwell, J. and Schelten, H. (eds), *Contemporary Research in Population Geography. A Comparison of the United Kingdom and The Netherlands*. Dordrecht: Kluwer Academic Publishers.

Salt, J. (1984) 'Labour migration within multi-locational organisations in Britain'. Economic and Social Research Council, *End of Grant Report*, F/00/23/0027, London.

Salt, J. (1987) 'Contemporary trends in international migration study'. *International Migration*, **25**, 241–51.

Salt, J. (1986) 'International migration: a spatial theoretical approach' in Pacione, M. (ed) *Population Geography: Progress and Prospect*. Beckenham: Croom Helm.

Whyte, W. H. (1957) *The Organisation Man*. London: Cape.

Woolwich Building Society (1988) *Cost of Moving Survey*. London.

CHAPTER 5

Regional Migration and Its Inter-relationship with the Journey to Work in The Netherlands

P. K. Doorn and A. van Rietbergen

Introduction

This chapter focuses especially on the changing distribution of the working population and employment, and the effects of the mobility of job-providing institutions on the behaviour of their employees. In fact, firms, like people, are mobile. New firms open their gates, existing ones expand or contract, seek new locations for their activities, or close down.

In The Netherlands there has been an aggregate shift of employment from city centres to newly developing locations on the urban fringe. Different rates in the deconcentration of the residential population and employment have resulted in a huge increase of commuting across municipal borders. In 1985 more than half of the labour-force was working outside its own municipality. Most studies that have been carried out in The Netherlands on the effects of relocating institutions were oriented towards the home/work distance and modal split. It has often been found that relocations away from large concentrations of population have resulted in an increase of commuter traffic. Commuting distances have tended to increase, and the use of the car as a means of transport has grown. This is caused by the fact that the new employment centres were often separated spatially from both existing residential areas and new housing locations. Moreover, such locations were usually difficult to reach by public transport (Nozeman, 1986).

The interrelation between living and working is, however, far more complex than the simple arithmetic of home/work distance and modal split before and after relocation. Hanemaayer *et al.* (1981) point out that the consequences of relocation depend on the type of employees, the type of new location, and the time interval over which changes are studied. The structure and functioning of the internal labour market is also of importance for the mobility behaviour shown by the personnel in response to a relocation of the organisation they work for. Moreover, the distance of the relocation in combination with the characteristics of a housing market will affect the decision whether or not to move to the new work place. If the distance is relatively short and it is difficult to obtain a house at the new location (or to get rid of the old house), migration is unlikely. Change in location of the workplace and other factors become increasingly important in explaining residential moves over a distance of more than 40 kilometres. Although there is no clear break in the reasons for mobility, a distinction can be made between work motivations for longer distances, and life-cycle and housing market motivations for shorter distances (Rima and v. Wissen, 1987). Mobility research in general is hindered by the empirical difficulty of disentangling the 'autonomous' mobility processes from the ones that directly originate from the relocation of the job-providing organisation.

Last but not least, the above-mentioned factors are likely to work out differently for contrasting individuals or groups of employees. The reaction pattern of employees to the relocation of their firms has been shown to vary in relation to their sex, age, and social status (Maas-Droogleever Fortuyn and v. Engelsdorp-Gastelaars, 1985; Freijsen et al., 1979).

In a study of the effects of relocating offices, Van Heelsbergen made a distinction between the mobility behaviour of people who started working (participation mobility), those who came from other firms, and those who stayed with the office. He demonstrated that the socio-economic and demographic characteristics of these three groups differed considerably. By using abbreviations of his variables he named his groups SODECs (Van Heelsbergen, 1981). We used this approach in a more general way with different data sets.

In this chapter we will present a general introduction on shifts in population and employment within the Dutch urban system and give some results of case studies of relocating employment institutions. We will focus especially on the mobility effects from the relocation of a hospital in the province of Utrecht.

The changing distribution of population and employment

Since the Second World War, there have been considerable shifts in the urbanisation of the Dutch municipalities. Comparing cross-sectional data for 1947, 1956, 1960 and 1971, it is apparent that the number of rural municipalities has strongly decreased, whereas the number of urbanised rural municipalities has considerably increased, and the number of urban municipalities grew slightly. Between 1947 and 1971 the total population of The Netherlands grew from less than 10 to over 13 million. In relative terms this meant that the rural population declined from nearly 30 per cent to just over 10 per cent, while the urban population remained pratically stable around 55 per cent and the intermediate groups more than doubled from 16 to 34 per cent. Since 1971 the total population has grown from 13 to 14.5 million.

Shifts in the distribution of the employed population within the urban system are mainly caused by internal migration and the selectivity of this process. Those in the 20–30 year age group were both most inclined to migrate and most fertile, so regions or urban categories receiving a net-inflow of migrants generally saw their birth-rates go up, while the reverse was the case in areas or settlements losing population. The propensity to migrate has considerably changed over the last fifteen years. Total internal migration has steadily risen during the sixties from about half a million to over 700,000 in the early seventies. After 1973/74 the tide turned and migration began to decrease. At the end of the decade, the number of internal migrants amounted to less than 550,000, at which level it seems to have stabilised. In relative terms, the migration rate reached a peak of 5.3 per cent in 1973 and dropped to 3.8 per cent in 1979. Since then, it has been less than 4 per cent of the population (Doorn, 1986).

The majority of the moves took place over relative short distances and could be characterised as suburbanisation. The urbanised rural municipalities (the commuter municipalities) grew very fast in this period, at the expense of bigger urban areas. For instance, the three largest cities (Amsterdam, The Hague and Rotterdam) lost more than 500,000 inhabitants in a period when the total Dutch population grew by 12 per cent (Buitendijk, 1987). As previously stated, the trend was accentuated by the age specificity of the migrants. The suburbanisation of people has now almost finished, but the outward shift of employment from the cities is still gaining in importance. Small municipalities near highways in 'The Randstad' are booming. Examples are the spectacular growth in the Amsterdam-South East area (for five years a deteriorating area), The Haarlemmermeer (a municipality near Schiphol airport), Nieuwegein and Houten (near Utrecht), and Zoetermeer (near The Hague).

The deconcentration of employment resulted again in an increasing average distance between residential areas and working areas in 'The Randstad'. For instance, in the period 1971–1981 the average distance between place of residence and employment increased from 0.2 kilometres in the Utrecht area to 1.4 kilometres in the agglomeration of Amsterdam (Beumer et al., 1983). This deconcentration of employment resulted again in a huge increase of commuting across municipal borders. The increase in commuting was even larger than the net effect of the diverging suburban-isation rates of residence and employment because of the selectivity in both processes. The figures are rather impressive. The number of people that worked outside their residential municipality increased from 27 per cent in 1960 to 52 per cent in 1985, so there are now more people working outside than inside their own municipality. This means that more than 3 million people each day have to cross a municipal border to reach their work. It is hardly surprising that this has resulted in congestion on the roads in 'The Randstad'. In fact, solving these problems is one of the main goals of the

Dutch central government. One calculation has already suggested that congestion problems cost Dutch society approximately 700 million guilders per year (McKinsey, 1986). We will now study the selectivity of mobility in more detail in the Utrecht urban area.

Mobility effect of a hospital relocation to Nieuwegein

Mobility has been studied using three data-sets. In the first place Doorn re-analysed data gathered by Van Heelsbergen. The data-set contained 857 completed and returned interviews from nineteen firms which had recently been resettled from The Hague to Zoetermeer (Doorn, 1985). The second data-set was the complete Labour-Force Sample of the Netherlands of 1981. This is a sample of dwellings comprising 170,000 records and a sample fraction of 2.5 per cent. We will use some of the outcomes of these earlier studies but focus in particular on the relocation of a hospital in the centre of The Netherlands. The hospital shifted from the old city of Utrecht to the new town of Nieuwegein, some 10 km to the south of the city. Despite the short distance of the move, it was expected to have a considerable effect within the context and small scale of The Netherlands (v. Rietbergen, 1987).

The municipality of Nieuwegein was created in 1971 by a fusion of the former municipalities of Jutphaas and Vreeswijk. The number of inhabitants has grown rapidly in the past decades, from about 13,000 in 1971, to 40,000 at the beginning of this decade, and to nearly 60,000 today. A large planned housing development was undertaken to absorb the overspill of the suburbanising population of the city of Utrecht. The housing stock increased by about 7,000 dwellings in the 1980s to over 21,000 houses in 1987. This new centre did attract many migrants from Utrecht, although new inhabitants from elsewhere also settled in Nieuwegein (Figure 5.1). In the past few years the proportion of migrants from the city of Utrecht has decreased while the proportion of migrants from elsewhere has grown. In 1980 about a quarter of the 13,000 out-migrants from the city resettled in Nieuwegein, while in 1985 a mere 13 per cent of the 10,500 out-migrants from Utrecht went to this growing town. The total number of people migrating to Nieuwegein has also fallen recently.

Employment remained concentrated in the central cities much longer than population. In 1980 the labour force of Nieuwegein amounted to 13,400 people, while there was local employment for only 7,500 people. Just before the move of the St Antonius Hospital, these numbers amounted to 18,700 and 9,200 respectively (Walen and Nozeman, 1985). The hospital, which provided nearly 2,000 jobs, would contribute substantially to employment in Nieuwegein.

The management of the St Antonius Hospital decided by the end of 1975 that it was more efficient to relocate the hospital in Nieuwegein than to modernise the old building in order to meet the standards of today. The hospital started to leave Utrecht in October 1983. The case was the subject of an earlier piece of research just after the relocation was completed in May

74

Figure 5.1 Migration to Nieuwegein according to origin, 1980–1985

Origin	1980		1982		1984		1985	
	number	%	number	%	number	%	number	%
City of Utrecht	3371	58.3	3408	51.9	1349	45.3	1376	42.3
Province of Utrecht*	491	8.5	925	14.1	447	15.0	442	13.6
Other provinces	1918	33.2	2229	34.0	1183	39.7	1435	44.1
Total	5780	100	6562	100	2979	100	3253	100

*Excluding the city of Utrecht
Source: Based on municipal data

1984 (Walen and Nozeman, 1985), and our survey at the end of 1986 would allow us to make some comparisons over time.

Walen and Nozeman presented the relocation of the hospital as a classic example of the more general trend towards relocating non-profitmaking institutions from central cities to suburban locations. They paid special attention to how these relocations fitted in with several aims of governmental spatial policy making. They gave attention to the mobility effects for both the employees of the hospital and its visitors. In their sample of 182 employees, 84 per cent had moved house in the period 1976–1984. Only a quarter of the movers had moved from elsewhere to Nieuwegein. A small minority mentioned the relocation of the hospital as the main motive for their move.

The relocation of the hospital brought about a small increase in the average home/work travelling distance for the employees, from 10.5 to 12.1 km. Car use increased from 38 per cent before to 46 per cent after the relocation, and the average travel time rose slightly from 26 to 29 minutes. The relatively small effect of the hospital relocation on decisions to move was an interim conclusion that could be used as a starting point for further research. Moreover, Walen and Nozeman expected that the effects of the relocation would become more influential after some years. The time and cost involved in finding a new house impose a barrier against a swift adaptation of the residential location to a change in work location. In a more general study, this has also been demonstrated in the case of Nieuwegein. Whereas only some 15 per cent of the employees of job-providing organisations that had recently relocated to Nieuwegein appeared to live there, this percentage for institutions which had been established in the town for some time was nearly 75 per cent (ETI, 1981).

Our research consisted of two parts. The purpose of the first part was to examine the effects of the relocation on the mobility behaviour of distinct groups of employees. The second part was used to place these reactions in a longitudinal framework of previous changes of home and work locations (for more details about this research see Doorn and v. Rietbergen, 1989). The first part consisted of a questionnaire survey of all 1,826 employees of the hospital. Because the response rate was rather low (36%), as is usual in postal surveys, we checked for a possible bias by comparing the survey data with figures provided by the hospital itself. For most control variables the sample did not seem to be seriously biased, though some misrepresentations of certain occupational groups appeared to exist (civil and technical personnel under-represented, medical staff and paramedical professions slightly over-represented). In order to correct for this bias the data were weighted.

Of the personnnel interviewed in our survey in 1986, 37 per cent lived in Nieuwegein, against 16 per cent in 1980 (cf. Walen and Nozeman: 18 per cent in February 1983, just before the relocation, and 26 per cent a year after the relocation in May 1984). In the period 1980–1986 54 per cent of the employees moved house (note that the crude mobility rate is much lower than in the research by Walen and Nozeman). However, a larger proportion than before of the movers had Nieuwegein as a destination (31%). The most important place of origin of these movers was, not surprisingly, the city of Utrecht, which generally saw a decrease in its share of hospital employee residences.

In general, the labour force of the hospital is relatively young and well educated, and there are many people working part-time. Moreover, contrary to most sectors of the economy, the majority of the personnel is female (72%). The large number of households with two or more working people is also remarkable (63%). The staffing of the hospital in Nieuwegein is therefore clearly very different from the composition of the personnel in our research in the office strip in Zoetermeer.

Just as in the Zoetermeer research and the research on the Labour Force Sample, we used a cluster technique to group the data. The purpose of this analysis was to find a representation of a limited number of groups with more or less homogeneous socio-economical and demographic characteristics, whose mobility behaviour could subsequently be studied. The variables used in this analysis were not strictly the same as in earlier research, though they are roughly comparable. Income data were not collected in the Nieuwegein case. On the other hand, information was available on the number of working people in the household, which is directly related to the household income. Together with educational attainment, occupational type and number of working hours, this variable was used as an indicator of socio-economic status.

With regard to demographic and household characteristics, marital status and having children at home were taken as indicators. Additional information was available on the composition of the household and whether the respondent was the main breadwinner or not, but these variables were not

---

Figure 5.2 Summarised description of Nieuwegein SODECs:

SODEC 1: Young working people living with their parents
SODEC 2: Unattached people
SODEC 3: Full-time working partners without children
SODEC 4: Part-time working partners with children
SODEC 5: Middle aged unskilled and semi-skilled personnel
SODEC 6: Medical staff and assistant doctors

included in the cluster analysis because of the overlap with the previous two. As in other researches, age and sex were the other demographic indicators.

A summary of the SODEC categorisation in Nieuwegein is presented in Figure 5.2, while a much more extensive description is presented in Figure 5.3.

- The first SODEC is formed by a small group of young people who are still living with their parents. Characteristically, they are working part-time. Because of the size of this group and because it must be expected that decisions to move are primarily made by the parents, the group will not be used in all comparisons.
- SODECs 2 and 3 are also relatively young (on average under thirty years old), but their household situations are rather different. SODEC 2 mainly consists of women living alone. The majority of them have had a higher vocational education. Typically, they are employed full-time as staff nurses or in paramedical occupations. SODEC 3 also consists largely of women, but in contrast to the previous group they are living with partners who are the main breadwinners. They do not have children and most of them are employed full-time as nurses, although a considerable proportion have not yet finished their training. SODEC 3 is the largest group, comprising almost one-third of the sample.
- SODEC 4 is almost entirely composed of women working part-time, most of whom are married and have children living at home. On average there are two working persons in the household here, of which SODEC 4 are secondary income earners. Their age is on average in the late thirties.
- SODEC 5 is the oldest group (on average 45 years); it is predominantly male, and the educational level is relatively low. More than half of these employees work in civil and technical occupations. Most of them are heads of households who work full-time.
- SODEC 6 consists largely of male members of the medical and paramedical staff. They are highly skilled and work a full working week or even more. Most of them are heads of households and more than 70 per cent have children.

In some respects, the SODECs of Nieuwegein and those of earlier research display similarities, but as expected there are differences as well. For instance, the office executives in Zoetermeer (SODEC 1) have characteristics comparable to those of the hospital staff in Nieuwegein (SODEC 6). And although in Nieuwegein four 'female' groups are identified as opposed to two in Zoetermeer, household conditions again appear to play an important role in their subdivision. Moreover, the two 'male' SODECs in Nieuwegein differ primarily with respect to socio-economic criteria. On the other hand, the dividing lines among the SODECs in both regional and sectoral submarkets obviously do not run exactly parallel. In particular, the discriminating power of the gender criterion seems to be less strong in Nieuwegein, where such a large proportion of the personnel are female.

Figure 5.3 Percentage frequencies of variables in Nieuwegein SODECs

Variable	SODEC 1 Category	(2.2%) Pct	SODEC 2 Category	(22.1%) Pct	SODEC 3 Category	(32.6%) Pct
Working hours	Mean	15.5	Mean	36.4	Mean	36.3
Occupational	Civil/techn	54.9	Staff nurse	52.5	Stud nurse	41.3
Type	Stud nurse	18.9	Paramedic	25.2	Staff nurse	22.1
	Other	13.5				
Sex	Female	63.4	Female	90.0	Female	78.8
Age	Mean	19.0	Mean	29.5	Mean	27.0
Education	Primary	36.6	Higher voc	51.0	Higher voc	40.3
	Secondary	63.4	Secondary	21.8	Secondary	36.5
			Primary	11.8	Primary	13.7
Household situation	Fam w chld	100.0	Unattached	75.8	Fam w/o chld	76.7
					Fam w chld	14.9
Main breadwin	No	100.0	Yes	94.9	No	87.1
Marital status	Unmarried	100.0	Unmarried	90.3	Married	79.7
Children	No	100.0	No	95.2	No	97.0
Empl persons	Mean	4.2	Mean	1.0	Mean	2.1

Variable	SODEC 4 Category	(18.0%) Pct	SODEC 5 Category	(13.8%) Pct	SODEC 6 Category	(11.3%) Pct
Working hours	Mean	16.2	Mean	36.5	Mean	43.9
Occupational	Staff nurse	36.6	Civil/techn	55.7	Med staff	46.0
Type	Civil/techn	18.1	Admin/autom	20.0	Paramedic	22.1
	Admin/autom	13.5	Paramedic	10.2	Civil/techn	10.9
Sex	Female	97.1	Male	61.6	Male	93.6
Age	Mean	37.2	Mean	44.5	Mean	39.8
Education	Primary	34.4	Primary	42.0	Academic	51.7
	Higher voc	31.0	Secondary	36.4	Higher voc	44.0
	Secondary	16.6				
Household situation	Fam w chld	85.7	Fam w chld	49.6	Fam w chld	68.3
			Unattached	29.6	Fam w/o chld	18.9
			Fam w/o chld	13.1		
Main breadwin	No	96.7	Yes	18.1	Yes	95.5
Marital status	Married	94.8	Married	62.7	Married	87.2
Children	Yes	87.1	Yes	56.5	Yes	72.0
Empl Persons	Mean	2.0	Mean	1.4	Mean	1.5

Note: number of working hours, age and number of employed persons in household are averages, not percentages.

Mobility profiles of Nieuwegein SODECs

The different SODEC categories showed considerable variations in their response to the relocation of the hospital, although there was a prevalent tendency among all groups of employees to follow their employer and to

78

move to Nieuwegein. Here we will examine the reactions of the personnel with respect to residential and labour mobility. It must be noted that the changes in travelling behaviour (modal split) did not display significant patterns, especially when compared to the data presented by Walen and Nozeman.

Residential mobility

The proportion of the employees living in Nieuwegein has risen over time for all groups, though in varying degrees. The general growth of Nieuwegein was, of course, greatly influenced by the fact that many newly-built houses of a relatively high quality became available, whereas in Utrecht there was a housing shortage. So the planned housing supply of Nieuwegein influenced demand to a large extent. Still, the life-style groups all appeared to have a rather well defined mobility profile. The motives for residential mobility also varied for different groups.

Considerable differences existed among the SODECs with respect to the rates of residential mobility between 1980 and 1986. While 60 per cent of the total sample moved to another house in this period, the percentage of movers was considerably below average in SODECs 1, 4, 5 and 6, and above average in SODECs 2 and 3. These differences are partly related to the socio-demographic and economic characteristics of the groups, but also to their existing spatial distribution (see maps in Figure 5.4 and 5.5).

Figure 5.4 Residential distribution of Nieuwegein SODECs after hospital relocation (1986)

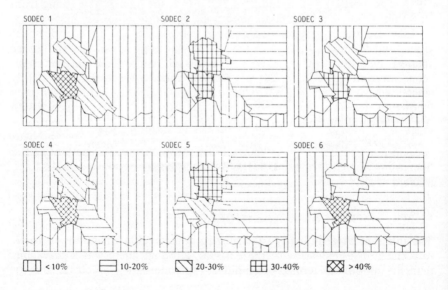

Figure 5.5 Residential relocation of Nieuwegein SODECs, 1980–1986

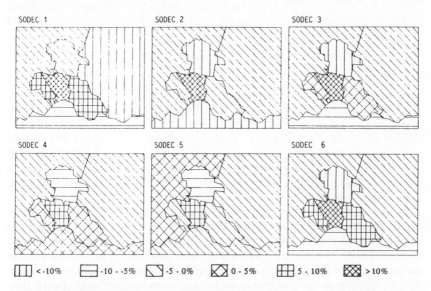

▥ < -10%	▤ -10 - -5%	◩ -5 - 0%	◪ 0 - 5%	▦ 5 - 10%	▨ > 10%

Of the employees living in and moving to Nieuwegein, SODEC 4 takes an outstanding position. In 1980, well before the relocation of the hospital, 40 per cent of the present-day part-time workers were already living in Nieuwegein, which is a much higher proportion than is found in any of the other groups, around 20 per cent of whom lived there at that time. It is also noteworthy that the suburbanisation of all groups had begun even before 1983. The increase was steepest for SODEC 2, the unattached, rising from less than 15 per cent in 1980 to almost 40 per cent in 1986 (Figure 5.6).

Likewise, the proportion of all groups living in Utrecht has dropped over time, and for SODECs 3, 4, 5 and 6 this was again already found in the period 1980-1983. Only SODEC 2 displayed a different pattern; their concentration in the city of Utrecht was well above average and even slightly increased from 1980 to 1983. After the hospital relocation, however, they showed a clear tendency to move out of the city. This is in accordance with earlier research findings that single people prefer to live close to their job.

The proportion of the employees living elsewhere (i.e. neither in Nieuwegein nor in Utrecht) has decreased for most groups. For SODEC 2 the increasing concentration in Utrecht that we have just observed appears to be related to a steep decline in the fraction living elsewhere. SODEC 6 still has the largest proportion living in attractive municipalities 'elsewhere', which is related to the low proportion of this group living in the city of Utrecht.

The motives for residential mobility also vary among the groups. A maximum of three motives was recorded in the survey. It should be noted that the motives mentioned refer to all removals, not just to migration from Utrecht to Nieuwegein. Work-related motives were divided into three

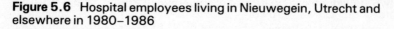

Figure 5.6 Hospital employees living in Nieuwegein, Utrecht and elsewhere in 1980–1986

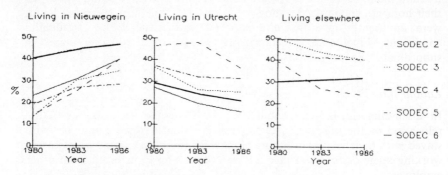

categories: change of work by the respondent; job mobility by the partner of the respondent; and home/work distance. In combination, these three motives were mentioned as important in the decision to move by 30 per cent of SODECs 2, 3, 4 and 5. For SODEC 6, the medical staff, work-related motives were mentioned in half of the cases. This is remarkable and at first sight contrary to what was found in, for instance, the Zoetermeer research, where labour-related motives did not play any role whatsoever in decisions to move made by the top executives.

However, this pattern can be explained by taking into account the differences in the specific geographic circumstances of the sectoral sub-markets for the top group in both regions. In Zoetermeer, the shift of work location generally brought about a reduction in travel time for the highest ranking SODEC, because the majority was living in a semicircle around Zoetermeer. In Nieuwegein, where nearly 20 per cent of the present hospital staff did not work in the St Antonius Hospital, but outside the province of Utrecht in 1983, the travel situation will have been much less favourable. The labour market for hospital staff is obviously more dispersed than for higher office employees. Since we recorded multiple motives for residential mobility, the group who worked and lived far away from Utrecht and Nieuwegein alone will have accounted for a considerable part of the labour-related motives for moving.

The importance of labour mobility by the partner of (female) second-income earners is clearly illustrated by SODECs 4 (part-timers) and 3 (full-timers). Especially with SODEC 4, the labour mobility of the partner has been much more important than that of the respondent in the decision to move. For the same groups, the home/work distance is hardly a reason to move, especially because they tend to accept work only in the neighbourhood of the dwelling.

A change in the household situation (especially marriage) has been an important cause for residential mobility for SODEC 3, which consists of recently formed couples. Dissatisfaction with existing housing conditions is also an important motive for some groups, most notably for SODECs 4 (40%) and 2 (35%). For growing families the need for more spacious dwellings, and for people living alone the option of improving the quality of their housing, encouraged a move of home. SODEC 6, on the other hand, were apparently already quite satisfied with their earlier residential conditions. Finally, it is remarkable that financial reasons played a subordinate role in decisions to move.

Labour mobility

In discussing the labour mobility of the personnel in response to the relocation of the hospital, a distinction is made between employees who stayed with their employer (going along with the move), those who started working anew or for the first time, and those who transferred from other employers.

Both in SODEC 1 and in SODEC 4 there is a high proportion of persons who started working at the hospital after its relocation. For SODEC 1, the young working people living with their parents, this is hardly surprising, since they are still very young. More interesting though is this phenomenon in SODEC 4, the older, part-time working women with children. Apparently, it is especially this group who have been replaced to a considerable extent. Although we did not collect information about the employees who have left the hospital, the explanation is clear. It was not worthwhile for part-time working women, who lived close to the hospital when it was still located in Utrecht, to join the relocation to Nieuwegein. Since they were only second-income earners, their influence on migration decisions was low anyway. The costs of travelling to Nieuwegein and the time involved made it difficult for them to combine child-care and work, so they must have given up their jobs (and maybe found other work closer to home). For women with children already living in Nieuwegien, however, the part-time vacancies offered an opportunity to re-enter the labour market.

A comparable argument can be set up for the high amount of job mobility in SODEC 3. Many young couples had already moved to Nieuwegein in the general wave of suburbanisation, independently from the relocation of the hospital. When new (full-time) employment became available in the new hospital, this was attractive for nurses working or training at other hospitals. Among SODECs 5 and 6 the percentages of new employees are relatively low. Most of the members of these groups stayed with their employer and joined in the relocation of the hospital. The rationale for their behaviour runs as follows: the middle-aged and moderately skilled SODEC 5 did not have too bright an outlook in the labour market in the early 1980s. As appeared in earlier research, this group tends not to be very mobile, the lack of mobility being related both to their age and to their level of skills, as well as to their household situation. For SODEC 6, the medical staff, the relocation of the hospital will not have been an important factor in decisions to take another job.

82

Conclusion: mobility effects of relocating institutions

Population and employment are being redistributed continually, but the pace and the direction of the relocation processes are changing over time and they differ, as demonstrated in this case study, along socio-economic and demographic dividing lines. As has been shown, this has resulted in a spectacular increase in the number of commuters in The Netherlands. The fact that in 1985 already 52 per cent of the employed people worked outside their own municipality can be seen as the accumulated expression of divergent trends in residential and labour mobility. Though blurring tendencies of various kinds of 'criss-cross relations' have come up, various trends in the mobility profile of social, demographic and economic groups can be observed.

We have focused in this chapter especially on three types of effects of the relocation of the St Antonius Hospital: the effects on labour mobility, on residential mobility, and on commuting. The effects on labour mobility are summarised and compared with earlier research in Zoetermeer in Figure 5.7. In Zoetermeer 44 per cent and in Nieuwegein 33 per cent of the employees were replaced in the few years following the relocation.

A proportion of the employees have stopped working with their employer in response to the relocation. Although we did not pursue this group, an impression of their characteristics can be obtained from inspecting the composition of the newly appointed personnel after the relocation. It can be deduced that part-time workers and women with children, in particular, have been replaced to a considerable extent as a consequence of the relocation of the offices and the hospital. These groups tend to look for work in the immediate surroundings of their home, and even a moderate increase in travel time impedes their economic activity.

On the other hand, new employees have been attracted at the new location itself. These include both beginners on the labour market and people who previously worked somewhere else. The general shortage of employment in dormitory towns is of particular significance for the groups just mentioned – i.e., people who want to work part-time, especially mothers with children. The new local demand for labour stimulated them to enter or re-enter the labour market. Others who were already working further away seized the opportunity to take a job closer to their homes. Apart from the effects on labour mobility there have been consequences for the residential distribution of the employees. In this respect also Zoetermeer and Nieuwegein offer an analogous pattern with nearly identical figures (Figure 5.8). The proportion

---

Figure 5.7 Summary of labour mobility after employment relocation (%)

	Zoetermeer	Nieuwegein
Participation mobility	10.7	12.4
Distribution mobility	33.3	20.5
No labour mobility	56.0	67.2
Total	100	100

Figure 5.8 Summary of effects of employment relocation on residential mobility (%)

	Pre-move location	Post-move location	Shift
Zoetermeer area (1972–1980)			
Zoetermeer	18.5	34.6	+ 16.1
Conurbation The Hague	36.0	25.8	– 10.2
Elsewhere	45.5	39.6	– 5.9
All	100	100	0
Nieuwegein area (1980–1986)			
Nieuwegein	20.6	38.0	+ 17.4
Utrecht	36.3	26.6	– 9.7
Elsewhere	43.1	35.4	– 7.7
All	100	100	0

of the employees living in the growth centre has increased over time at the cost of the central city. The percentage living elsewhere has also declined. It was demonstrated that different SODEC categories responded differently to the relocation of their employer and that the motives for moving varied substantially. As a result of the relocation of the offices and the hospital, in combination with the partial adaptation of the residential situation, there have been important changes in home/work travel flows. In the Nieuwegein case, the commuting rate immediately after the relocation amounted to 74 per cent (Walen and Nozeman 1985). In 1986 the percentage of employees who did not live in the municipality where they worked had dropped to 62 per cent. In Zoetermeer a comparable commuting rate of 65 per cent was found. Since we do not know the addresses of all employees before the relocation of their employers, the pre-location commuting rates are hard to assess. Still, the ratio of the employees who were living in the central city to those who were working there before the relocation gives some indication of the size-order of the earlier commuting rate. In the case of Utrecht this estimated commuting rate was nearly 60 per cent. In the case of The Hague the estimated rate for the whole agglomeration (including the municipalities of Leidschendam, Rijswijk, Voorburg and Wassenaar) was just over 40 per cent. Thus, the relocation brought about a considerable increase in commuter traffic, although this increase was subsequently somewhat reduced due to removals towards the municipality in which employment was located.

There has also been a clear contribution to the phenomenon of 'cross commuting', that is, the flow of commuters living in the central city and working elsewhere and which is in contrast with the mainstream. In both researches in Nieuwegein and Zoetermeer this group amounted to more than a quarter of all employees. This phenomenon also shows an inclination to subside with the increasing resettlement of employees in the place where they work.

The effects on average travel time and modal split appear to have been rather small in both instances. The combined effect of labour and residential

84

mobility has tended to keep the average travel time fairly constant. To conclude, it seems that the SODEC approach can also be of use in mobility studies within regional and sectoral sub-markets. The fact that the exact delimitation of the groups will be dependent on the prevailing conditions in the relevant segments of the labour and housing markets does not detract from the insights that can be gained.

References

Baker, D. de; Ottens, H. (1983) *Wonen en werken in Midden-Utrecht.* Utrecht: UGS nr. 28.

Beumer, R. J., Harts, J. J. and Ottens, H. F. L. (1983) *Ontwikkeling ruimtelijke structuur en ruimtelijke functieverschuivingen in de vier grote stadsgewesten.* Utrecht: Geografisch Instituut.

Buitendijk, D. (1987) 'Terug naar de stad'. *Intermediair* 6 November.

Doorn, P. K. (1985) 'Problems of categorization of actors and the inter relation of labour mobility and residential mobility: A case study of mobility effects of office relocation'. *Tijdschrift voor Economische en Sociale Geografie,* **76**, 3: 163–179.

Doorn, P. K. (1986) 'Migration, Employment and the Composition of the Dutch Urban System'. *The Netherlands Journal of Housing and Environmental Research,* **1**, 4: 379–408.

Doorn, P. K. and Rietbergen, A. van (1989) 'Life Time Mobility: The interrelations between labour mobility, residential mobility and the household-cycle'. *Canadian Geographer* (forthcoming).

Engelsdorp-Gastelaars, R. van and Maas-Droogleever Fortuijn, J. C. (1985) 'Personeel op Drift: Hoe reageren personeelsleden op een verplaatsing van hun bedrijf.' *Geografisch Tijdschrift,* **19**, 3: 181–91.

Economisch Technologisch Instituut (1981) *De structuur en ontwikkeling van de werkgelegenheid in Nieuwegein.* Utrecht.

Freijsen, G., Kuyper, N., Straten, E. van and Taal, F. (1979) *Ongelijkheid op de arbeidsmarkt; een sociaal-geografisch analyse.* Utrecht: Geografische Instituut.

Hanemaayer, D. E., Heelsbergen, K. M. van, Kasteleijn, F. C. H. and de Smidt, M. (1981) *Kantoren en ruimte; vestigingstendenzen van kantoren en ruimtelijk beleid in een aantal Nederlandse steden.* Utrecht: Geografisch Instituut.

Heelsbergen, K. M. van (1981) *Relokatie van kantoren en woon-werkrelaties; de kantorenstrook te Zoetermeer.* Utrecht: Geografisch Instituut.

McKinsey & Company (1986) *Afrekenen met files.* Amsterdam.

Nozeman, E. F. (1986) *Nieuwe bouwlocaties in het licht van enkele doelstellingen van ruimtelijke ordening,* (Planologische Studies 1) Amsterdam; University van Amsterdam.

Rietbergen, A. van (1987) 'Files en hun achtergronden; een aanzet tot een geografische verklaring' in *Planologische discussiebijdragen,* **2**, 621–30.

Rima, A. and Wissen, L. G. J. van (1987), *A dynamic model of household relocation. A case study for the Amsterdam Region.* PhD Thesis, Free University Amsterdam.

Walen, B. J. and Nozeman, E. S. (1985) Evaluatie van een ziekenhuisverplaatsing. *Stedebouw en Volkshuisvesting,* **66**, 383–391.

CHAPTER 6

Individual and Organisational Dimensions in the Migration of School Teachers

Brian Schofield

Introduction

An understanding of the factors influencing the geographical mobility of teachers is of considerable importance in the evaluation of Government educational policies. The study of this topic also has a much wider significance in that it stresses and attempts to specify interrelationships betweeen the individual and the organisational dimensions of migration. Career-related migration (that is, residential relocation necessitated by change in place of employment) is viewed as being the outcome of two sets of interacting factors. On the one hand, factors working at the organisational and stuctural level govern the opportunities presented for migration, the constraints imposed upon migration and the specific policies aimed to favour certain prescribed spatial goals. On the other hand, factors working at the level of the individual teacher influence the propensity to engage in career-related migration and the nature and direction of migration.

This chapter has two main objectives. First, it explores the ways in which the characteristics of the state education system operating in England in the early 1980s set a spatial framework within which individual migration could take place. More specifically, it focuses attention on spatial variations in the supply and demand relationship for secondary school teachers and assesses the effectiveness of policies aimed at certain spatial goals.

Second, it considers the ways in which the characteristics of the state education system set a framework for career advancement which influenced the frequency and types of move made by teachers. A major concern in this section is the relationship between promotion and migration. Other factors of an individual nature will be shown to be important in influencing the ability to engage in career-related migration and the type and direction of move made.

The organisational dimension

Prior to 1987 the Burnham Committee was the statutory body responsible for the organisation and structure of the teaching profession in England and Wales. Via reports and recommendations which it passed to the Department of Education and Science, the Committee had effective control over the number and distribution of teaching posts, the provision of additional allowances and the negotiation of salary levels.

The structure of the profession underwent several radical changes in the post-war period which had considerable importance for career development and consequently for teacher mobility and migration. Restructuring produced increased differentiation in status, with the result that teachers could see promotional prospects in terms of a series of clearly defined steps, each of which brought both financial and status rewards. Between 1972 and 1987 five teacher scales were in operation – the basic teacher grade of Scale 1 and the higher promotional scales of Scale 2, Scale 3, Scale 4 and Senior Teacher. These were in addition to the posts of Deputy and Head Teacher. The importance of the increased differentiation was stressed by Hilsum and Start (1974). The new structure, it was suggested, would result in teachers searching out higher scaled posts, thereby generating greater teacher movement between schools. The effect of this might be seen as advantageous or detrimental to the quality of education, depending upon one's point of view.

Alongside moves to increase structural differentiation were moves to maintain or even increase organisational uniformity. The principle of a nationally uniform salary structure was retained and the equalisation of pay for men and women was completed in 1961. Departures from a spatially uniform salary were only made in the cases of the London area and areas of social deprivation. Teachers in schools in these areas received allowances in order to make teaching there more attractive.

Teachers in England and Wales thus faced a radically different institutional organisation from that faced by their colleagues in the United States of America. The tradition in the United States of high levels of local autonomy and decentralised decision-making had resulted in each community playing a major role in determining its educational provision, both in terms of its quality and its organisation. Bowman (1979) notes that a major distinction between the two systems was that teachers in the United States could move to a higher salaried post by transferring to another school district without necessarily being promoted to a higher scale. This stands in very marked contrast to the uniform salary system operated in England and Wales.

The State Education System in the period 1972 to 1987 was thus characterised by two main features. First, it was distinctly hierarchical in structure, with clearly defined promotional steps. Second, it was centralised in organisation and spatially uniform with a national salary structure.

The individual dimension

The observed behaviour of teachers within the profession cannot be fully explained by considering the organisation and structure alone. Every teacher is eligible to apply for any advertised vacant teaching post for which he or she is qualified. That teachers do not apply for every vacancy implies selectivity on their part.

Actual behaviour is influenced by a number of factors. First, there is the individual's knowledge of vacancies. Vacancies are normally 'open' to all qualified teachers and are advertised in the national press. A survey of Local Education Authorities (LEAs) conducted in 1981 (Schofield, 1986) found that slightly over 50 per cent of LEAs always advertise posts nationally irrespective of subject and scale. Departures from this norm occurred in LEAs operating a redeployment scheme but these were of a temporary nature. Second, behaviour is influenced by the perceived attractiveness of the vacant post. This would include considerations of the duties of the post itself, the type and age range of the school and the area in which the school is located. Third, behaviour reflects the constraints imposed upon the individual by, for example, family considerations. One would therefore expect married women to exhibit occupationally-related mobility patterns quite different from those of male or single female colleagues.

These factors would affect the individual teacher's propensity to engage in career-related migration, the type of move made (whether a lateral move at the same scale of appointment or a promotional move from a lower to a higher scale of appointment) and the frequency and direction of such moves.

Teacher supply and demand

The teacher labour market reflects the interaction of the individual and organisational dimensions. As far as the individual teacher in Britain in concerned, teaching posts are ubiquitous and salaries spatially uniform. Any qualified teacher should therefore be able to gain employment in any part of the country which he or she chooses without salary penalty or reward.

From the employers' point of view, the demand for teachers is largely dependent upon the number of children of school age and, because of the uniform salary structure, is independent of teacher salaries.

During the 1970s and 1980s, as a result of cuts in expenditure made by LEAs, falling school rolls and the closure of smaller schools, the demand for teachers fell. The surplus of teachers which had started to develop in the middle 1970s grew in size and by the late 1970s concern was being expressed about 'the teacher surplus' and the efficiency of the prevailing teacher labour market.

Though in aggregate there was a surplus of teachers, certain schools experienced difficulty filling some vacancies. Market surpluses and deficiencies appeared to vary geographically, with some more favoured areas attracting a greater supply of teachers than other less fortunate areas. Despite its importance comparatively little work had been conducted on the choice of work area of teachers and the factors affecting such choices.

A Department of Education and Science Report (1964) found a high association between the location of a student teacher's home and his or her place of first teaching appointment. Jay (1965) also noted the tendency for teachers to gravitate towards those areas with which they were already acquainted prior to the start of their teaching career. In a much more extensive study Duggan and Stewart (1970) revealed a distinct drift of teachers towards their home areas at the beginning of and also during their careers.

In the United States the findings of two studies are of particular note. Greenberg and McCall conducted a number of studies on the teacher labour market (1973a, 1973b, 1974). Their conclusions stress the importance of non-salary factors in the movement of teachers between teaching appointments. Pederson (1973) also showed that teachers move in response to area dispar-ities, not only from low to high salary areas but also from areas of low pupil affluence to areas of high pupil affluence.

Number of applicants

The notion that teacher movement is responsive to area differentials of a non-salary nature formed the basis of a study into variations in teacher supply conducted in 1980 (Schofield, 1986). This study measured teacher supply in the secondary state education sector by recording the number of applicants received for teaching vacancies advertised nationally in the summer of 1980. In total a sample of 1,328 vacancies was surveyed and these attracted 15,971 applicants. This gave a national average figure of 12.03 applicants per vacancy.

Vacancies were categorised by subject area and by scale of post as well as by Local Education Authority area since it was thought that the labour market for teachers was internally partitioned. Movement in the profession is normally within a scale level or between adjacent scale levels. It would be rare, for example, for a scale 1 teacher to move to a scale 3 post. Movement is also normally within the same subject area. Both aspects of partitioning are supported by the work of Hilsum and Start (1974).

Subject specialism

Considerable variation in teacher supply was shown to exist between the subject areas. Vacancies in mathematics, technology, office skills and the physical sciences attracted fewest with respective means of 4.06, 3.38 and 3.34 applicants per vacancy. At the other extreme vacancies in history attracted most applicants with a mean of 42.33 per vacancy.

A note of caution in interpreting these results is needed. One cannot infer equivalence between the number of applicants and the number of teachers seeking appointments. Teachers in those subject areas experiencing a high number of applicants per post may well appreciate that they face a tighter job market than do their colleagues in other subjects and may therefore apply for a greater number of vacancies. However, the results do clearly demonstrate that, at a time when concern was being expressed about a national surplus of teachers, the surplus was far from uniform.

The opportunities for career-related migration are dependent upon the prevailing market conditions and are therefore influenced by subject specialism. Teachers of shortage subjects have a greater choice or work area than do their colleagues. Faced with less competition for vacant posts they stand a greater chance of securing a favoured post.

Scale of appointment

The relationship between scale of vacancy and number of applicants is more complex. Vacancies at scales 3 and 4 attracted a higher number of applicants than did the lower scale vacancies. However, on average, scale 2 vacancies attracted far fewer applicants than did scale 1 vacancies (7.20 compared with 11.56). If higher scale posts are generally preferred to lower scale posts (as a result of salary and status rewards) one would have expected a positive relationship between scale and number of applicants at all levels. One plausible explanation of the higher than expected value for scale 1 vacancies is that there existed a pool of qualified people unable to secure employment as teachers. The majority would be newly or recently qualified and therefore only eligible to apply for scale 1 vacancies. Their job-seeking activity would in consequence swell the number of applicants for scale 1 vacancies.

The teacher surplus which existed in 1980 was concentrated not only in certain subjects but also at the lower end of the teacher market, especially at the point of entry to the profession.

New entrants, in particular, would be greatly constrained in their choice of work area. Similarly, teachers seeking promotion posts at the higher scales faced greater competition and would have a reduced chance of securing a post in a preferred work area. For both these groups the desire to secure an appointment may well weigh far higher than any consideration of locational advantages.

Spatial differentials

If spatial differentials exist, whether they be of a monetary or non-monetary nature, schools located within favoured areas ought to attract a greater teacher supply than schools in less favoured areas. The analysis was conducted on scale 1 vacancies only (in order to eliminate the effect of scale vacancy) and on standardised scores (in order to eliminate the effect of subject). These data show the presence in 1980 of very large differences in teacher supply. Metropolitan areas tended to receive far fewer applicants than did non-metropolitan areas. The lowest area mean values were recorded by the metropolitan area of the North (− 49.16 per cent) and the South East (− 40.51 per cent). The West Midlands metropolitan area also recorded a negative mean value of − 19.69 per cent. However, the metropolitan areas of the North West and Yorkshire and Humberside went against the trend and gave positive values of + 8.38 per cent and + 28.45 per cent respectively.

East Anglia recorded the lowest value of any non-metropolitan area of − 12.08 per cent and non-metropolitan South East also gave a negative value. The South West and non-metropolitan Yorkshire and Humberside recorded the highest area values of + 59.9 per cent and + 32.31 per cent respectively. The South West in particular emerges as a region where the supply of teachers is typically well above the national average.

It is difficult to account for such large differences in teacher supply by variations in the organisation and structure of the teaching profession. Centralisation of decision making, as we have already noted, produced a nationally uniform system with little local flexibility. With the exception of certain area allowances (which we shall consider shortly) the salary structure was uniform. Similarly, the local demand for teachers reflected the pupil/teacher ratio which was also nationally directed. Some areas would undoubtedly be experiencing a greater fall in school rolls than other areas but it seems unlikely that this would be of sufficient magnitude to influence the pattern of supply to the observed extent.

The effect of special allowances

Areas with disadvantages, such as a higher than average cost of living or expensive housing will, other things being equal, be less attractive to teachers. In a free market wage differentials would emerge to offset these differences. However, since teacher salaries are negotiated and applied nationally, wage differentials cannot naturally develop.

In response to this problem two policy implements are used to influence teacher supply on an area basis. These are the London Area allowances and the Social Priority School allowance. London teachers have been paid an allowance for many years and in 1981 the payments stood at £939 for schools in the inner-London area, £615 for the 'outer area' and £246 for the 'fringe area'.

The Social Priority School allowance differs from the London allowances in that it is applied to individual schools and not uniformly over a given area. When first introduced in 1968 as the School of Exceptional Difficulty allowance it gave explicit recognition to the difficulties faced by teachers working in socially deprived areas. In 1981 the allowance stood at £201, increasing to £276 on completion of $2\frac{1}{2}$ years qualifying service.

If the payment of an allowance, or allowances, fully compensates for differences between areas, we should expect to find that vacancies arising in schools receiving allowances attract a corresponding number of applicants to similar vacancies in schools not in receipt of an allowance.

The evidence suggests that the payment of special allowances falls far short of its objective. Zabalza, using data from the 1970s, noted that the level of both allowances appeared to be inadequate to equalise teacher supply (Zabalza et al., 1979). The position in 1980/81 leads one to the same conclusion (Schofield, 1986). The lowest mean number of applicants was recorded by those vacancies in which both a London Area allowance and a Social Priority School allowance was payable (6.5 applicants compared with

13.04 applicants per vacancy where no allowance was payable).

This conclusion suggests that the organisation and structure of the profession has been such as to make the teachers' choice of work area, and thereby the direction of career-related migration, largely dependent upon non-salary factors. Factors, such as regional variations in house prices, would appear to offer more promising explanations of the observed large spatial differences in teacher supply than would the organisational dimension.

Choice of work area

The notion that teachers gravitate towards their home area appears well documented. However, it is unlikely that the tendency would produce large variations in teacher supply since there is no evidence of marked area differences in the choice of teaching as a career or large differences in the provision of places for teacher training.

The suggestion that the attractiveness of the countryside in which the post is situated and the availability of facilities for cultural and recreational pursuits are important factors was put forward by Duggan and Stewart (1970). Results of questionnaire surveys (Schofield, 1980) would lend support to this view.

Movement of teachers in the San Diego school system (Greenberg and McCall, 1973a, 1973b) was shown to be from schools with a low status (as measured by a high percentage of minority group students, a high proportion of students with parents on welfare and students with below average IQ and reading ability) to schools with a higher status. This tendency would seem more influential at the local level than at the national level since it presupposes quite detailed knowledge about a school and its catchment area.

It is very tempting to suggest that the large variation in the supply of teachers for scale 1 posts in England reflects variations in the cost of housing. Indeed there is much circumstantial evidence to support this view as many teachers have commented on the difficulty facing teachers in securing accommodation in the South East and Greater London in particular.

Though an excellent medium term investment, the high cost of housing in certain parts of the country would be a strong disincentive to move to these areas in the short term. This would be especially true for newly qualified teachers attempting to gain a first foothold in the housing market.

Teacher mobility

The pattern of teacher supply discussed in the previous section provides the backcloth against which actual migration within the profession may be viewed. Much of the empirical evidence presented in this section is based on a survey of mobile teachers conducted in the summer of 1980 (Schofield, 1986). It is important to note that the survey intentionally targeted only those teachers who were changing appointments at the time of the survey or who had just gained an appointment on first entering or re-entering the profession. The behaviour of new entrants to the profession is considered first.

The mobility of new entrants

Slightly over half of all initial appointments necessitated a change in place of residence (as defined by the individual teachers) – 51.8 compared with 48.2 per cent Figure 6.1. This high initial rate of migration is not surprising since the majority of new entrants would be newly qualified teachers in their early 20s.

Figure 6.1 Mobility of new entrants

	Male %	Female %	All %
Prior to 1970			
Change in residence	46.8	44.2	45.9
No change in residence	53.2	55.8	54.1
1970 to 1975			
Change in residence	56.3	41.7	51.0
No change in residence	43.7	58.3	49.0
1975 to 1980			
Change in residence	60.6	51.4	55.2
No change in residence	39.4	48.6	44.8
Totals			
Change in residence	55.0	48.4	51.8
No change in residence	45.0	51.6	48.2

Source: Schofield, 1986

Males are shown to be more mobile than are their female colleagues although the difference is small. The total figures show that 55 per cent of males compared with 48.4 per cent of females moved place of residence on taking up their first teaching appointment.

The rate of initial migration increased over the time period considered in the study. This increase is reflected in the figures both for men and women but is more uniform and larger in the case of men. The data suggest the persistence of, even a widening between, rates for men and women.

Explanations of the differences between male and female migration and the trend towards increasing initial migration are many and various. Societal changes in status and norms would undoubtedly affect the behaviour of newly qualified teachers and one would expect teachers to mirror trends prevalent in wider society. Some market forces, however, are particular to teachers. The mid- to late-1970s marked an important watershed in the supply/demand relationship for teachers. The teacher shortage rapidly turned into a teacher surplus and for the first time in the post-war period teacher unemployment became a reality. The teacher surplus was not a

Figure 6.2 The effect of subject specialism

	Change in residence %	No change %
Subjects in high over-supply	57.1	42.9
Subjects in low over-supply	49.2	50.8
All subjects	51.8	48.2

Source: Schofield, 1986

uniform phenomenon. As we have seen earlier, marked variations existed in teacher supply among geographical areas and among subjects.

Spatial variations in supply would have the effect of raising the level of initial migration amongst new entrants resident in the areas of teacher surplus. Faced with a shortage of locally available vacancies, many would be forced to widen their search horizon and apply for posts outside daily commuting distance. The effect would be strongest for prospective teachers in those subjects with the greatest surplus of applicants.

The data lend support to this view (Figure 6.2). A higher percentage of teachers in subjects with high over-supply migrated than did teachers in other subjects. Initial rates of migration seem to respond to market changes in the supply/demand relationship for teachers such that the higher the supply of teachers the higher the rate of migration.

There are several factors which could help explain the lower rates of initial migration for women. A significant number of women are already married on entering the profession. These women are highly constrained in their choice of work area because of their husbands' place of work and also possibly because of family commitments. For them mobility may not be a practical possibility. Further, a proportion of women may view teaching as a temporary career prior to acquiring a family. Zabalza et al. (1979) found that married women remained in the profession for a shorter time than did men. Some women may feel that the benefits accruing from mobility are less than the benefits as assessed by their male colleagues and hence are less inclined to move to obtain their first teaching post.

Movement within the profession

There is much evidence to suggest a strong relationship in the teaching profession between career advancement and migration. However, much of the literature on teacher mobility has focused on movement between teaching appointments and has given little explicit attention to career-related migration – that is, to residential relocation consequential upon taking up a new appointment.

In the survey of mobile teachers conducted in 1980 moves between appointments were categorised as being either lateral (at the same scale level) or promotional (to a higher scale level). Moves were further split into those that did or did not necessitate migration (Figure 6.3).

Figure 6.3 Lateral and promotional moves

	Lateral moves %	Promotional moves %
Single males	17.5	82.5
Married males	15.0	85.0
All males	17.0	83.0
Single females	21.9	78.1
Married females	33.0	67.0
All females	23.6	76.4
All teachers	20.1	79.9

Source: Schofield, 1986

Figure 6.4 Migration and type of move

	Change in residence %	No change %
Lateral moves:		
Single males	52.5	47.5
Married males	44.8	55.2
All males	51.0	49.0
Single females	29.1	70.9
Married females	15.8	84.2
All females	26.3	73.7
All teachers	37.4	62.6
Promotional moves:		
Single males	45.0	55.0
Married males	38.8	61.2
All males	43.6	56.4
Single females	39.8	60.2
Married females	23.4	76.6
All females	37.7	62.3
All teachers	41.0	59.0

Source: Schofield, 1986

Lateral moves accounted for a much smaller proportion of moves than did promotional moves (20.1 per cent compared with 79.9 per cent). Females, especially married females, made a considerably greater proportion of lateral moves than did their male colleagues. Lateral moves accounted for 33 per cent of all moves made by married females – a figure more than double that of married males. Males made a larger proportion of promotional moves than did females, especially married females.

When the data are classified according to whether there was a need to relocate place of residence some interesting contrasts emerge. The figures clearly demonstrate differences in migratory behaviour between male and female teachers and between single and married teachers.

Male teachers made a much higher proportion of lateral relocations than did females (51 per cent compared with 23.6 per cent). Just as striking is the effect of marital status on the level of migration. For both males and females, marriage is associated with a reduction in the proportion of lateral relocations.

The figures for promotional relocations confirm the importance of sex and marital status. Single males recorded the highest proportion of this type of move (45 per cent) whereas married females recorded the lowest proportion (23.4 per cent). The promotional chances of married women appear to be reduced as a result of the constraints on their migration.

Career profiles

An area of some interest is the teacher's present scale of appointment and how this scale is related to career history, as described by length of service and mobility. Before discussing career profiles it is instructive to consider the proportion of teachers attaining the various scale levels.

Figure 6.5 Distribution of current posts

Scale of current post	Males	Females	All teachers
1	27.4	54.9	40.7
2	21.0	18.1	19.6
3	21.5	17.6	19.6
4	25.6	8.3	17.3
Senior teacher	4.6	0.9	2.8

Source: Schofield, 1986

40.7 per cent of the sample of mobile teachers had remained on scale 1 appointments throughout their teaching career. 59.3 per cent had obtained at least one promotion. Figure 6.5 clearly demonstrates that the distribution of promotion posts is unequal. Men are over-represented in the promotion grades, especially in the higher scales of scale 4 and Senior Teacher, whereas women are over-represented in the basic teaching grade of scale 1.

Figure 6.6 Average years of service

Scale of current post	Males	Females	All teachers
1	2.23	2.71	2.55
2	4.74	7.14	5.81
3	10.83	11.17	10.98
4	13.59	15.12	13.95
Senior teacher	12.60	14.50	12.92

Source: Schofield, 1986

A comparison of length of service (Figure 6.6) also makes an interesting contrast between males and females. The average length of service of women is, at all scale levels, greater than that of their male colleagues and, in the case of scale 2 appointments, is considerably greater.

Figure 6.7 Average number of years between career-related migrations

Scale of current post	Males	Females	All teachers
1	2.06	3.34	2.81
2	3.30	7.54	4.77
3	6.06	13.86	8.07
4	10.01	12.24	10.49
Senior teacher	7.25	8.40	8.16

Source: Schofield, 1986

The figures for length of time between career-related migrations (Figure 6.7) indicate that the majority of such moves occur in the early stages of a teacher's career – on initially entering the profession and on promotion to scale 2. (The grade of Senior Teacher is unusual in that there are very few such posts which carry an additional responsibility of an administrative nature.) This conclusion is consistent with the view that migration decreases with age and is higher for single than for married teachers. The figures also show that women are, on average, less mobile. Since, in theory at least, the pay and opportunities of men and women are equal, an explanation of the unequal distribution of promotion posts would seem to lie in the relative immobility of many women.

Summary and concluding comments

The basic thesis of this chapter has been that, if migration is to be understood, then both the organisational context within which migration occurs as well as individual factors must be considered. In the instance of career-related migration a major context is the organisation and structure of the appropriate profession. Attention has focused on one profession at one moment in time. The state education system operating in England was shown to have a distinctive organisation and structure which served to distinguish it from the previously existing system and from the system operating in the United States of America. Of particular importance were the presence of a strongly hierarchical structure with clearly defined promotional steps and a nationally uniform salary structure.

Individual factors, it has been suggested, influence the teachers' ability to engage in career-related migration and the type, frequency and direction of migration. Married women in particular are highly constrained in their ability to engage in this type of migration and in consequence this appears to reduce their chances of gaining promotion. Research has also stressed the importance of non-salary factors in the choice of work locations by teachers.

The view that migration is context dependent emphasises the dynamics of the process and calls for, in conclusion, comments on the situation prevailing in the late 1980s. Much has changed. The teacher surplus appears to be rapidly developing into a teacher shortage and a radical reorganisation and restructuring of the teaching profession is underway.

In 1980 there existed a national surplus of teachers. This surplus was, however, far from uniformly distributed either across all subjects or across all areas of the country. It was at its lowest in subjects such as the physical sciences and in the south-east of England. In 1988 Essex is, according to a report in the *Teachers' Weekly* (14 March 1988), 'facing a desperate shortage of teachers'. So severe is the shortage that many vacancies are said to be attracting no applicants. The 'shortage' has prompted calls for a massive increase in salaries to raise teacher supply. Under the uniform salary system, a salary increase would do little to improve the supply in Essex since it would be applied nationally. It seems likely that the inadequate supply of teachers in Essex reflects the non-salary disadvantages of the area, namely, escalating house price inflation. A more flexible policy which recognises the existence of local differentials in the attractiveness of areas would be a more appropriate policy response than a national increase in salaries.

The notion of increased local flexibility to reflect differing local circumstances is at the heart of Kenneth Baker's educational reforms. The exact form that the education system will take in the 1990s is, as yet, uncertain. What is clear is that in structure and organisation it will be quite different from that which prevailed in 1980.

In organisation it will reflect a decentralisation of decision-making, with governing bodies taking a significant responsibility for the allocation of school funds or, if they wished and with parental consent, leaving local government support and becoming directly maintained by central government.

Alongside this and other organisational changes important structural changes have already been introduced. The Burnham Committee has been abolished and a new less hierarchical salary structure introduced with effect from October 1987. This consists of a single professional grade for all teachers (except heads and deputies) with incentive allowances paid as additions. These allowances may be paid to teachers for a variety of reasons. Significantly these include the need to employ teachers for shortage subjects and for posts which have proved difficult to fill (AMMA, 1987).

The impact of these changes on the future migration of school teachers is difficult to predict. What does seem certain is that area-differences will increase. The organisation and structure of state education in England in the 1990s may well have more in common with the system in the United States, than with that operating in the 1980s.

98

References

AMMA (1987) *The New Salary Structure, 1987 – a guide for AMMA members to the salary parts of the school teachers' pay and conditions document 1987.* London: Assistant Masters and Mistresses Association.

Bowman, L. A. (1979) 'Some Transatlantic Comparisons' in Zabalza, A., Turnbull, P. and Williams, G., (1979) *The Economics of Teacher Supply* pp. 193-222. Cambridge: Cambridge University Press.

Department of Education and Science (1964) *Factors Influencing the "Production" of Teachers.* DES Analysis of Education Students. Unpublished Report.

Duggan, E. P. and Stewart, W. A. C. (1970) 'The Choice of Work Area of Teachers'. *The Sociological Review,* Monograph No. 15.

Greenberg, D, and McCall, J. (1973a) '1 Teacher Mobility in San Diego'; (1973b) '2 A Theory of Labour Mobility with Applications to the Teacher Market'; (1974) '7 Teacher Mobility in Michigan'. *Analysis of the Educational Personnel System.* Santa Monica: The Rand Corporation.

Hilsum, S. and Start K. B. (1974) *Promotion and Careers in Teaching.* Slough: NFER.

Jay, L. T. (1965) *The Mobility of Teachers.* Sheffield: University of Sheffield.

Pederson, K. G. (1973) *The Itinerant Schoolmaster.* Chicago: Midwest Administrative Centre, University of Chicago.

Schofield, B. (1986) *Mobility and Career-Related Migration in the Teaching Profession.* Unpublished M. Phil. dissertation, University of Lancaster.

'Teacher shortage hits Essex'. *Teachers' Weekly,* 14 March 1988.

Zabalza, A., Turnbull, P. and Williams, G., (1979) *The Economics of Teacher Supply.* Cambridge: Cambridge University Press.

CHAPTER 7

Labour Migration and Counter-Urbanisation in France

Paul White

Introduction

In the ten years since Vining and Kontuly (1978) produced the first attempts at an international comparison of population dispersal, or 'counter-urbanising' trends, a vast output of literature on the topic has occurred, of which contributions on France form a significant component (Berger *et al.*, 1980; Boudoul and Faur, 1982; Fielding, 1986; Ogden, 1985; Winchester, 1989; Winchester and Ogden, in press). Much of the work of French scholars has been highly empirical, consisting of in-depth local case studies. In particular, there has been little real attempt to relate the French experience to general theories on the causation of the rural revival, nor to evaluate rural population changes in France in the context of wider issues of demographic, social and economic change in the country as a whole.

One of the commonest theories underlying attempts to explain counter-urbanisation relates to the concept of a new spatial division of labour in which the locations of economic activities are restructured, providing new employment growth in more peripheral regions and thereby resulting in population growth there, both through the retention of labour that might otherwise have moved away, and through the in-movement of certain key personnel such as branch managers and technicians to run the newly decentralised enterprises (Fielding, 1985; Winchester, 1989). The implication of the operation of such a process should be a profound alteration in established patterns of labour migration, producing changes in the composition of the migrants and a reversal of various long-standing flows which, in net terms, have contributed to urban growth and reflected the dominance of metropolitan economies.

Figure 7.1 The planning regions and principal cities of France

Recent research by Winchester (1989) and Winchester and Ogden (in press) has cast doubt on the new spatial division of labour theory as an adequate explanation of counter-urbanisation at the level of France as a whole. There is little real evidence of employment decentralisation to genuinely remote areas, although certain more peri-urban regions (for example, and most notably, the outer parts of the Paris Basin) have benefited in recent years from new employment growth. This appears to support the claims made by Noin and Chauviré (1987) that what France has recently experienced is a wider spread of the wave of sub-urbanisation, rather than a real turn around in the spatial patterns of economic and population change. However, most of the research upon which such conclusions are based is concerned with aggregate population or employment change, with little specific attention being paid to spatial patterns of labour flows.

This chapter considers the recent history of labour migration in France in the context of the apparent revival of traditionally relatively impoverished areas of the country. The scale chosen for analysis is that of the planning region, of which there are 22 within France (see Figure 7.1), although Corsica is omitted from discussion here because of certain inadequacies in the data for that region. Concentration on the regional scale permits an evaluation of the extent to which the processes of population flow involved in the evolution of the new pattern of growth within France may be operating at a sub-regional or at a wider scale. The data used originate in the population censuses carried out in France at irregular intervals – in 1962, 1968, 1975 and 1982 – with particular emphasis placed here on comparisions between labour flows during the periods of 1962–8 (of continued urbanisation in France) and 1975–82 (of counter-urbanisation).

Levels of migration

One of the most commented upon results of the 1982 French census was the appearance of a reduction in the mobility levels of the French population (Courgeau and Pumain, 1984; Boudoul and Faur, 1985), reversing a century or more of mobility increase (White, 1989). The annual inter-regional mobility rate declined from 1.9 per cent in the period of 1968–75 to 1.72 per cent, a reduction of just under 10 per cent. Nevertheless, the rate still stood considerably above that of 1962–8 when it had been 1.59 per cent per annum. In terms of labour flow, it is interesting to note that the rate of inter-regional labour movement in 1975–82 stood at 91.3 per cent of that during the previous inter-censal interval, whilst the rate for those not in the labour force was only 89.7 per cent of its earlier level. Although inter-regional flow has been reduced in recent years, the labour component in the flow has increased in proportion, from 40.6 per cent in 1962–8, to 42.7 per cent in 1968–75 and 45.2 per cent in 1975–82.

Occupational mobility has diminished in France in recent years, bearing a close relationship to the fortunes of the economy. Amongst publicly-employed tertiary sector employees of both sexes annual job mobility rates of between 15 and 16 per cent per annum were the norm in the early 1970s, falling to 10 and 11 per cent during the recession of the later years of that decade and standing at around 9 per cent per annum by the mid 1980s (Cézard and Rault, 1986). Amongst male private sector tertiary employees the fall in job mobility rates over the same period has been from around 23 per cent per annum to 17 per cent and then 12 to 13 per cent in the mid 1980s, with female rates at between two-thirds and three-quarters of male rates.

In common with recent experience in other countries, there are clear indications of change in the profile of those involved in job mobility, whether also involving geographical mobility or not (Jayet, 1988). It was during the decade of the 1970s that the skilled labour force took over from the unskilled as the more occupationally mobile (Beret, 1966, p. 57). This feature is partly related to the significance of internal labour markets within large employing organisations. In 1986, in establishments employing more than 50 people, 7.3 per cent of those leaving their current position went to another establishment of the same enterprise (Perreaux, 1987). There was a considerable gender differential at work, with 9.0 per cent of males moving within internal labour markets as against only 5.1 per cent of women. It is the sectoral differences, however, that are the most important. Internal labour markets accounted for only 1.5 per cent of moves by unskilled white collar workers in 1986, and only 2.2 per cent of moves by unskilled manual workers: at the other end of the scale such movement encompassed 28.1 per cent of manager mobility and 21.7 per cent of moves by specialist skilled white collar workers. Because of this socio-professional selectivity the average age of those moving within internal labour markets was high: whilst less than 2 per cent of the moves of the under-25s were transfers, over 23 per cent of moves by the over-50s were of this type.

The emerging picture of French labour migration given by data from the early to mid 1980s is therefore that it is declining slightly in level, but changing considerably in composition, with an increase in migration by high level manpower, and with a growing importance of internal labour markets for larger enterprises. These are conclusions that could be in accord with any proposition that labour migration is now both a major cause and a reflection of the counter-urbanisation trends seen in France as a whole. However, the data so far discussed, drawn from national sample surveys carried out by the Institut National de la Statistique et des Etudes Economiques, do not permit any spatial analysis. Further validation of the labour migration and counter-urbanisation proportion must depend on consideration of the spatial pattern of labour flows, using census materials.

Inter-regional labour flows

If comparison is made between the last inter-censal interval of major urbanisation in France (1962–8) and the most recent period of counter-urbanisation (the inter-censal interval 1975–82), the net pattern of labour flows can be seen to have changed in several respects (see Figure 7.2). Had there been no changes in net labour flows all the regions could have points plotted on the diagonal. In fact in eight regions there had been a worsening of the labour migration balance (points above the diagonal), whilst in thirteen there had been an improvement (points below the diagonal).

Between 1962 and 1968 only five regions experienced net labour inflow, of which the strongest was to the Île-de-France region around Paris. Four of these regions retained net labour inflow during 1975–82, although in only two cases – those of the Centre region and of Provence – had there been any strengthening of the net balance. In the Île-de-France there had been a total reversal, producing a significant net labour outflow on a regional scale.

Between 1975 and 1982, in addition to four of the regions that had experienced net labour inflow during the earlier period, six other regions of earlier loss were attracting labour migrants on balance. The most interesting of these reversals are arguably the Pays de la Loire, Brittany and Limousin – all of them regions of traditional out-movement and with a strongly rural character. Other rural regions that improved their position between the mid 1960s and the late 1970s, but which had still not moved into balance on inter-

Figure 7.2 Annual net flows of inter-regional labour migrants, per 1000 members of the labour force, 1963–8 and 1975–82.

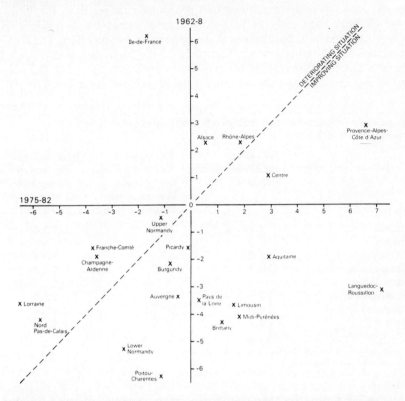

Data sources: Recensement Général de la Population de 1982, Principaux Résultats, Sondage au 1/20, France Métropolitaine. The 1975–82 figures take account of the erratum slip issued in 1988.

regional labour migration, included Lower Normandy, Poitou-Charentes and the Auvergne. On the other hand, two predominantly rural regions – Franche-Comté and Champagne – actually worsened their labour migration balance between the two periods.

Indeed, looking at labour migration at the regional scale, what stands out is not so much the attraction of rural regions (though that is clearly present) as the division of France into an eastern sector of labour out-movement and a western sector of labour gain. Eleven regions lie to the east of an imaginary line drawn from the mouth of the Rhône to the mouth of the Seine; amongst these eleven regions are all eight of those (Figure 7.2) whose labour migration position worsened between 1962–8 and 1975–82. The only three regions to the east of this imaginary line to improve their migration balance were Picardy, Burgundy and Provence.

Migrant characteristics

It is clear, therefore, that the labour migration patterns of France, at a regional scale, have undergone certain profound changes since the 1960s. These changes apparently fit to a considerable extent the hypothesis of counter-urbanisation; but there is also a need to know something about the characteristics of the migrants. According to the 'new spatial division of labour' argument, there should be an excess of managers and/of skilled non-manual workers amongst the movers for the most recent intercensal period.

Figure 7.3 Employment characteristics of inter-regional migrants, France, 1975–82

	Per cent of total inter-regional migrants	All migrants 1975–82 as per cent of total in employment category, 1982	Inter-regional migrants as per cent of all migrants, 1975–82
Farmers	1.1	14.8	10.4
Artisans, self-employed	6.5	42.0	16.9
Management	16.1	60.3	29.2
Intermediate professions	23.9	59.2	20.6
Employees	32.3	57.3	18.4
Workers	20.1	50.3	10.6
	100.0		

Data sources: See Figure 7.2

Figure 7.3 shows the characteristics of inter-regional migrants between 1975 and 1982. The first column shows that management and intermediate employees together made up 40 per cent of inter-regional migrants for the period, although the 1982 census also recorded the fact that these two groups made up only 25.2 per cent of the labour force. Employees were also slightly over-represented amongst inter-regional migrants, whilst the other occupational categories were under-represented. From the second column it is clear that, for all internal migration within France (including intra-commune, inter-commune, inter-*département*, and inter-regional scales), the managerial category had the highest migration rate over this period, followed by those in the intermediate professions. The third column shows that migratory managers were far more likely to make an inter-regional move than were other employment categories. Comparison of these last two columns shows that at the time of the 1982 census 17.6 per cent of managers had made an inter-regional move since 1975, against 12.2 per cent of those in the intermediate professions and 10.5 per cent of those in the employee category. Caution is necessary in ascribing too much significance in these figures since the 316,000 managers who moved between regions still amounted to far fewer such movers than amongst employees (635,000), the intermediate professions (469,000), workers (395,000) or even the retired (369,000). Even so, it is clear that inter-regional labour migration during the period considered was disproportionately composed of the more skilled elements in the workforce.

However, when consideration is given to the distribution of these inter-regional migrants between destinations at different levels in the settlement hierarchy the hypothesis linking inter-regional migration to counter-urbanisation trends via the new spatial division of labour begins to break down.

Figure 7.4 shows the destination within the urban hierarchy of different types of inter-regional labour migrant. Ogden (1985, p. 33) has drawn particular attention to the role of the ZPIU (urbanised rural zones) and of smaller urban centres with populations of up to 100,000 in the recent experience of rural revival. If such revival is brought about by labour migration dependent on a new spatial division of labour then there might be the expectation that these levels in the settlement hierarchy would have witnessed significant in-movement by skilled white-collar workers. This is not, in fact, the case. As Figure 7.4 makes clear, such migrants are only over-represented in inter-regional moves to the highest levels in the hierarchy, namely to cities of over 100,000 population and to the Paris agglomeration. Amongst inter-regional labour movers to rural *communes* within ZPIU all three white-collar groups were under-represented (a total of 64.8 per cent, against 72.3 per cent of all inter-regional labour migrants).

It might be suggested that if the scale of analysis is moved down to the sub-regional level, skilled white-collar movement may be found to be the significant factor in the rural revival but operating on a more local level. This is not the case. White-collar movement is again under-represented amongst new arrivals in settlements below 100,000 in size.

It appears, therefore, that whilst inter-regional labour migration in France has recently undergone certain significant changes in the direction of net flows, there is doubt about the extent to which such changes are the result of growing rural employment opportunities halting the emigration of the unskilled and producing inflows of the skilled. Whilst white collar migrants are over-represented in inter-regional flows, their destinations are predominantly the bigger urban centres. The significance of the Paris region for such movers is scarcely dimmed. Indeed it is probably being enhanced through the increase in the importance of internal labour markets within large organisations: in comparison with the country as a whole almost twice as many moves into and out of the Île-de-France region are internal labour market moves (Corbel et al., 1987).

Inter-regional moves into the more urbanised rural zones and into smaller urban settlements (the crucial *loci* of counter-urbanisation) actually show a high significance of movement by manual labour, a somewhat unexpected finding, at least at the national scale. Winchester (1989), commenting on a similar result from her anlaysis of the rural revival in the *département* of the Isère, ascribes it to a general suburbanisation of all employment oppor-

Figure 7.4 Characteristics of regional in-migration by size of settlement, 1975–82

| | Percentage of regional in-migrants to: | | | | | |
| | Rural *communes* | | Urban *communes* | | | |
	Not in a ZPIU*	In a ZPIU*	Population less than 20,000	20,000 to 99,999	100,000 to 1.9 million	Paris agglomeration
Farmers	7.6	1.9	0.7	0.2	0.1	0.1
Artisans, self-employed	11.2	9.2	8.8	5.9	5.2	2.3
Management	9.2	12.9	13.4	16.1	19.3	18.5
Intermediate professions	21.2	24.2	23.2	23.5	25.4	22.7
Employees	25.1	27.7	29.0	32.8	32.5	41.3
Workers	25.8	24.2	24.9	21.5	17.5	15.3
Retired per 100 labour migrants	40	29	25	16	14	5

* Zone de Peuplement Industriel ou Urbain

Data sources: Recensement Général de la Population de 1982: Résultats du Sondage au 1/4, France Métropolitaine (Par Catégorie de Commune) tunities and puts a major emphasis on the role of housing, with better-paid manual labour at last able, after decades of restricted housing choice, to express preferences for specific housing types and locations. Whether such conclusions for a single *département* can be extended to the whole of France, and to inter-regional as well as local migration, is problematic.

In addition to information about the employment characteristics of inter-regional migrants, Figure 7.4 also indicates the variable significance of retirement moves. Here there is a very clear decrease in significance with increasing level in the urban hierarchy. In rural *communes* not in urbanised zones there were, in 1982, 40 recent arrivals of retired people to every 100 movers currently in employment: for *communes* in a ZPIU and for small towns the ratios were 29: 100 and 25: 100 respectively.

These facts are a reminder that counter-urbanisation is a complex process in which labour flow is but one component. Comparison of the net figures of inter-regional migration for both the labour force component and the inactive component (consisting both of retired labour and of all others without employment) for the period 1975–82 enables a typology of regions to be derived. Aubry (1988) has suggested a four-fold typology but closer inspection of the data indicates that six categories are more appropriate (see Figure 7.5).

Figure 7.5 A typology of regions in terms of inter-regional migration, France, 1975–82

1.	Net in-migration, labour-led	Rhône-Alpes
2.	Net in-migration, not labour-led	Centre
		Pays de la Loire
		Brittany
		Languedoc
		Aquitaine
		Midi-Pyrénées
		Limousin
		Provence-Alpes-Côte d'Azur
3.	Net labour outflow outweighed by gain of inactive migrants	Picardy
		Burgundy
		Poitou-Charentes
		Auvergne
4.	Net out-migration, labour led	Haute-Normandie
		Basse-Normandie
		Nord-Pas de Calais
		Lorraine
		Franche-Comté
5.	Net labour inflow outweighed by loss of inactive migrants	Alsace
6.	Net out-migration, not labour-led	Île-de-France
		Champagne

There is only one region in which there is clear evidence of the employment-led attraction of inter-regional migrants, that of the Rhône-Alpes. Here 65 per cent of the total net inflow of 45,000 between 1975 and 1982 were composed of labour migrants. The attraction of this region is not a new phenomenon; as a whole, Rhône-Alpes has consistently been a successful region for economic growth over the last thirty years. Figure 7.2 showed that it was attracting labour migrants during the 1960s but that, in fact, its pulling power has weakened slightly in recent years.

Eight regions experienced net population growth through inter-regional migration between 1975 and 1982, but with the labour component outweighed by the inflow of the inactive. All of these regions except Provence are in the western part of France where, from Figure 7.2, it was earlier seen that the balance of labour migration had recently improved. It seems clear, however, that the employment attractions of these regions are secondary (and possibly subservient) to their attractions in other terms – most notably as retirement locations. The labour force component in net in-migration was highest in Provence (36 per cent) and Limousin (18 per cent). The high figure for the region of the Centre possibly reflects general suburbanising trends affecting both employment and residences in an area generally accessible to Paris.

Four regions experienced a net loss of labour through inter-regional movement, but more than compensated by gains in non-active movers. Clearly here employment considerations were working in the opposite direction to the other factors attracting migrants.

Five regions showed labour-led out-migration, with the labour component in the net outflow as high as 99.8 per cent in the case of Lower-Normandy. Clearly here moves of inactive migrants were almost in balance whilst labour movement was predominantly outwards. Of the other regions in this category, the labour-force component made up between 48 and 74 per cent of the net population outflow.

In the single case of Alsace an inflow of labour was more than compensated by an outflow of the inactive population component. Finally, in the cases of Île-de-France and of Champagne there was clear out-migration but with the non-labour-force component being dominant. In Île-de-France, for example, the deficit on labour movement accounted for only 13 per cent of the total net deficit on inter-regional migration.

It is clear from this typology that consideration of employment opportunities needs to be supplemented by discussion of other aspects of attraction in the search for the causes of counter-urbanisation and of total inter-regional migration flows. Labour movement, although accounting for 45.2 per cent of all inter-regional movement, has not been the driving force behind net in- or out-flow in most regions.

Examination of the characteristics of the labour flow into regions in different classes of the typology (Figure 7.6) shows the existence of variations in the composition of the migrants. Unfortunately it is only possible to consider here the characteristics of in-migrants and not of those who left the region during the period. Migrants arriving in Brittany and

Figure 7.6 Characteristics of labour in-migrants, selected regions, 1975–82

	Rhône-A.	Brittany	Poitou-C.	Nord	Alsace	Île-de-France
Farmers	0.7	1.2	1.7	0.4	0.2	0.1
Artisans, self-employed	5.7	8.0	8.3	5.3	2.9	2.5
Management	17.3	14.9	14.1	21.6	17.7	18.1
Intermediate professions	25.7	24.8	24.0	24.1	24.5	22.8
Employees	29.3	31.9	31.6	26.8	32.1	40.6
Workers	21.3	19.2	20.3	21.9	22.7	15.9
Retired per 100 labour migrants	12	28	27	11	9	6

Data sources: Recensement Général de la Population de 1982: Résultats du Sondage au 1/4, France Métropolitaine

Poitou-Charentes, where counter-urbanisation and the rural revival have been accompanied by recent improvements in the pattern of labour migration, actually consist of a smaller proportion of white-collar movers than do migrants arriving in the other four example regions. These two regions show high ratios of retirement to labour migrants, again indicating the significance of considerations other than employment for the rural revival. In contrast, inter-regional labour migration to the Île-de-France region is very much dominated by white-collar movement (particularly of the less skilled), whilst that to the economically declining region of the Nord shows the strongest over-representation of the managerial class in an area where various government-sponsored industrial initiatives were under way to seek to reduce unemployment.

Conclusions

Examination of the regional dimension of labour migration in contemporary France produces interesting, and in some ways equivocal, observations. Labour migration in France has recently been diminishing in intensity, with a close relationship apparent with overall economic circumstances in the country at large. The migration balances of different regions within the country have changed quite profoundly between the 1960s and the 1980s, with regions in the west of the country improving their fortunes at the expense of regions in the east. At the regional level this east-west divide in labour migration is more pronounced than any distinction between more urban and more rural regions. Thus rural regions in the east of France (such as Franche-Comté or Champagne) have paradoxically seen their labour migration balances worsen since the days of large-scale urbanisation in the 1960s, whilst similarly rural regions in the west (such as Brittany or the Pays de la Loire) have seen an improvement.

110

The analysis presented in this chapter supplements the consideration of explanations of counter-urbanisation elsewhere (Winchester, 1989; Ogden and Winchester, in press) by highlighting the role of long-distance labour migration, a factor so far largely neglected. It appears that such migration has contributed to counter-urbanisation trends in France in recent years, but only in certain regions and to a limited extent. Detailed examination of the results of the 1982 census suggest that any hypothesis of new employment growth in rural areas attracting technical and managerial staff over long distances and thus setting up counter-urbanisation forces is far too simplistic. The truth is much more complex. Skilled labour is certainly more migratory than unskilled labour in contemporary France, but skilled labour is still being predominantly drawn into urban centres. Within regions it is possible that skilled labour moves do contribute to the growth of smaller settlement, but at this scale such movements could equally well be suburbanising moves producing longer-distance commuting patterns: the examination of such possibilities has anyway lain outside the scope of this chapter.

The role of inter-regional labour migration in counter-urbanisation in France has generally been a subsidiary one. For the country as a whole, the rural revival has been brought about much more by movement unrelated to local job availability, and a crucial role has been played by retirement movement. Certainly there have been variations from one region to another in the balance of forces at work, but where labour migration has occurred in conjunction with the rural revival, as in much of the west of France, it can be suggested that such labour migration has occurred within the context of general counter-urbanisation trends, rather than as their cause.

References

Aubry, B. (1988) 'Les migrations interrégionales depuis 30 ans: de l'attirance à l'indifférence . . . et vice versa'. *Economie et Statistique*, **212**, 13–21.
Beret, P. (1986) 'Les evolutions des systèmes de mobilité dans la crise et les stratégies des offreurs de travail'. *Travail et Emploi*, **28**, 57–68.
Berger, M. *et al.* (1980) 'Rurbanisation et analyse des espaces ruraux péri-urbains'. *Espace Géographique*, **4** 303–313.
Boudoul, J. and Faur, J-P. (1982) 'Renaissance des communes rurales ou nouvelle forme d'urbanisation' *Economie et Statistique*, **149**.
Boudoul, J. and Faur, J-P. (1985) 'Depuis 1975, les migrations interrégionales sont moins nombreuses'. *Economie et Statistique*, **180**, 11–21.
Cézard, M. and Rault, D. (1986) 'La crise a freiné la mobilité sectorielle'. *Economie et Statistique*, **184**, 41–62.
Corbel, P., Guergoat, J-C. and Laulhé, M-C. (1987) 'Les mouvements de main-d'oeuvre en 1985: nouvelle progression des contrats à durée déterminée'. *Dossiers Statistiques du Travail et de l'Emploi*, **30**, 5–41.
Courgeau, D. and Pumain, D. (1984) 'Baisse de la mobilité résidentielle'. *Population et Sociétés*, **179**.

Fielding, A. (1985) 'Migration and the new spatial division of labour' in White, P. E. and van der Knaap, G. A. (eds) *Contemporary Studies of Migration*, pp. 173–180. Norwich: Geo Books.

Fielding, A. (1987) 'Counterurbanisation in Western Europe' in Findlay, A. M. and White, P. E. (eds) *West European Population Change*, pp. 35–49. London: Croom Helm.

Jayet, H. (1988) 'Mobilité professionelle et mobilité géographique en France entre 1976 et 1980'. *Espace, Populations, Sociétés*, 3, 477–486.

Noin, D. and Chauviré, Y. (1987) *La Population de la France*. Paris: Masson.

Ogden, P. E. (1985) 'Counterurbanisation in France: the results of the 1982 population census'. *Geography*, 70, 24–35.

Perreaux, P. (1987) 'Les mouvements de main d'oeuvre en 1986: augmentation de la rotation des effectifs'. *Dossiers Statistiques du Travail et de l'Emploi*, 34–5, 137–148.

Vining, D. and Kontuly, T. (1978) 'Population dispersal from major metropolitan regions'. *International Regional Science Review*, 3, 49–74.

White, P. E. (1989) 'Internal migration in the nineteenth and twentieth centuries' in Ogden, P. E. and White, P. E. (eds), *Migrants in Modern France: Population Mobility in the Later Nineteenth and Twentieth Centuries*, pp. 13–33. London: Unwin Hyman.

Winchester, H. P. M. (1989) 'The structure and impact of the postwar rural revival: Isère' in Ogden, P. E. and White, P. E. (eds), *Migrants in Modern France: Population Mobility in the Later Nineteenth and Twentieth Centuries*, pp. 142–59. London: Unwin Hyman.

Winchester, H. P. M. and Ogden, P. E. (in press) 'The rise and fall of counterurbanization: France' in Champion, A. G. (ed) *Counterurbanisation: The Changing Pace and Nature of Population Deconcentration*. London: Edward Arnold.

PART II
Decision-making and information

CHAPTER 8

The Economics of Information in the Context of Migration

Gunther Maier

Introduction

The well known fact that 'distance acts as a serious deterrent to migration – perhaps even the single most important deterrent –' (de Jong and Fawcett, 1981, p. 22) has often been seen as the result of information effects (e.g. Sjaastad, 1962; Vanderkamp, 1971; Levy and Wadycki, 1974; Greenwood, 1975; Kau and Sirmans, 1979). As Greenwood (1975, p. 405) notes 'one reason for the finding that migration decreases perceptibly with distance is that information decreases, and hence uncertainty increases, with increased distance from a person's home'. Vanderkamp (1971, p. 1015) lists four reasons for the distance decay of migration rates, among them 'uncertainty about income prospects due to lack of information'. Despite its early recognition the influence of information was used in an *ad hoc* fashion for the interpretation of empirical results or it was merely added on to the basic framework (Sjaastad, 1962).

A more rigorous treatment of the relationship between information, uncertainty and migration started with some researchers importing concepts from the economics of information into the theory of migration decision-making (e.g. David, 1974; Flowerdew, 1976; Miron, 1978, Smith *et al.*, 1979; Rogerson and MacKinnon, 1981; Rogerson, 1982; Maier, 1985). As it turned out the relationship was not as simple as had been assumed in some of the previous literature. When using simple concepts of information the resulting migration models are dull and quite uninteresting, while more complicated (and more realistic) concepts appear to be cumbersome and in some cases even intractable.

115

In the first section of this chapter a general framework linking migration and the labour market is discussed to provide a conceptual basis for what follows. This section examines the inter-relation between people's decisions about their place of residence and place of work. It also explains the relationship between migration and commuting. We will also make some simplifying assumptions about the spatial structure of the problem, in order to keep it at a manageable size.

The following section discusses neo-classical labour market theory and its relationship to migration. We will analyse the assumptions about the decision-making process, about information, and will discuss the causes and consequences of migration.

Then we turn to the economics of information. We discuss the concept of 'job-search' and analyse its behavioural basis. We then apply the 'standard search model' to our multi-regional problem, discuss its implications for migration and underline some of its advantages and limitations. The concluding section presents a more sophisticated search model which leads to more realistic implications for migration. Information channels and their spatial and organisational structure become important elements in the migration decision. We give examples of how frequently observed phenomena in migration can be explained by such a framework.

Migration and labour market: a general framework

Each person who is working has a place of residence (R) and a place of work (W), probably coinciding. If W and R do not coincide the spatial gap between them has to be covered by commuting. Since commuting is costly not only in terms of monetary expenses but also in terms of time and effort, R and W cannot fall too far apart and the individual's decisions about them are interdependent. When changing the place of residence the individual has to take into account his place of work (or other available working opportunities) and vice versa.

Commuters are those people who have to leave their place of residence to get to their place of work. However, the distinction between commuters and non-commuters depends on the spatial scale we apply and on the individual's location within a basic spatial unit. This is sketched in Figure 8.1 where each R indicates an individual's place of residence and the connected W the respective place of work. We have thirteen individuals each facing the same distance between R and W. If we consider the circle surrounded by the solid line as our basic spatial unit we get ten non-commuters and three commuters (one in-commuter and two out-commuters). When breaking down the circle along the dashed lines into three basic spatial units we get seven non-commuters and six commuters. With successive reductions of the spatial scale we can increase the percentage of commuters further until we may end up with all thirteen individuals being commuters. For a specific definition of the basic spatial unit the chance of an individual being a commuter decreases with his distance from the border. In Figure 8.1 only individuals with R close to the solid circle have a chance of working at a location outside the basic spatial unit. Only they can become commuters in this setup.

Figure 8.1 Relationship between location, scale and definition of commuters and non-commuters

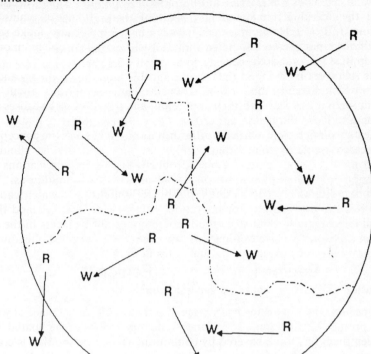

The situation sketched in Figure 8.1 is already a considerable simplification of reality since we only take into account the activities 'living' and 'working'. In reality when making location decisions people also have to consider opportunities for other activities like shopping, recreation, schools, kindergartens. So, by concentrating on 'living' and 'working' we reduce a multivariate problem to two activities.

Migration can be defined as a change in the place of residence usually without any reference to the place of work. Since this definition depends on the choice of the basic spatial unit as well, the same ambiguity applies as with commuting.

Since choices of R and W are interdependent as we have noted above, migration and commuting are inter-related processes. However, they can be complementary, substitutive, or neutral. This is sketched in Figure 8.2, where we start with an individual living and working in region I (R,W). So, this person is initially a non-commuter. If the individual moves his place of residence to R^1 in region II he becomes a migrant and a commuter at the same time, since he has to commute from R^1 to W. Migration and commuting are complementary processes in this case. On the other hand, if the individual moves his place of work from W to W^1 he substitutes commuting for migration. He does not migrate but becomes a commuter. The third possibility is the individual moves both his place of residence and his place of work to region II (R^1W^1). He becomes a migrant but does not become a commuter. These three types can be associated with different spatial contexts. The first one is typical for a suburbanising agglomeration where people increase commuting distances by living in the urban ring. The second is associated with regions which are short of workplaces. Their inhabitants have to work outside the region anyway and their only choice is either to commute or to migrate and leave the region altogether. The third possibility is typical for long-distance-migration, where the distance to the old place of work is too large to be covered by commuting.

Figure 8.2 Inter-relation of migration and commuting

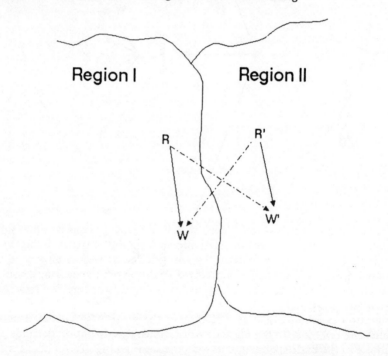

It is this third type of migration we will concentrate upon in this chapter. To be more specific, we assume a set of distinct regional labour markets (Schubert *et al.*, 1987) with no commuting between them, so that commuting occurs solely within the regions. Migration is defined in this context as a relocation of people between regions. Since commuting across boundaries is prohibited by assumption, people migrating from one region to another also have to move their place of work to that region. With this assumption we are

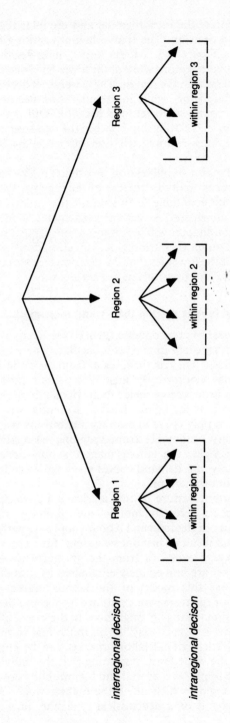

Figure 8.3 Spatial lay-out assuming distinct regional labour markets with no commuting between them.

The basic spatial layout

120

able to separate the intra-regional and the inter-regional component of an inter-related decision. The spatial layout resulting from this assumption is sketched in Figure 8.3. At the upper, inter-regional level the individual chooses between regions while at the lower level decides about the opportunities available within the region. The lower level decision is conditional on the choice of the region, while in the migration decision the individual has to take into account the lower level decision. Our main interest in this contribution lies in the relationship between the two levels: How do the opportunities for the intra-regional decision influence the inter-regional migration decision?

A second major simplification we will use in this contribution is concerned with the internal spatial structure of the regions. We treat them in the usual way, as 'point economies'. This means the regions themselves do not have any spatial dimension. All activities take place in one point. Only in the final section of the chapter will we discuss some departure from this assumption. With this assumption intra-regional location decisions become meaningless. Therefore at the lower level of the decision tree we concentrate on the choice of workplace and treat this in a spaceless way.

Neoclassical labour market theory and migration

In neoclassical microeconomic theory (see Kreps *et al.* 1974; Baumol and Blinder, 1979) the labour market is the place where the supply of and demand for labour meet. They, in turn, result from the optimising behaviour of firms and potential workers. By maximising their profit function (subject to constraints) firms derive their labour demand curve, which adds up to the demand curve of the labour market. Potential workers on the other hand derive their supply curve in a utility maximising way by trading off income (or the utility obtainable from spending it) against leisure time. Again aggregation yields the labour market supply curve. The intersection of market supply and demand curves gives the wage level and the amount of work used in production.

An important feature of this market is its transparency. All agents are assumed to be perfectly mobile and to know all relevant parameters. Therefore labour demand and labour supply are perfectly elastic. This yields the important result of just one wage level for a specific type of labour in the whole market. Deviations from the normal wage level determined in the labour market are immediately eliminated by mobility.

We can use this model of the labour market for the intra-regional component of the framework outlined above and derive its implications for the inter-regional part, i.e. migration. In the world of the neoclassical labour market model it is very easy for an individual to make rational migration decisions. Each regional labour market can be characterised by just one parameter, the wage level. Assuming that the individual aims to maximise utility at the upper level as well and that mobility costs are negligible, he will choose the region which offers the highest wage level. Since the regional labour market is of a neoclassical type, the intra-regional decision is no problem at all. The individual can randomly choose a job, because all employers offer exactly the same wage.

The process described above is of central importance in the neoclassical regional growth model (see Richardson, 1973; Armstrong and Taylor, 1985). Whenever inter-regional differences in wage levels occur they bring about migration flows from low wage to high wage regions, thus reducing labour supply in the former and increasing it in the latter. Provided migration costs are negligible migration continues until the inter-regional wage differentials are eliminated. When mobility costs are significant, however, wage differentials will not vanish completely (Cebula, 1979). They will only be eliminated up to the point where mobility costs equal the wage differential. However, in this theory they are the only element which is sensitive to distance moved. So, the distance decay in migration rates can only be attributed to migration costs.

The mechanism driving migration in this model is the labour market, in which resources seek their most productive utilisation and are guided by price signals.

One of the central elements of the theory is the assumption of rational agents. The rationality assumption of economics has been the subject of discussion for a long time (e.g. Simon, 1957; Hogarth and Reder, 1986). In the standard neoclassical model rationality not only means that individuals choose the best available alternative they are aware of, but also that they are aware of all alternatives and know all their relevant parameters with certainty (objective rationality).

As Simon (1986) observes it is the latter set of assumptions which brings about the conclusions that are reached by neoclassical reasoning. 'Almost all the action, all the ability to reach non-trivial conclusions comes from the factual assumptions and very little from the assumption of optimisation'. (Simon, 1986, p. S212) It is therefore this set of assumptions about the 'decision-making environment' (Maier and Weiss, 1987) which has to be inspected critically. The optimisation assumption alone – 'substantive rationality' as termed by Simon – is a useful theoretical tool rather than a strong behavioural assumption.

The assumptions about the decision-making environment cause a number of conceptual problems in neoclassical theory, particularly with respect to adjustment mechanisms (Arrow, 1986). An interesting question in this context is where perfect information comes from. If we consider information a commodity – and this is what economists should do – perfect information means that people always consume all the information available. Whatever economic problem comes up, neoclassical theory assumes, people have all the knowledge to deal with it. This implies that information has a zero price and accumulating it does not require any time and effort (i.e. information is completely costless). We all know that reality is not this way. Moreover, some of the information which the theory assumes people to have is not even available. Nobody can have perfect knowledge of future economic conditions, which nevertheless must be taken into account in current decisions. Success or failure of an investment project, for example, depends to a considerable amount on future prices. Money can buy sophisticated estimates but not perfect knowledge.

It is often argued by defenders of a neoclassical approach that, although reality is not that simple, people act as if it were, and that the effects of deviations from optimal rationality are eliminated by aggregation and competition. Recent theoretical work, however, demonstrates that this type of behaviour (often termed 'quasi-rational') can have a significant and persistent impact upon aggregate parameters such as prices (e.g. Akerlof and Yellen, 1985; Conlisk, 1980).

The economics of information, the labour market, and migration

The economics of information was stimulated mainly by the problem of uncertainty about the future we have mentioned above. Two of its major inter-related concepts are *expected utility* and *search*.

The concept of expected utility was introduced by von Neumann and Morgenstern (1944). We will illustrate it by the use of Figure 8.4. Suppose a decision-maker can choose between two actions, a_1 and a_2, the results of which depend also on the future state of the world. For simplicity we assume two possible states, s_1 and s_2. So, there are four results the decision-maker can get ($r_{11} - r_{22}$), two for each action. If he chooses action a_1 he can then only wait to see which state of the world occurs. With s_1 he will receive r_{11}, with s_2 it will be r_{12}. It is assumed that the decision-maker can assign (subjective) probabilities to the chance that the various states of the world will occur. In Figure 8.4 these probabilities are denoted p_1 and p_2.

Figure 8.4 Concept of expected utility: probable states of the world and choice of action

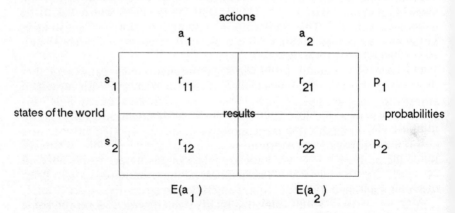

With this set of parameters the decision-maker can calculate the returns he can expect from his actions. For action i (i = 1,2) the expected return is

$$E(a_i) = r_{i1}p_1 + r_{i2}p_2$$

In general, the expected return is *not* the adequate measure on which to base the choice of action. It does not take into account the decision-maker's evaluation of the two returns. To integrate the utility function von Neumann and Morgenstern have proposed the expected utility as a criterion. Suppose the decision-maker's evaluation can be described by a utility function $U(r)$ defined over the returns. Expected utility of the i-th action is then defined as

$$EU(a_i) = U(r_{i1})p_1 + U(r_{i2})p_2$$

Or more general

$$EU(a_i) = \Sigma_l U(r_{il})p_l$$

It is essential to understand that, in general, expected utility is *not* equal to the utility of the expected return. In the former the decision-maker evaluates each possible outcome and then forms the expectation while in the latter he substitutes the expected return, a measure without any behavioural meaning, into his ultility function.

The only case where these two measures coincide is when the individual is risk neutral. In this case the individual has a linear utility function $(U(r) = \alpha + \beta r)$ and $EU(a) = U(E(a))$. A risk neutral decision-maker is indifferent between a certain event and a lottery with the same expected value. The two other cases follow immediately: a person preferring the certain event is said to be risk averse, while a risk preferring individual values the lottery higher than the certain event. The difference between the three cases is illustrated in Figure 8.5. From a specific action the individual can get returns r_1 and r_2 which yield utility $U(r_1)$ and $U(r_2)$ respectively. The expected return of this action lies somewhere between r_1 and r_2, the exact position depending on the probabilities. If p_1 is close to zero the expected return lies close to r_2; if it is close to one the expected return is near r_1. Similarly the expected utility of the action lies on the straight line connecting $U(r_1)$ and $U(r_2)$. In Figure 8.5 one possible pair of points is denoted $E(r)$ and $EU(a)$. According to the definition of risk aversion the utility of $E(r)$ must be higher than $EU(a)$ for all possible probabilities. The utility function of a risk averse decision-maker is therefore shaped like U^1 in Figure 8.5. A similar argument leads to U^2 for a risk preferring individual. The risk neutral individual has a linear utility function which coincides with the line representing the expected utilities.

It is quite obvious that, in a situation with risk, maximisation of expected utility plays the same role which utility maximisation plays in a decision with certainty. The rational decision-maker will choose the action which maximises his expected utility.

After choosing the appropriate action the decision-maker in this model is completely passive. He just waits for the state of the world to occur and has to accept whatever return he gets. This might be appropriate for a number of economic decisions but it is definitely not adequate for the labour market. In the labour market people can bargain, quit jobs and change jobs when they dislike the result they get.

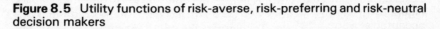

Figure 8.5 Utility functions of risk-averse, risk-preferring and risk-neutral decision makers

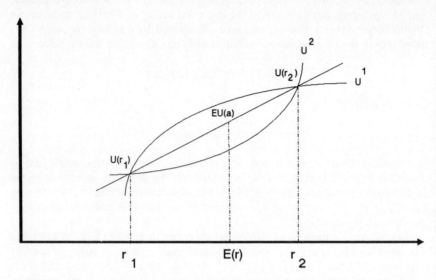

An attempt to capture at least some of these possibilities is provided by the theory of job search. As we will see later, it is closely related to the concept of expected utility maximisation. Job search theory focuses on the worker trying to find the 'best' job in the labour market. The main focus of job search theory is to determine what the 'best' job is and by which strategy it can be found. For simplicity the 'quality' of the job is usually described by the wage it offers, although introducing other characteristics should not bring about any major problem. The supply side of the labour market is viewed as a random number generator producing just these wage offers according to a given distribution.

Starting with the pioneering work by Stigler (1961; 1962) search theory has been developed in numerous variants. We will first present a basic variant – 'standard search model' (Lippman and McCall, 1976; 1979) – and then discuss some of the modifications. In the standard search model the individual is assumed to be risk-neutral and to draw randomly from the infinitely large pool of wage offers. The distribution which generated the wage offers is assumed to be known to the individual. We denote the cumulative density of this distribution by F. F(y) gives the probability that the individual draws a wage offer below the value y. The draws from the wage offer distribution are not free. For each draw the individual has to bear costs of c. These consist of two elements: '(1) direct costs or out-of-pocket expenses, and (2) opportunity costs, that is, whatever is forgone because of the search.' (Goodman, 1981, p. 143)

So, at the beginning the individual pays c to be allowed to draw from the wage offer distribution, draws one wage offer and then has to decide whether

Figure 8.6 The decision-making tree used in the search process for an acceptable wage offer

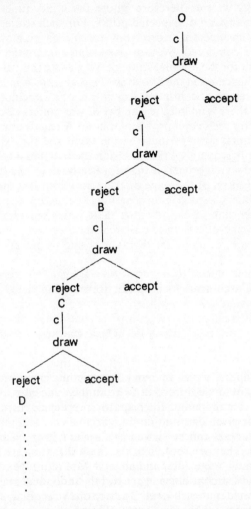

to accept this wage offer and stop searching or to reject it and draw additional offers. If he rejects the wage offer the individual again pays c, draws and decides whether to accept or reject. This process is sketched in Figure 8.6. The individual moves down the tree and at each level he has to decide about accepting or rejecting the wage offer. The major problem is just to determine acceptable and unacceptable wage offers. If the individual is too choosy he will pay too high search costs. If he is too modest he will accept an offer which is too low.

A simple argument will help us to solve this problem. Since we have assumed the individual to be risk-neutral, expected utility and expected return are related by a positive linear transformation. When determining the optimal strategy we can therefore ignore the utility function and use the expected return instead of expected utility. For each strategy the individual applies there is an expected return from search, and from our set of assumptions it can be computed. We are particularly interested in the expected return of search for the optimal strategy. We denote this value as y*. Now, if the individual has rejected the first draw (he is at point A in Figure 8.6), there is an expected return of continued search, i.e. of a search process starting at point A. Since there is an infinite number of wage offers all coming from the same distribution the search problem at point A equals exactly that at point O. So, the optimal strategy must be the same and the expected return of search at point A is again y*. The decision the individual has to make at the first level of the search process is therefore between y* and the wage offer x_1, which is a realisation of the wage offer distribution. It is quite obvious that the optimal strategy is to give up searching (i.e. accept the wage offer) only when x_1 is larger than y*. So, y* is the value which separates acceptable and unacceptable wage offers. In the search literature this point is known as 'reservation wage'. A model of this type is said to possess the 'reservation wage property'.

The numerical value of the reservation wage can be determined implicitly from the above argument. Its algebraic formulation yields after some basic transformations

$$c = \int_{y*}^{\infty} (x - y*) \, dF(x)$$

This relationship has a well known economic interpretation. The left hand side is the costs of an additional draw from the wage offer distribution while the right hand side represents the respective expected return. So, the reservation wage is determined by equating marginal cost and marginal return.

The search process can be viewed as a series of von Neumann /Morgenstern decisions. They are specific in the sense that they are between a given number, the drawn wage offer, and an uncertain return of continued search. However, in the search process in general the individual plays a more active role, since he decides at each level. The optimal strategy is quite simple. The individual searches for the first wage offer to exceed the reservation wage (McCall, 1970; Telser, 1973; Lippman and McCall, 1976, 1979).

The standard search model has some important properties which are a direct consequence of the simplifying assumptions. They also have important consequences on the migration level.

As we have seen already the reservation wage equals the expected return of search. Moreover, in the standard search model it is constant throughout the search process. This results from the assumption of an infinite number of wage offers, which implies that the searcher cannot run out of chances during the search process and from the assumption of risk-neutrality. The latter implies that the amount the individual has already paid in search costs does not have any impact on the evaluation. They are sunk investments which do not influence the future strategy. Search models with a finite number of wage offers or with more general utility functions usually do not have this property.

So, with the assumptions of the standard search model the expected return of the intra-regional decision can be described by a single parameter, the reservation wage of the respective regional labour market. This is very similar to the neoclassical model, where 'the wage level' served this purpose. The main difference is that the reservation wage in the standard search model is a function of the wage offer distribution as a whole and of search costs. For example, an increase in the variance of the distribution leads to an increase in the reservation wage (Hall, Lippman and McCall, 1979). In practical terms for a migration model it is therefore more difficult to derive estimates for regional reservation wages than the regional wage level. Conceptually, however, there is no fundamental difference between a migration model based on the neoclassical labour market theory and one based on the standard search model. The regional reservation wage simply replaces the regional wage level. Again, migration costs are the only distance sensitive element in the model. The migration decision itself is again a decision under perfect information. Although the individual does not know which wage he will finally get in a specific region nevertheless he has the same amount of information for choosing between the regions as in the neoclassical model. It is impossible in this model that during the search process the individual will have to revise his migration decision as long as the parameters remain the same. This results directly from the fact that the reservation wage remains constant through search.

This property, however, results from rather restrictive assumptions (infinite number of wage offers, risk neutrality). When the search process is limited, each rejected wage offer reduces the pool from which to choose. So, when the individual has rejected all but one of the wage offers he will accept the last one irrespective of its value since the only alternative is to have no income at all. The optimal search strategy has to take this into account and the reservation wage will decline through the search process. Risk-aversion may yield a similar result even with an infinite number of wage offers. The expenses for search costs which accumulate through the search process reduce the individual's wealth. When risk-aversion increases with decreasing wealth, as is usually argued, the individual becomes more and more risk-averse during the search process, i.e. the reservation wage declines.

At the migration level a decline in the reservation wage may have important implications. A region may become suboptimal during the search process when its reservation wage falls below that of another region. So, an individual may react to unsuccessful search by (further) migration, something which is impossible in the standard search model. A clear distinction has to be made in this context between region specific and individual specific influences. In the first case (e.g. a restricted number of employment opportunities in the region) the reservation wages of all the other regions remain unchanged. In the second (e.g. decreasing wealth, ageing) the reservation wages of all other regions will decline as well. Migration after unsuccessful search is clearly more likely in the first case. Also the size of a region becomes an important factor. For otherwise identical search problems the expected return of search is higher for a larger number of wage offers. The larger region will therefore be preferred over the smaller one.

Another major simplification we have used until now is the assumption of regional point economies, i.e. our regions lack any internal spatial dimension. What happens if we relax this assumption? For simplicity let us assume all the other simplifications of the standard search model (perfect information about the distribution, risk neutrality, infinite number of wage offers). Let us assume further that the location of the individual within the region is fixed. The internal spatial structure of the region influences the individual's search behaviour in two ways: search costs differ between firms, and, more important, commuting costs differ. Because of risk-neutrality we can aggregate search costs and the present value of commuting costs into one cost figure and use it as (generalised) search costs. In this framework the number of wage offers is restricted endogenously. Since search costs increase with the distance from the individual's location there is a distance beyond which search costs will exceed the mean of the wage offer distribution. There will be no search beyond this distance since it implies expected losses. This maximum search distance restricts the number of wage offers. Within this area the optimal strategy is to search for wage offers in increasing order of search costs (Maier, 1986). Any deviation from this sequence leads to a decrease in the expected return from search. Also the spatial distribution of wage offers within the area is important. A higher concentration of wage offers around the individual's point of residence implies, other things being equal, a higher expected return from search. The reason is that in this case the individual has a better chance to find an acceptable wage offer close by (for a more formal treatment see Maier, 1986).

The standard search model has been modified in a number of additional ways including discounting (Lippman and McCall, 1976), uncertain recall of previously rejected wage offers (Landsberger and Peled, 1977), uncertain arrival of wage offers (Flinn and Heckman, 1982), and intensity of search (Benhabib and Bull, 1983; Morgan 1986). We do not pursue these variants any further.

To summarise this section, migration is influenced by different factors according to the assumptions we apply for the intra-regional (job search) decision. In all variants except the one with risk aversion the migration decision is guided by the return an individual can expect from searching for a job in a specific region. With risk aversion the expected utility becomes the appropriate measure. We did not discuss this aspect in this contribution.

● In the standard search model the expected return of search is determined by the wage offer distribution and the level of search costs. It is constant throughout the search process. There are no internal factors in the model which may lead to a change in the migration decision.

● When there is only a limited number of wage offers available or when the individual is risk averse the reservation wage declines during search. This may lead to a revision of the migration decision. However, it is important to distinguish between region-specific and individual-specific factors in this context. Also the number of wage offers in a region influences its attractiveness for migration.

● Relaxation of the assumption of point economies yields the insight that the internal spatial structure of the region is an important factor. Search occurs only within an internally determined maximum search distance and the number of wage offers within this distance and their spatial distribution has an influence upon the expected return from search and consequently upon migration. Regions with more wage offers and regions with a more concentrated distribution yield, other things being equal, a higher expected return and are therefore more attractive for migrants.

Search models with learning and migration

So far the limitations and conceptual problems of the standard search model and its variants have not been discussed. We have mainly concentrated upon their implications for the level of migration.

One of the most important limitations of the standard search model is its treatment of labour demand (Rothschild, 1973). In the model employers simply generate wage offers and have no real intention of filling vacancies. In reality they are searching for workers just in the same way as workers are searching for jobs. Their search costs are costs of interviews, newspaper advertisement, losses in production, etc. They can partly control these costs by the wages they offer. With high wage offers their vacancies will be filled faster than with low offers, at the expense of higher labour costs. There have been a number of attempts in the literature to extend the standard search model and its variants into a labour-market model operating on the basis of search (e.g. Carlson and McAfee, 1983; Reinganum, 1979). All these models have the problem that the wage offer distribution must be determined endogenously, since it is now the result of the search behaviour of employers. This leads to potential conceptual problems with the search model, particularly with the information assumption. Assuming that workers have perfect knowledge the wage offer distribution really means that they know with certainty which behaviour the employers as a group will display. There is no reason why the same should not hold for employers as well. When labour is homogeneous (i.e. all workers have identical reservation wages), employers will only offer wages identical to the reservation wage. Lower wage offers will be rejected by all workers, higher wage offers are a waste of resources since the same labour can be hired at the reservation wage. With homogeneous labour (or homogeneous employment) the wage offer distribution will therefore collapse to the reservation wage. All attempts to extend the concept of search to a labour market model rely therefore on the assumption of workers differing in terms of search costs and employers having different cost functions (see Carlson and McAfee, 1983). This, however, is not a very satisfactory solution. It is difficult to see why workers, who all know the wage offer distribution (or the behaviour of labour demand) equally well, should differ in search efficiency.

The source of this conceptual problem lies again in the assumption made about information. As a matter of fact, the assumption of perfect knowledge of the wage offer distribution is not much weaker than the perfect information assumption of neoclassical theory. Only if information about the wage offer distribution is free, will an optimising individual acquire full knowledge about the wage offer distribution. Otherwise he will try to balance the cost of additional information with its marginal value. The latter depends crucially upon the purpose for which the information is needed.

Perfect knowledge of the wage offer distribution implies some strange behaviour by the decision-maker. In the standard search model, even when he is offered the lowest possible wage a number of times in a row, he will not change his beliefs about the wage offer distribution and lower his aspiration level. In reality we would doubt the psychic health of such a person.

Also, the assumption itself appears to be a rather strange breed. When doing empirical work no economist has ever had perfect knowledge about the price distribution in a market. All he has had were observations and parameter estimates. Nevertheless, assumptions of perfect information or perfect knowledge of some distribution are quite common in the economics profession.

The reason for the popularity of this assumption lies in the fact that it simplifies the model structure and brings about an optimal search strategy which has the reservation wage property. With this property the set of possible wage offers can be divided into two convex subsets, acceptable and non-acceptable wage offers. If the assumption of perfect knowledge of the wage offer distribution is dropped 'the problem becomes more complex, and search strategies become less well behaved' (Rosenfield and Shapiro, 1981, p. 1). Search models with learning, where wage offers not only characterise employment opportunities but also provide additional information about the wage offer distribution which the searcher uses to update his prior beliefs, do not necessarily have the reservation wage property. Consider, for example, the following situation (adapted from Rothschild, 1974, p. 701):

> Suppose there are three wages, $1.00, $2.00, and $3.00, and that the cost of search is $0.01. Prior beliefs admit the possibility of only two distributions of wages. Either all wages are $1.00 or they are distributed between $2.00 and $3.00 in the proportions 1 to 99. A man with these beliefs should accept a wage of $1.00 (as this is a signal that no higher wages are to be had) and reject a quote of $2.00 (which indicates that the likelihood is high that a much better wage will be obtained at another draw) (Lippman and McCall, 1976, p. 174).

Obviously there is no reservation wage in this example. What makes this example work is that the wage offer contains an enormous amount of information, since it allows the individual to discriminate between the two possible distributions. In more reasonable situations, however, this search model with learning also usually has the reservation wage property (Rothschild, 1974; Rosenfield and Shapiro, 1981).

In this contribution we want to restrict ourselves to a model which has the reservation wage property. Moreover, we only want to give an intuitive outline of this model type and to discuss the consequences for migration. (For a more formal treatment see Rothschild, 1974; Rosenfield and Shapiro, 1981; Maier, 1983, 1985; Morgan, 1985.) Again, for the sake of simplicity we will retain the basic assumptions of the standard search model and only modify this single element.

In a search model with learning the individual starts with some prior beliefs about the respective distribution. These beliefs can originate from sources like friends, relatives, media, special reports, etc. They are a by-product of everyday life, which means there were no resources devoted especially to the acquisition of that information. Nevertheless, the prior beliefs held by an individual play an important role in the model. Only when they indicate a chance for success will a rational (risk-neutral) individual invest resources into the acquisition of additional information or job search. This prior knowledge not only has a content but also a specific reliability. In a modelling context the prior knowledge is usually expressed as a sample and its reliability by the sample size. In reality, however, judgment of the reliability of information is a quite complicated task for the decision-maker influenced by a number of factors.

When the individual acquires additional information, it has to be merged with his prior beliefs. Prior knowledge and additional information together form the individual's new state of information. In the models this updating is usually done by Bayes' rule, which weights all the information equally. When the individual's prior beliefs only have low reliability, additional information will have a strong influence upon the updated (posterior) knowledge. When the reliability is high, it will only have a small impact. At the limit, when reliability goes to infinity, the individual has perfect knowledge about the distribution and we are back at the standard search model. The standard search model is therefore a limiting case of this search model with learning. The expected (marginal) return of an additional unit of information, which is high for prior beliefs with low reliability, converges to zero in the case of the standard search model.

Additional information to be added to the prior beliefs may come from information activities or search activities. The first only attempt to improve the individual's state of knowledge about the wage offer distribution, while the latter also carry the right to accept the investigated job. Search differs between the standard search model and the model with learning. In the search model with learning each search not only provides an employment opportunity but also gives additional information about the wage offer distribution. So, the decision-maker has to decide about accepting or rejecting the offer, but also has to incorporate additional information into his state of knowledge.

This has consequences for the search process itself. Contrary to the standard search model, observing a sequence of unacceptable wage offers influences the individual's perception of the wage offer distribution. Intuitively, the influence should be such that, with each additional unacceptable wage offer obtained, the decision-maker will consider that an acceptable wage offer is less likely to be made. The decision-maker realises that high wages are more difficult to get than he has initially thought. This will tend to lower the reservation wage. The wage offers observed during the search process have an asymmetric effect upon the updated beliefs. The decision-maker can only grow less selective, since the wage offers which are able to raise his reservation wage immediately stop the search process. As a consequence, a search activity based on more reliable prior beliefs yields a higher expected return than one based on identical but less reliable prior beliefs. This is true even for a risk-neutral decision-maker.

Another consequence is that acquiring information, although costly, may be a profitable activity. It is usually modelled analogously to search. The individual again has to pay some fee and is then allowed to draw one wage offer from the distribution. Its sole purpose is to improve the reliability of the individual's beliefs about the wage offer distribution. Updating is performed in the same way as above. In reality there may be great differences between the information one gets from job search and from collecting information (Hugo, 1981; Gustavus and Brown, 1977). They may differ in terms of reliability and also in terms of content, although it is hard to judge in theory which activity might provide the more reliable information.

In our modelling framework information activities are specific to the search model with learning. In the standard search model and its variants information activities are suboptimal. They are simply a waste of resources, since the searcher has all information about the distribution by assumption.

Now, let us turn to the migration level. The return an individual can expect from searching for a job in a specific region (the intra-regional component) is again the relevant measure for choosing among the regions. Now it depends on the individual's perception of the respective wage offer distribution, its content as well as its reliability, rather than the distribution itself. The perceptions result from the individual's prior knowledge and additional information about the wage offer distribution which he has gained through information or search activities. The individual's prior beliefs are a key factor in this model, as they provide the basis for any further decisions. The rational decision-maker will migrate or acquire additional information only when he can expect a net gain on the basis of his prior knowledge. Important cost components influencing the net return of the various strategies are information costs, migration costs, and search costs.

This differs markedly from the migration model resulting from the standard search framework, where search and migration costs are the only relevant cost components and migration costs alone are distance sensitive. In the migration model based on search with learning, spatial factors play a much more prominent role. Physical distance increases all cost components. Language barriers, cultural differences, etc. have an impact by limiting the flow of information. Radio, TV and newspapers may lead to a biased distri-

133

bution of information and thus structure migration flows (for an empirical investigation see Saunders and Flowerdew, 1987). Friends and relatives who have migrated earlier provide access to information about specific regions. They improve the prior knowledge of those who stay behind and also provide a cheap source for additional information. Past migrants will therefore increase the chance of current and future migration. Improved prior knowledge and lower information costs establish 'beaten paths' of migrants (Morrison, 1977).

The model also allows for differences between individuals in the ability to acquire information. People with higher education, specific social groups, particular professions, etc. may have better access to information. They will have more reliable prior beliefs as well as being able to get additional information at lower cost. Therefore, they will more likely respond to inter-regional differentials by migration. So, differences in information costs and prior knowledge can also serve as an argument for demographic and socio-economic differences in the level of spatial mobility. These phenomena are well documented in the empirical literature (see Greenwood, 1975).

We have already pointed out that a major weakness of most job-search models is their limitation to the supply side of the labour market and that the concept should be extended to the labour market as a whole. In the context of search models with learning such an attempt causes considerably higher technical problems as in the case of the standard search model. On the other hand, the less restrictive framework will allow more substantial insights into the decision-making process. The simultaneous attempts of supply and demand to find the optimal partner at the other side of the market and mutual feedback processes via learning may bring about theoretical arguments for the establishment of new strategies and labour market institutions. Search and information costs can be saved in a considerable amount when both sides of the market 'agree' to use specific information channels. Once established these

> ... institutions have the potential to structure the market. They can filter information, specialise on some specific area (in terms of content and space) or favor one side of the market. Even when biased in one way or the other they are not necessarily challenged by competing institutions, since establishing a new institution requires cooperation from both sides of the market. (Maier and Weiss, 1987, p. 13)

The spatial layout and operation of information channels and labour market institutions may have considerable impact upon migration via the mechanisms mentioned in this section.

References

Akerlof, G. A. and Yellen, J. L. (1985) 'Can small deviations from rationality make significant differences to economic equilibria?' *American Economic Review*, **75**, 708-20.

Armstrong, Harvey and Taylor, Jim (1985) *Regional economics and policy.* Oxford: Philip Allan.

Arrow, Kenneth J. (1986) 'Rationality of self and others in an economic system'. *The Journal of Business*, **59**, 4, Pt.2, 5385-400.

Baumol, William J. and Blinder, Alan S. (1979) *Economics principles and policy.* New York: Harcourt Brace Jovanovich.

Benhabib, Jess and Bull, Clive (1983) 'Job search: the choice of intensity'. *Journal of Political Economy*, **91**, 747-64.

Carlson, John A. and Preston McAfee, R. (1983) 'Discrete equilibrium price dispersion'. *Journal of Political Economy*, **91**, 480-93.

Cebula, Richard J. (1979) *Determinants of human migration.* Lexington: Lexington Books.

Conlisk, John (1980) 'Costly optimizers versus cheap imitators'. *Journal of Economic Behavior and Organization*, **1**, 275-93.

David, Paul A. (1974) 'Fortune, risk and the microeconomics of migration' in David, Paul A and Reder, Melvin W. (eds) *Nations and Households in Economic Growth.* New York: Academic Press.

De Jong, Gordon F. and Fawcett, James T. (1981) 'Motivations for migration: An assessment and a value-expectancy research model' in De Jong, Gordon F. and Gardner, Robert W. (eds) *Migration Decision Making, Multidisciplinary Approaches to Microlevel Studies in Developed and Developing Countries.* New York: Pergamon Press.

Flinn, Christopher J. and Heckman, James J. (1982) 'New methods for analyzing structural models of labor force dynamics' *Journal of Econometrics*, **24**, 115-68.

Flowerdew, Robin (1976) 'Search strategies and stopping rules in residential mobility'. *Institute of British Geographers Transactions*, New Series **1**, 47-57.

Goodman, John L. (1981) 'Information, uncertainty, and the micro-economic model of migration decision making' in De Jong, Gordon F. and Gardner, Robert W. (eds), *Migration Decision Making, Multidisciplinary Approaches to Microlevel Studies in Developed and Developing Countries.* New York: Pergamon Press.

Greenwood, Michael, J. (1975) 'Research on internal migration in the United States: A survey'. *Journal of Economic Literature*, **8**, 397-433.

Gustavus, Susan D. and Brown, Lawrence A. (1977) 'Place attributes in a migration decision context. *Environment and Planning*, **9**, 529-48.

Hall, Jeffrey, R., Lippman, Steven A. and McCall, John J. (1979) 'Expected utility maximizing job search' in Lippman, Steven A. and McCall, John J. (eds) (1979) *Studies in the Economics of Search.* Amsterdam: North Holland.

Hogarth, Robin M. and Reder, Melvin W. (eds) (1986) 'The Behavioral Foundations of Economic Theory'. *The Journal of Business*, **59**, 4, Pt.2.

Hugo, Graeme J. (1981) 'Village-community ties, village norms, and ethnic and social networks: a review of evidence from the third world' in De Jong, Gordon F. and Gardner, Robert W. (eds) *Migration Decision Making, Multidisciplinary Approaches to Microlevel Studies in Developed and Developing Countries.* New York: Pergamon Press.

Kau, James B. and Sirmans, C. F. (1977) 'The influence of information cost, and uncertainty on migration: A comparison of migrant types. *Journal of Regional Science*, **17**, 89–96.

Kreps, Juanita M., Somers, Gerald G. and Perlman, Richard (1974) *Contemporary labour economics: issues, analysis, and policies*. Belmont: Wadsworth Publishing.

Landsberger, Michael and Peled, Dan (1977) 'Duration of offers, price structure and the gain from search'. *Journal of Economic Theory*, **16**, 17–37.

Levy, M. B. and Wadycki, W. J. (1974) 'Education and the decision to migrate: An econometric analysis of migration in Venezuela'. *Econometrica*, **42**, 377–88.

Lippman, Steven A. and McCall, John J. (1976) 'The economics of job search: A survey. *Economic Inquiry*, **14**, 2, 155–189 and **14**, 3, 347–68.

Lippman, Steven A. and McCall John J. (1979) *Studies in the Economics of Search*. Amsterdam: North Holland.

Maier, Gunther (1983) 'Migration decision with imperfect information'. IIR-Discussion No. 16. Vienna: University of Economics.

Maier, Gunther (1985) 'Cumulative causation and selectivity in labour market oriented migration caused by imperfect information'. *Regional Studies*, **19**, 231–41.

Maier, Gunther (1986) 'The impact of optimal search models on the modelling of migration behavior'. IIR-Discussion No. 29. Vienna: University of Economics.

Maier, Gunther and Weiss, Peter (1987) 'Rationality and qualitative choice in an institutionalist framework: will much "cruder and simpler arguments" really suffice?'. Paper for the workshop on Institutional Choice and Design, 2–4 June 1987. Vienna: University of Economics.

McCall, John J. (1970) 'Economics of information and job search'. *Quarterly Journal of Economics*, **84**, 113–26.

Miron, J. R. (1978) 'Job search perspectives on migration behavior'. *Environment and Planning A*, **10**, 519–36.

Morgan, Peter B. (1985) 'Distributions of the durations and value of search with learning'. *Econometrica*, **53**, 1199–232.

Morgan, Peter B. (1986) 'A note on job search: The choice of intensity'. *Journal of Political Economy*, **94**, 439–42.

Morrison, Peter (1977) 'The functions and dynamics of the migration process' in Brown, Alan and Neuberger, Egon (eds) *Internal Migration: A Comparative Perspective*. New York: Academic Press.

Reinganum, Jennifer F. (1979) 'A simple model of equilibrium price dispersion'. *Journal of Political Economy*, **87**, 851–858.

Richardson, Harry W. (1973) *Regional growth theory*. London: Macmillan.

Rogerson, Peter and MacKinnon, Ross D. (1981) 'A geographical model of job search, migration and unemployment'. *Papers of the Regional Science Association*, **48**, 89–102.

Rogerson, Peter (1982) 'Spatial models of search'. *Geographical Analysis*, **14**, 217–28.

Rosenfield, Donald, Shapiro, B. and Roy, D. (1981) 'Optimal adaptive price search'. *Journal of Economic Theory*, **25**, 1–20.

Rothschild, Michael (1973) 'Models of market organization with imperfect information: a survey. *Journal of Political Economy*, **81**, 1283–308.

Rothschild, Michael (1974) 'Searching for the lowest price when the distribution of prices is unknown'. *Journal of Political Economy*, **82**, 689–711.

Saunders, M. N. K. and Flowerdew, R. (1987) 'Spatial aspects of the provision of job information' in Fischer, M. M. and Nijkamp, P. (eds) *Regional Labour Markets* pp.205–28. Amsterdam: North Holland.

Schubert, U., Gerking, S., Isserman, A. and Taylor, C. (1987) 'Regional labour market modelling: a state of the art review' in Fischer, Manfred M. and Nijkamp, Peter (eds) *Regional labour markets*. Amsterdam: North Holland.

Simon, Herbert (1957) *Models of Man*. New York: Wiley.

Simon, Herbert (1986) 'Rationality in psychology and economics'. *The Journal of Business*, **59**, 4, Pt.2, S209–224.

Sjaastad, Larry A. (1962) 'The costs and returns of human migration'. *Journal of Political Economy*, **70**, 80–93.

Smith, Terence R., Clark, W. A. V., Huff, J. O. and Shapiro, P. (1979) A decision making and search model for intra-urban migration'. *Geographical Analysis*, **11**, 1–22.

Stigler, George J. (1961) 'The economics of information'. *Journal of Political Economy*, **69**, 3, 213–25.

Stigler, George J. (1962) 'Information in the labor market'. *Journal of Political Economy*, **70**, 1, 94–105.

Telser, L. G. (1973) 'Searching for the lowest price'. *American Economic Review*, **63**, 40–9.

Vanderkamp, John (1971) 'Migration, flows, their determinants and the effects of return migration'. *Journal of Political Economy*, **79**, 1012–32.

von Neumann, John and Morgenstern, Oskar (1944) *Theory of Games and Economic Behavior*. Princeton: Princeton University Press.

CHAPTER 9

Migration and Job Vacancy Information

Mark N. K. Saunders

Introduction: job search and migration

Some labour migration is initiated by employers as multi-locational companies move their employees between various sites. McKay and Whitelaw (1977) inferred an important role for this type of migration through their study of those occupational categories closely associated with large firms in Australia. In the United States, Lansing and Mueller (1967) found that 25 per cent of their sample moving for economic, presumably job related, reasons were transferred by their employer.

Utilising data from their 1970–71 Housing and Labour Mobility Study, Johnson and Salt (1980) found that a slightly larger proportion (28 per cent) of British migrants moving for job reasons had remained with the same employer. Of these, over two-thirds had been asked to move by their employer. Those transferred tended to be males in managerial, professional and related occupations. Thus migration as a result of transfer within an organisation consists primarily, although not exclusively, of those in managerial, professional and technical occupations. More recent work by Salt (Salt and Flowerdew, 1986) suggests that employer initiated moves form a still higher proportion accounting for nearly 60 per cent of inter-regional moves.

However it seems probable that at least half of all job related moves will also involve a change of employer. Once again the majority of these migrants will be professional or technical workers (Bonnar, 1979), employment being arranged prior to migration. As a group such occupations have an overall high mobility rate, although there is considerable between-profession

137

variation (McKay and Whitelaw, 1977). Correspondingly junior non-manual and manual occupations have been shown to have a lower propensity to migrate (Gleave and Palmer, 1980).

Silvers (1977) suggests that migrants can be classified into two types:

(1) Those moving to an area to look for work (speculative migrants).
(2) Those searching for work and moving to an area only after they have found and accepted an offer (contracted migrants).

The latter will include employees moved by their employer. Lansing and Mueller (1967) found that 51 per cent of migrants moving for employment reasons already had a new job arranged prior to moving, with another 20 per cent moving but remaining with the same employer. Only 21 per cent were found to have migrated on speculation. When only workers who migrated to work for a new employer were considered, 85 per cent of professional and technical workers were found to have prearranged their jobs. In contrast only 61 per cent of other non-manual and 49 per cent of manual employees had a job prior to moving, these occupations producing far fewer migrants in proportion.

The migration process as experienced by the majority of workers involves a number of steps. A job seeker becomes aware of a specific post whose pay, working conditions and general environment appear preferable. He or she then applies for the job, migration being dependent upon a successful application and the need to move in order to undertake the job. In most cases such moves will be the result of the job being outside daily commuting distance, although for some posts a condition of employment may be residence in accommodation provided by the employer. The key factors in this process are therefore the means by which the employer notifies the vacancy, and the way the job seeker becomes aware of the vacancy; in other words, the role of information.

Empirical literature reveals little about the relationship between information job search and migration. Models of varying degrees of complexity have been produced (for example Rogerson and MacKinnon, 1982; Pickles and Rogerson, 1984; Amrhein and MacKinnon, 1984; Maier 1987), but their calibration and a real understanding of the process have been limited by a lack of results from empirical research.

The process by which people first hear about the vacancy which they later take up has been studied from the job seeker's viewpoint for a variety of occupations (for example Bradshaw, 1973; Granovetter, 1974). However, these studies have usually concentrated on the relative importance of different types of vacancy information source. Occasionally, as in the housing and labour mobility survey (Johnson, Salt and Wood, no date), data are available about how migrants first heard about their current jobs. This suggests that information is important in the migration process, thereby supporting theoretical work, but still leaves doubts about how this process operates. Salt's (1983) work on employee moves in multi-locational firms has shown the importance of such moves within the overall migration process. However, research has not considered moves between single location firms.

For such cases external notification is likely to be far more important.
Palm's (1976) housing mobility research supports the idea that information will be important, and showed that the way that a realtor provided information on vacant houses influenced the set of potential buyers. The exact
way such a process would operate in job search, and how this would then
influence migration is less certain. Different information will be provided by
the employer for different occupations through different information
channels, with certain ones more appropriate for particular jobs
(Braithwaite, 1976). Legislation or union agreements may also compel the
employer to provide vacancy information in a specified way, or through
stated channels (Clark, 1983). The characteristics of the area in which the
firm is located may also influence the recruitment pattern. Whilst these
factors have been recognised (for example Flowerdew, 1982) their effect on
recruitment and subsequent employee mobility is not known.

This paper considers the impact of vacancy information outlet choice on
migration from both the employer and employee viewpoints. The findings
have obvious policy implications for the employer and job seeker, as well as
for central government. Migration literature has shown certain occupation
and age groups to be more migratory which suggests that the effect of recruitment methods may well differ between various sub-groups of the population
(Ladinsky, 1967; Gleave and Palmer, 1980; Devis 1983). External factors are
also considered so as to provide a holistic study which places the role of the
recruitment process in the context of other factors influencing migration.

The application of a soft systems approach

The systems approach incorporates a method for conceptualising the system
of interest, in this case vacancy information and job related migration, as a
series of components. Many of these are related to one another, and some are
also coupled to other systems or components of interest outside the system of
interest (Wilson, 1981). The methodology emphasises the linkages between
the various components within the system as well as their interdependence
with components outside the system's boundary (Jenkins, 1969). This is
important as it is necessary to conceptualise and understand how job search,
information provision and migration are interlinked. A systems approach
therefore provides a series of guidelines by which the exact focus of the
research can be identified and clearly expressed, and the relevant systems and
their interactions defined (Checkland, 1981).

Two separate but interlinked systems can be used to express the overall
situation. These are an 'employer's attraction system' and a 'job search and
migration system'. The former of these can be said to be under the
employer's control, and the latter under that of the job searcher, who may as
a product of job search also become a migrant. Inevitably both systems are
subject to external influences. The employer's attraction system affects the
way in which the job search and migration system operate. An employer's
choice of notification outlets will at least partially determine who receives
information about vacancies. This and other factors, such as the provision

of mobility incentives, may also affect the likelihood of job related migration. In a similar manner a variety of external bodies outside the employer's control (including government agencies) may also influence job search and the subsequent migration pattern of the job seeker. It is within the confines of this subsystem that the potential employee receives and acts upon vacancy information, as well as being influenced by other factors. In summary:

- The **employer's attraction system** can be described as a system through which the vacancy information provided, the way it is distributed, and the level of mobility assistance offered by the employer are defined, subject to the characteristics of the vacant post, the characteristics of the firm, and a variety of external factors outside the employer's control.

- The **job search and migration system** can be summarized as that which decides whether or not a job seeker will consult vacancy information channels and apply for a vacancy which he or she has heard about. If successful it will affect whether or not he or she will need to migrate to take up the post. This is subject to the way the employer has notified the vacancy, the mobility assistance offered by the firm, the nature of the vacancy, the characteristics of the job seeker, and a variety of external factors outside both the employer's and job seeker's control.

A conceptual model can then be constructed from these summaries. The links within the model can be represented by one or a series of verbs. In their simplest form these links can be characterised by the verb 'affects', and an influence diagram constructed (Figure 9.1). This model illustrates how the two systems are linked, and how the external influences operate on them. Because the model is firmly based upon the migration and job search literature the influence diagram incorporates all these factors, rather than just the role of information. Through this it is hoped a better representation of the real world has been obtained. Each of these factors, represented by oval boxes, can be visualised as having some form of influence (represented by the arrows) over the way in which the overall employment-related migration system operates.

Three distinct areas of control are immediately visible in the job search/recruitment/migration process. Each of these may be controlled by different factors in the process. The factors over which the employer has some control centre upon the outlets chosen to disseminate information about vacancies and the level of migration assistance offered. Control may take the form of a recruitment policy which states how and when difficult vacant posts should be advertised, although this will differ between firms. The type of vacancy information provided by employers will also be subject to external factors which are outside their control. Government legislation may influence or even specify the recruitment procedure used for a particular post, as could an agreement between the employer and a union. The characteristics of the local labour market may also influence the way an employer notifies vacancies, and the type of information provided. Between them these factors will result

Figure 9.1 Influence diagram showing factors affecting the provision of vacancy information and subsequent likelihood of migration

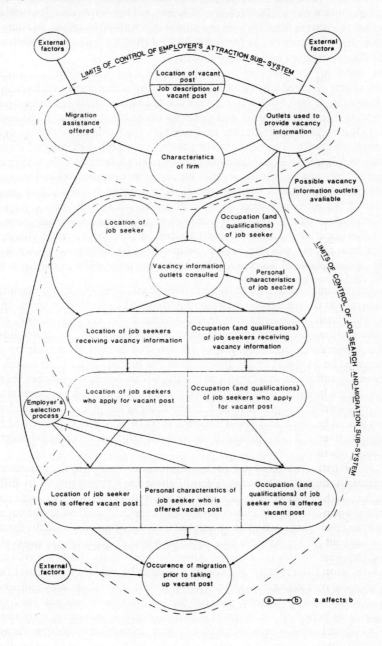

in a particular population sub-group. The type of vacancy information provided by the employer should therefore dictate, to a large extent, the location and personal characteristics of the job seekers who receive information about a particular vacancy. This means that employers can influence whether the post is filled by a migrant by their choice of vacancy notification media. An employer could further influence the likelihood of migration by providing incentives to facilitate moving.

In contrast job seekers control the amount and type of vacancy information received through their choice of information media to consult. By choosing certain outlets the job seeker will immediately restrict search to vacancies in a specific area, and perhaps range of occupations (Saunders, 1986). Job seekers can therefore predetermine their probability of migration through the choice of information channels. Inevitably the choice of whether or not to migrate will have already been partially affected by the employer's decision on how to provide the vacancy information (Rogerson and MacKinnon, 1982), and whether or not the employer decides to hire the job seeker at the interview stage. The location of job seekers who receive the vacancy information, and their occupational and personal characteristics, are influenced by the outlets used to advertise the existence of vacancies. Local newspapers will only reach people in a limited geographical area, whereas professional journals tend only to be read by the professions they serve (Braithwaite, 1976).

Through their choice of methods to disseminate information employers partially control the location of those who receive details about vacancies. This has further implications, as it also affects the subsequent likelihood of migration to take up the post. If informal contacts only are used, then few people will be reached (Granovetter, 1974). Providing the information through formal media increases the number of potential applicants considerably. If national circulation outlets are used then information will be available over a large geographical area. This means that the job seeker, and thus the successful applicant, may be located outside his or her threshold commuting distance (Dasgupta, 1983). If this is the case then he or she will either have to migrate or not take up the post. If only local circulation media are used to notify vacancies then this situation will be less likely. The relationship is unlikely to be the same for all occupations, as some are more migratory than others (Gleave and Palmer, 1980) and so migration will also be related to occupation. The job seeker also controls his or her decision to search, and thus whether he or she is receptive to vacancy information. This is related, at least partially, to personal characteristics such as age, sex, and life-cycle stage, which are also related to the likelihood of migration (Clark WAV 1982; Devis, 1983).

External incentives will also influence the probability of migration. The employer may provide mobility assistance for the employees which will increase the likelihood of migration by significantly reducing the inertia impeding moving. In a similar manner accommodation assistance will reduce the inertia caused by the need to find somewhere to live (Johnson et al., 1974). Government mobility schemes may encourage prospective employees to take up a post where acceptance necessitates migration, with mobility assistance for movements within the same firm having a similar effect. Less obvious, although still important, are the potential applicants' perceptions of the relative attractiveness of the source and destination areas (Gould and White, 1974). These may influence not only the decision to apply, but also the decision to take up the offered job where migration if necessary. However, it is likely that these factors are less important, because without vacancy information the job seeker could never have heard about the post in the first place.

Methods of disseminating information are not just a product of the nature of the vacant post (Figure 9.2), since the outlets used in effect summarise a range of factors. Thus overall a discernible 'information effect' (due in part to these other factors) should still be noticeable even after controlling for different occupations and personal characteristics. This 'effect' will summarise aspects of both the employer's and the job seeker's influence over the process. The former will choose which outlets to use from those available, and the latter will decide (consciously or subconsciously) whether or not to search each of the available recruitment media outlets for vacancies. The job seeker's choice may in some cases preclude the possibility of migration. Thus the occurrence of migration will also be related to the outlet through which the job seeker first heard of the vacancy. It is the importance of this 'information effect' upon migration that will now be addressed using the example of local government employment in England and Wales.

The aggregate pattern of local government vacancy information

To investigate the effects of the choice of vacancy notification outlets on employee location and any subsequent migration, the recruitment practices of Non-Metropolitan District Councils (NMDCs) in England and Wales were examined. These constitute a lower tier of local government; each provides essentially the same diverse range of services to a population of approximately 100,000. Each is an independent entity, but they all have the same statutory responsibilities and hence similar needs for labour. These cover a wide range of occupations including professional, managerial, technical, clerical and manual. A postal questionnaire was used to obtain data about which information outlets were used by NMDCs to notify a range of occupation types. This questionnaire resulted in 217 responses, a 66.6 per cent response rate, and tests carried out suggest that the sample was representative of NMDCs in England and Wales in terms of the areas they served. The results discussed relate to the way in which a NMDC would normally advertise a vacancy of the specified type. As such they do not represent the number of outlets used or the frequency of notification, but rather the relative importance of local and national outlet types for different posts.

Considerable differences were found in the use of local and national recruitment media over the range of occupations. Manual posts are notified, almost without exception, through local circulation outlets. Internal recruitment and word-of-mouth both decline in importance as the skill level increases, but local newspaper advertisements are more important for notifying skilled vacancies. As suggested by other studies (for example Bradshaw, 1973), notification by word of mouth is more frequent for manual than non-manual posts. 25 per cent of responding districts said that they would normally use this method for manual jobs compared with 6.5 per cent for non-manual posts.

Fewer councils used local free newspapers than local traditional newspapers for their recruitment notification presumably because fewer free papers were available at that time (British Rate and Data, 1983). Internal circulars were important for notifying all manual vacancies, and were normally used by 68.5 per cent of all responding councils. They were more widely used for non-manual posts, where they were mentioned by 85.4 per cent of responding councils.

Considerable variation existed in the type and range of outlets that were usually used to notify non-manual posts. For posts not requiring professional qualifications local outlets, in particular newspapers, were most frequently used (99.5 per cent of cases). Some employers used job centres only because the services they provided were free, and so further publicity for a vacancy could be gained at little extra cost. Limited notification through national outlets (used by 36 per cent of councils) was concentrated in local government related journals, in particular those provided free of charge to employees.

Those posts which required professional qualifications were advertised nationally by the majority of NMDCs. The most widely used outlets were local government free publications such as *Opportunities*, professional journals such as *The Planner*, and other local government related publications such as the *Municipal Journal*. These were used by over three-quarters of respondents. Other national outlets such as daily newspapers, weekly magazines, and the state administered Professional Executive Register (PER) were used by less than 5 per cent of responding NMDCs.

Internal notification of vacancies was important for all non-manual posts, although not as important for those which require professional qualifications. This must be due in part to the various agreements between employers and unions. It may also be a result of the recommendation in the Bains' Report (1972) that each local authority should provide a career structure and training. As a consequence councils were able to replace the skills and expertise of leaving and retiring employees internally, and so notification of possible internal candidates was sensible (Fowler, 1980), especially if job savings could be made at the same time.

A signficant difference in use of local and national media existed between posts (see Figure 9.2). Local media were always used for manual, trainee, and junior non-manual posts. National media were rarely used for manual posts, and less than a quarter of trainee and a third of junior non-manual posts were notified in this way. In contrast (and as suggested by Braithwaite, 1976) virtually all professional posts were notified nationally. In summary the more qualifications a post required, the more likely it was to be notified

Figure 9.2 Use of advertisements in local and national media for different types of post

A LOCAL MEDIA

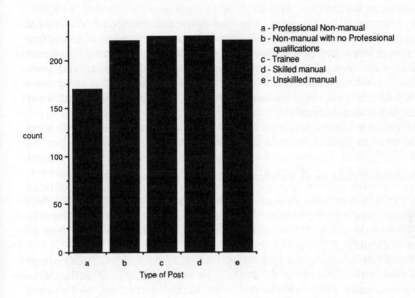

a - Professional Non-manual
b - Non-manual with no Professional
     qualifications
c - Trainee
d - Skilled manual
e - Unskillled manual

B NATIONAL MEDIA

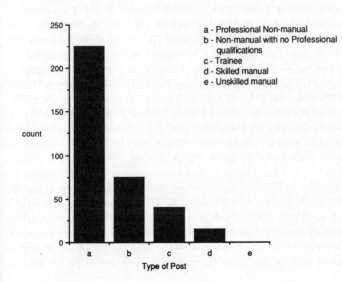

a - Professional Non-manual
b - Non-manual with no Professional
     qualifications
c - Trainee
d - Skilled manual
e - Unskilled manual

nationally, and the fewer qualifications the less likely. The relationship with local media notification was the reverse of this, although it was not so pronounced.

It therefore seems probable that, as suggested earlier, the types of media used by NMDCs to notify a vacancy were related to the occupation type involved. As the skill and responsibility levels increased so did the likelihood of national notification. However, recruitment policy is not only related to the vacancy, as there were pronounced differences between NMDCs in how they notified similar vacancies. A series of tests were conducted to discover if there was any significant difference in the local area characteristics between NMDCs which notified a particular type of post nationally and those which did not. NMDCs which served large populations were significantly less likely to notify junior technical and administrative posts nationally than those with small populations. Similarly where unemployment rates were relatively high national notification was significantly less likely for technical and administrative posts than in areas of low unemployment.

The detailed pattern of vacancy notification and migration

Four NMDCs allowed their personnel records to be used to obtain further information about the linkages between job vacancy information and migration: namely Alyn and Deeside (Clwyd), Lancaster City (Lancashire), Tonbridge and Malling Borough (Kent) and the Vale of the White Horse (Oxfordshire). Data were extracted for every externally recruited vacancy since each council's inception in 1974, including the type of post, methods used to notify the vacancy, how the employee was recruited, whether migration was involved, and personal details for each employee. The data included all employees from the Vale of the White Horse, and all non-manual employees for the other NMDCs.

For all four councils professional vacancies such as architects/town planners and accountants were notified nationally in professional and trade journals, and often in occupation sector publications (Figure 9.3). In the case of professional and trade journals, particular journals concentrated on particular job types such as *Building* or *The Surveyor* for surveyors' posts. Most nationally notified vacancies including the professions were also placed in a local government journal such as *Opportunities*. These occupation sector publications were also used for those occupations which do not have a well-established professional journal, such as chief executive and other more general administrative posts. Use of local newspapers, including free sheets, were shown to be inversely correlated with use of national notification methods.

In contrast, clerical and manual vacancies were rarely notified outside local circulation media (Figure 9.3). Within this pattern the differences in the use of local newspapers, job centres, and circulation of adjacent authorities appeared to be based on two closely related factors: the notification policy decided upon by the council's personnel department, and the extent to which this has been affected by local branches of the two local government unions

Figure 9.3 Percentage of occupational groups notified of vacancy using various methods, by all four district councils, 1974–1983

Occupational group	National journals and magazines	National papers	Regional papers	Local papers	Job Centres	Circulars to adjacent district councils	Internal notification	Other methods	Total number of jobs involved
Managers	83	12	7	42	97	74	100	5	127
Professional employees	96	4	9	31	96	69	97	4	75
Ancillary workers	57	2	14	70	98	59	99	10	244
Foremen (non-manual)	39	3	10	82	94	63	99	1	67
Junior non-manual	1	0	1	84	95	68	98	12	660
Personal services	19	0	1	94	94	40	99	7	95
Foremen (manual)**	55	0	2	73	98	67	100	2	45
Skilled manual*	0	0	0	98	98	16	100	2	57
Semi-skilled manual*	0	0	4	91	96	10	100	3	69
Unskilled manual*	0	0	0	91	90	0	100	9	152

Source: Analysis of personnel records for Alyn and Deeside, Lancaster City, Tonbridge and Malling Borough, and the Vale of White Horse District Councils.

**These values are distorted by sports centre supervisors

*These values refer predominantly to the Vale of White Horse District Centre

(National Association of Local Government Officers and National Union of Public Employees). Differences between councils also occurred due to the availability or lack of established media within their districts. In particular this was evident for local free newspapers. Whereas free papers were well established in the Vale of the White Horse district this was not the case for the local area served by Lancaster City.

The effect of notification on applicant location

Inevitably, as suggested in the marketing and recruitment literature (Braithwaite, 1976; Armstrong and Hackett, 1979), the choice of notification methods also affected the location of potential candidates. Unfortunately data were only available locating the successful applicant for each post along with those outlets through which the council had notified the vacancy. For Lancaster City and Tonbridge and Malling Borough, data were also available about how the successful applicant first heard of the vacancy; that is, the process of recruitment (Ford *et al.*, 1982). Thus the effect of notifying a vacancy could not be measured in terms of applicant response. Similarly the importance of informal sources would only be known where the applicant had stated that he or she had heard of the vacancy in this way.

The radius of local newspaper circulation was calculated for each NMDC by taking the mean distance from the council's main office to the limits of local media circulation areas as defined by the rate cards (British Rate and Data, 1983). This definition, although perhaps an underestimate, had the advantage of compensating for the probable exaggeration in the circulation areas as defined by each local newspaper. In each case the local circulation radius was approximately 30 kilometres. Over 95 per cent of successful applicants who were recuited via local media by Alyn and Deeside District Council came from within this radius, and very similar patterns were noted for the other three NMDCs. In the two NMDCs where data on how the successful applicant first heard of the vacancy were available a similar pattern was evident. The area from which the successful applicant for a local post was recruited was dependent upon the circulation area of the outlet in which he or she first saw the vacancy.

Data collected from the Vale of the White Horse also included information about manual employees. Over 95 per cent of those recruited via local media lived locally. This suggests that the effect of only notifying a vacancy locally is to attract applicants and thus recuit a successful applicant from the local area. The results from the Vale of the White Horse District Council's data show that this was also true for manual vacancies which are only notified locally.

A pattern was evident in the location of successful applicants of nationally notified vacancies to the four NMDCs. There was a higher density of applicants in the immediate area of each of the four council's offices and in nearby population centres. However, as nearly 50 per cent of nationally notified vacancies had also been notified at the local level, this would increase the likelihood of locals hearing about a vacancy relative to non-locals. This in turn would affect the likelihood of a local applying, and thus of a local applicant being recruited to fill the vacant post. The likelihood of locals hearing about nationally notified vacancies would also be increased where the council had circulated adjacent local authorities and perhaps notified job centres. Locals would also be more likely to apply, as success would result in less disruption since a residential move (migration) would be unnecessary (Rossi, 1980). A distance decay effect was observed, the number of successful applicants declining with distance from the workplace. This was presumably partly the result of the disruption that moving could cause.

The way in which a successful applicant first heard of a vacancy differs significantly between those who had migrated and those who had not (see Figures 9.4 and 9.5). At both Lancaster City and Tonbridge and Malling Borough (the two NMDCs for which these data were available) the proportion of non-migrants who first heard of vacancies informally or via local information sources was very similar: migrants formed approximately 15 per cent of successful applicants who used informal channels and 4 per cent of those who used local media. In contrast the effects of recruitment

Figure 9.4 How successful applicants to Lancaster City first heard of the vacancy by migration

First heard of vacancy:	Non-migrants (per cent)	Migrants (per cent)	Total (count)
Informally	84	16	25
Local media	96	4	218
Regional media	0	0	0
National media	29	71	82
All vacancies	79	21	325

Note: Values are correct to the nearest percent
Source: Analysis of personnel records from Lancaster City Council

Figure 9.5 How successful applicants to Tonbridge and Malling Borough first heard of the vacancy by migration

First heard of vacancy:	Non-migrants (per cent)	Migrants (per cent)	Total (count)
Informally	86	14	7
Local media*	96	4	157
Regional media	0	0	0
National media	51	49	70
All vacancies	86	14	224

*Includes 9 applicants via the Job Centre, and 1 through the Professional Executive Register (PER)
Note: Values are correct to the nearest percent, although the data appear to be biased towards non-migrants
Source: Analysis of personnel records from Tonbridge and Malling Borough Council

through national media were very different. Nearly three-quarters of those recruited through national media to work for Lancaster City were migrants, whereas less than half those recruited in this manner to work for Tonbridge and Malling Borough were migrants. Thus in the latter case the effect of national recruitment upon migration appears to be less pronounced. This is likely to have been due to a number of factors suggested earlier, including the employer's location close to a large conurbation and the relatively high cost of living in that council's area.

The effect of notification upon migration

The evidence that has been discussed supports the hypothesis that the way in which an employer notifies a vacancy will affect who hears about it, and hence who applies and is appointed. In turn the method of notification will affect whether or not the appointee has to migrate to take up the vacancy, but it is difficult to disentangle the effect of information from other factors relating to migration. Earlier discussion has shown that the employer's choice of vacancy notification media outlets appears to be related to the location of the successful applicant and it seems probably that this will be related to the likelihood of subsequent migration (Figure 9.1). However it is possible that this effect is subsumed by the relationship between occupation and notification media used, or the relationship between occupation and migration (Gleave and Palmer, 1980; Brown and Belcher, 1966; Jones, 1981). Other factors such as age (Schwarzkopf and Miller, 1980; Long, 1973) and gender have also been shown to be significant in the migration process, but gender is also closely correlated with occupation.

The log-linear modelling technique as discussed generally by Wrigley (1985) and in its current context by Saunders (1986) was used to disentangle the data. It enables, for example, the effect of any interaction between notification media and migration to be assessed, controlling for the interaction between socio-economic group and notification media. This means that the significance of the effect of media upon migration independent of socio-economic group can be established. In a similar manner the significance of other factors on migration can also be assessed, independently of their relationship with some other factor.

In the construction of models to explain the data, a number of important findings were made regarding the job search/migration process. The most significant interaction with migration was the media used by the employer to notify the vacancy. When only national media were used migration was more likely to occur than where both national and local, or only local media were used. The socio-economic group of the vacancy filled, and the new employee's age and gender were also important factors influencing whether or not migration took place. Employees who had taken managerial or professional posts were the most likely to have migrated, whereas those in junior non-manual jobs were the least likely. Male employees were more likely to have moved than females, and those in the 25 to 34 age group more likely that those outside it.

As suggested by the influence diagram (Figure 9.1) the media used to notify a vacancy were found to be closely related to the post type (socio-economic group) as well as migration. However, even after the effect of this and other interactions had been taken into account other factors were still significant. In particular the choice of media used to notify the vacancy still influenced whether or not the successful applicant migrated. It therefore appears probably that both socio-economic group and vacancy information influences upon migration are, to a certain extent independent. The effects are mutually reinforcing. In a similar way a prospective employee's search pattern is likely to be related to the occupation sought, although with an independent effect on the likelihood of migration.

The vacancy notification media used were also related to the personal characteristics of the successful applicants, after the effects of socio-economic group (occupation) had been taken into account. Those vacancies which were advertised nationally were more likely to be filled by males, and those advertised locally by females, perhaps because the career patterns of wives are generally subservient to their husbands (Brzeskwinski, 1984 and see also Chapter 10). Vacancies advertised locally were also slightly less likely to be filled by people inside the 25 to 34 age group than those advertised both locally and nationally or just nationally.

The media through which an employer recruits new employees can therefore be seen to be important in the migration process. They enable the employer to pre-select the location of his or her potential applicants (that is, whether or not the successful applicant is likely to migrate to take up the vacancy), as well as their socio-economic group. A strong sex discrimination between occupations is apparent within NMDCs although this does not appear to affect migration directly. The employee, although having a choice of vacancy notification outlets to consult, is still constrained by the employer's initial choice. However it seems probably that if vacancies which an employer notifies nationally are more likely to be filled by migrants, then those job seekers who are searching in the national media are also more likely to be migrants.

Conclusions

These findings show that a NMDC's choice of media through which to recruit new employees affects the location of the successful applicant, and thus the likelihood of migration occurring. This is independent of vacancy type (in this case classified by socio-economic group) and the age and sex of the person who fills the post. However, obvious interactions do exist, such as between type of vacancy and the way it is advertised by an employer. It can be seen that the choice of recruitment media is important in the migration process. It provides a means by which the employer can pre-select the location of his or her applicants (and thus whether or not they will be likely to migrate), as well as their likely qualifications. The employee, although having a choice of vacancy information media, is constrained by the employer's initial choice, rather than by distance from the source region for the information. It still seems likely that employees deciding to consult national media are more likely to migrate than those who choose only to look at local media. Inevitably differences will occur between different areas of the country, dependent upon proximity to large urban areas, unemployment levels, and union agreements, to mention just a few factors.

More generally a conscious recruitment policy decision only to advertise posts locally, due perhaps to high local unemployment, would reduce the likelihood of any posts being filled by migrants, and so labour migration into the district. Conversely a decision to recruit from outside the local area and therefore to provide vacancy information over a wider area would increase the likelihood of such information reaching those for whom migration would be necessary to take up the post. This in turn would increase mobility into the area. These results apply only to NMDCs, which as public institutions may not be representative of private sector employers. Even if this is the case, local government in Britain employs some 3.1 million people or 12.3 per cent of the labour force (Lomas, 1980). Results from the questionnaire survey of 217 NMDCs suggest that the findings of the detailed examination of personnel records are representative. It therefore seems probably that a change in recruitment policy could affect the amount and direction of worker movement, although further empirical research is needed to establish the impact of this in the private sector.

References

Amrhein, C. G. and MacKinnon, R. D. (1984) 'Interregional Labour Migration and Information Flows'. Paper presented at the Association of American Geographers' Annual Meeting, Washington D.C.

Armstrong, M. and Hackett, P. (1979) *The Daily Telegraph Recruitment Handbook*. London: Kogan Page.

Bains, M. A. (1972) *The New Local Authorities: Management and Structure*. London: HMSO.

Bonnar, D. S. (1979) 'Migration in the South East of England: An Analysis of the Interrelationship of Housing, Socio-economic Status and Labour Demand'. *Regional Studies* 13: 345–359.

Bradshaw, T. F. (1973) 'Jobseeking Methods used by Unemployed Workers'. *Monthly Labour Review* 96: 35–40.

Braithwaite, R. (1976) *Communications and the Job Seeker*. London: Advertising Association.

British Rate and Data (1983) *British Rate and Data* 30: 4.

Brown, L. A. and Belcher, J. C. (1966) 'Residential mobility of physicians in Georgia'. *Rural Sociology* 31: 439–48.

Breskwinski, J. (1984) 'The Geographical Mobility of Graduate Women: Some Determinants and Consequences'. Unpublished Ph.D. thesis, University of Lancaster.

Checkland, P. (1981) *Systems Thinking, Systems Practice*. Chichester: Wiley.

Clark, G. L. (1983) *Interregional Migration, National Policy, and Social Justice*. Totowa, New Jersey: Rowman and Allanheld.

153

Clark, W. A. V. (ed) (1982) *Modelling Information Use in a Spatial Context*. London: Croom Helm.

Dasgupta, M. (1983) 'Employment and work travel in an inner urban context'. *Transport and Road Research Laboratory, Supplementary Report* no. 780.

Devis, T. (1983) 'People Changing Address: 1971 and 1981'. *Population Trends* 32: 15–20.

Dunnell, K. and Head, E. (1974) *Employers and Employment Services*. London: OPCS Social Survey Division.

Flowerdew, R. (1982) 'Institutional effects on Internal Migration' in Flowerdew, R. (ed) (1982) *Institutions and Geographical Patterns* pp. 209–227. London: Croom Helm.

Ford, J., Keil, E. T., Bryman, E. and Beardsworth, A. (1982) 'How employers see the Public Employment Service'. *Employment Gazette* p̈p. 466–72.

Fowler, A. (1980) *Personnel Management in Local Government* 2nd edition. London: Institute of Personnel Management.

Gleave, D. and Palmer, D. (1980) 'The Relationship between Geographic and Occupational Mobility in the context of Regional Economic Growth' in Hobcroft, J. and Rees, P. (1980) *Regional Demograhic Development* pp. 188–210. London: Croom Helm.

Gould, P. and White, R. (1974) *Mental Maps*. Harmondsworth: Penguin.

Granovetter, M. S. (1974) *Getting a Job – a Study of Contacts and Careers*. Cambridge, Massachusetts: Harvard University Press.

Guttridge, M. (1984) 'Manpower-regulations on employing the disabled'. *Local Government Chronicle*, **674**.

Jenkins, G. M. (1969) 'The systems approach'. *Journal of Systems Engineering* **1**: 3–49.

Johnson, J. H. and Salt, J. S. (1980) 'Labour Migration within Organisations: an Introductory Study'. *Tijdschrift voor Economische en Sociale Geografie* **71**: 277–84.

Johnson, J. H., Salt, J. and Wood, P. A. (no date) Unpublished tables from the Housing and the Migration of Labour survey 1970–71.

Jones, H. R. (1981) *Population Geography*. London: Harper and Row.

Ladinsky, J. (1967) 'Occupational Determinants of Geographic Mobility among Professional Workers'. *American Sociological Review* **32**: 253–64.

Lansing, J. B. and Mueller, E. (1967) *The Geographic Mobility of Labour*. Michigan: Institute for Social Research.

Lomas, E. (1980) Employment in the Public and Private Sectors 1974–1980. CSO *Economic Trends*, **325**: 101–9.

Long, L. H. (1973) 'Migration differentials by education and occupation: trends and variations'. *Demography* **10**: 243–58.

Long, L. H. and Hansen, K. (1979) *Reasons for Interstate Migration*. Washington D.C.: United States Bureau of the Census.

Maier, G. (1987) 'Job Search and Migration' in Fischer, M. M. and Nijkamp, P. *Regional Labour Markets*. pp. 189–204 Amsterdam: North Holland.

Mazie, S. M. (1972) 'The commission on population growth and the American future'. *Research report no. 5: Population distribution and policy*. Washington D.C.: Government Printing Office.

McKay, J. and Whitelaw, J. S. (1977) 'The Role of Large Private and Government Organisations in generating flows of Inter-regional Migrants: the case of Australia'. *Economic Geography* **53**: 28–44.

OPCS (1979) *The General Household Survey 1977*. London: HMSO.

OPCS and Registrar General (Scotland) (1983) *Census 1981: National Migration Great Britain, Part 1* (100% tables). London: HMSO.

Palm, R. (1976) 'Real estate agents and geographical information'. *Geographical Review* **66**: 266–80.

Pickles, A. and Rogerson, P. (1984) 'Wage Distributions and Spatial Preferences in Competitive Job Search and Migration'. *Regional Studies* **18**: 131–42.

Rogerson, P. and MacKinnon, R. D. (1981) 'A Geographical Model of Job Search, Migration and Unemployment'. *Papers of the Regional Science Association* **48**: 89–102.

Rossi, P. (1980) *Why Families Move* 2nd edition. London: Sage.

Salt, J. (1983) 'High Level Manpower Movements in Northwest Europe and the Role of Careers: An Explanatory Framework'. *International Migration Review* **17**: 633–52.

Salt, J. and Flowerdew, R. (1986) 'Occupational selectivity in labour migration'. Paper presented to the conference on comparative population geography of the UK and the Netherlands, Oxford.

Saunders, M. N. K. (1985) 'The Influence of Job Vacancy Advertising upon Migration'. *Environment and Planning A* **17**: 1581–89.

Saunders, M. N. K. (1986) 'The role of information in employment related migration in contemporary Britain'. Unpublished Ph.D. thesis, Department of Geography, University of Lancaster.

Saunders, M. N. K. and Flowerdew, R. (1987) 'Spatial Aspects of the provision of job information' in Fischer, M. M. and Nijkamp, P. *Regional Labour Markets* pp. 205–228. Amsterdam: North Holland.

Schwarzkopf, E. A. and Miller, E. A. (1980) 'Exploring the male mobility myth'. *Business Horizons* **23**: 38–44.

Silvers, A. (1977) 'Probabilistic Income-Maximising Behaviour in Regional Migration'. *International Regional Science Review* **2**: 29–40.

Wilson, A. G. (1981) *Geography and the Environment – Systems Analytical Methods*. London: Wiley.

Wrigley, N. (1985) *Categorical data analysis for geographers and environmental scientists*. London: Longman.

CHAPTER 10

Migration and Dual Career Households

Janina Snaith

Introduction

Labour migration, and the role of institutions (both public and private) in influencing and directing it, has come to occupy a central place in the geographical study of contemporary human migration. To date, though, a rather disturbing feature of most of this work has been the implicit assumption that household moves are made within the context of a single career. The apparent neglect of the phenomenon of the 'dual career' household (i.e. households where both husband and wife are engaged in professional careers) has not, however, been confined to geography.

In the light of the steady rise in the labour force participation of married women over recent years, and their increased career commitment, it is clearly an area which is deserving of research attention. This chapter will focus on the interplay between a wife's career and the geographical mobility of her household. This interplay raises a number of issues (Brzeskwinski, 1984).

- The first concerns the effect of marriage upon the determinants of a woman's geographical mobility. In particular, how far do married women make geographical moves in pursuit of their own career advancement and how does this compare with the proportion of career related moves undertaken by single women?
- Second, what are the overall consequences of occupationally induced household migration for the employment status of married women? This includes the need for some assessment of both the immediate and directly measurable effects of household migration on a wife's labour force participation and income contribution, and women's own subjective assessment of the longer term effects of this type of movement on their careers.

● The third issue is the location choices of dual career households and the possible influence of a wife's career on these. In particular, are dual career couples more likely to concentrate on larger labour markets so as to maximise their opportunities of employment? Is there any indication that the consequences for a wife's employment of a household move resulting from the demands of a husband's career vary with the relative size of the destination? How does family life cycle stage impact upon the migration behaviour in these households and what are the associated consequences for wives' employment? Of particular concern is the extent to which the presence of children might alter the relative weighting of the wife's career in household migration decisions.

● Finally, what is the range of issues surrounding locational conflict and decision making in households committed to the pursuit of two careers?

The chapter begins by proposing a model of mobility decision making in dual career households. It then uses empirical evidence from a survey carried out in 1980 amongst women graduates to test the applicability of the model. It concludes that in the majority of cases within dual career households, moves due to the demands of a husband's occupation take clear precedence over moves for a wife's career. Furthermore, these moves are highly likely to have a detrimental impact upon the career of his partner.

Modelling mobility decisions in the dual career household.

The range of variables which may weigh in a mobility decision and the possible consequences that can follow as a result of such decisions are described in Figure 1.

Before considering this model in greater detail two important 'qualifications' should be noted. First, it assumes the absence of any dependants in the household and so removes the possibility that other family considerations might influence a mobility decision. Whilst this may approximate reasonably closely to the situation in many childless households, it is obviously less likely to hold in households where dependants are present.

Second, for each individual these career variables are not likely to remain static through time so that the probability of a certain type of mobility decision is strictly a function of the career characteristics pertaining at the time the mobility option occurs.

The model

The model therefore firstly assumes a childless dual career household in which both partners (A and B) are currently in professional employment. It should be noted that A and B are interchangeable with regard to their sex.

A mobility option arises for A and the household is faced with a decision over whether or not to accept it. As may be seen from the model, a range of career-related factors may work to predispose the household towards making a move. The first of these concerns pressure from A's employer. Is the move a voluntary change of employer or is it an organisational transfer? In the latter case we may reasonably expect the degree of employer pressure to be stronger than for the former. In the case of a voluntary change of employer the degree of pressure emanating from A's employer is likely to differ if the company is experiencing contraction, as a result of economic difficulties for example, than if the mobility option is merely the result of A's desire for a change. The second box, relating to the possible gains to A from a move, is also likely to have a direct bearing on the final decision, whether those gains are viewed purely in financial terms (e.g. higher salary at new destination) or whether they are measured in terms of increased status or job satisfaction. However, in the case of our dual career household, gains to A must of course be offset against losses to B. Thirdly, a high level of work attachment by A, expressed either in terms of stated career commitment or of A's previous labour force participation record, will also act as a factor favouring a move. In addition to these three factors a number of characteristics pertaining to B's employment may serve to facilitate the likelihood of a move. The first is the case where B's level of work attachment is weak, either because he/she has a weak career orientation overall or because at a particular point in time other circumstances, for example family life cycle considerations, intervene and act to suppress the importance of B's career, albeit temporarily. Either way, the widely hypothesised braking effect of a second career in a household is drastically reduced under these conditions. Secondly, even where B has a strong attachment to work, it may be that he/she is in a field of employment which is relatively easily transferable so that a move is less likely to result in any income loss or change of status.

In some households the relatively low contribution of B's income to overall household income might also serve to weaken his/her influence in a particular migration decision. Finally, the probability of B obtaining work in a new area will vary, not only with the transferability of the job involved, but also with the characteristics of the likely destination area itself. For example, a move to a large labour market is likely to offer greater opportunities of employment for B than a move to a smaller one.

In contrast, on the right-hand side of the model are a number of career characteristics (largely those relating to B's employment) which may act as powerful brakes on mobility and predispose the households towards staying put. In many cases these are simply the reverse of those characteristics likely to encourage the decision to move. For example, just as pressure from A's employer can provide a powerful incentive to move, so pressure from B's employer may push a household towards staying. In the second box, the likelihood of heavy losses to B resulting from the move, in terms of income (which may well affect the entire household seriously), status or job satisfaction, may weigh heavily in reaching a decision to turn down A's mobility option. Moreover the chances of B's losses being heavy are obviously very high if B is strongly attached to work. Similarly, if A ranks career or work low in relation to other life spheres it is more likely that he/she will agree to

Figure 10.1 Mobility and the dual career family: a model to show decision making

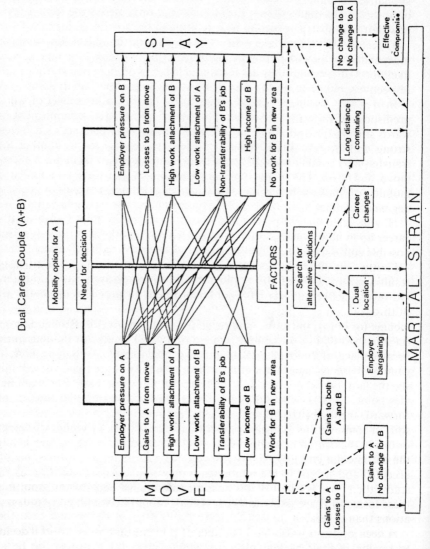

pass up a mobility option in the face of opposition from a partner. Finally, just as the transferability of B's job, the low income contribution of B's work and/or the strong probability of employment for B in the new destination are viewed as factors predisposing a household towards moving, so when these factors are found to be operating in reverse – in that B is in a highly specialised and location-specific job, contributes a relatively high proportion of household income and/or has a poor chance of finding employment in the new destination – the pressure to stay increases.

Therefore it can be hypothesised that these characteristics working independently on either the left or right of the model will increase the likelihood of a mobility option being resolved with a move or a non-move respectively, without any serious conflicts arising.

In reality, however, what often seems to happen is that factors predisposing A towards moving are in conflict with those predisposing B towards staying. For example, as can be seen from the model, it may be that strong employer pressure from A, as in the case of an organisational transfer, may conflict with the likely losses to B which would result from the move, and so on. The range of permutations may be seen from the model. A mobility option in a dual career household can, therefore, give rise to a high degree of conflict.

Having examined the likely career factors influencing a job move in a dual career household, the second part of the model focuses on the decisions and possible consequences of various strategies.

Firstly, it is clear that a decision to move in our dual career household, resulting from A's mobility option, should undoubtedly bring gains to A. However, the likely effect on B's employment will be less clear cut. For B, one of three outcomes is possible: he/she may lose out in employment status or income (or both); the move may result in no change to B's status or income (in other words B is successful in acquiring a job similar to the one in the former place of residence); B might also be successful, along with A, in gaining an improvement in status or income in the new destination. Obviously the last two outcomes are likely to be the most desirable from B's viewpoint. The case where B's career is damaged by the move is less straightforward. It may be that B will come to terms with this, either because of a shift in commitment to other spheres (e.g. family work or voluntary work), or due to the overall household gain resulting from the move. Alternatively, the detrimental effect of A's job move on B's career may not be so readily accepted and strains in the relationship may result. An important area for study, therefore, is whether it is possible to establish under what conditions these losses to B are likely to occur. Is this more likely with certain destinations than others?

A decision to stay also has a number of possible outcomes. If both decide to remain in their present places of employment there is likely to be no immediate change of status for either. This outcome may, then, represent a compromise in which both partners effectively elect to forgo individual promotions for the sake of a common good. However, this outcome may eventually lead to frustration on the part of A with regard to a missed opportunity and strains in the relationship may ensue. Similarly, an alternative outcome of a decision to stay might be that one partner (in this case A) would take up a long distance commuting in order to take advantage of the new employment option without necessitating the disruption of B's employment.

The model suggests that the choices facing our household are not limited to simply moving or staying. A number of alternative solutions exist. For example, it may be that in the case of an organisational transfer, an employee can 'bargain' with his employers over either the timing or destination of the move or, indeed, the necessity of it at all. Another possibility is that the household is unable to resolve the conflict arising from the mobility option and splits up either on a permanent basis through divorce or separation, or alternatively as a temporary measure until partner B can find suitable employment in the new location or until partner A moves on again to a more mutually acceptable location. Meanwhile the household becomes a 'dual location' family. Yet another solution is for one or both partners to change career. An example may be where a couple decide to go into business together or one changes so that the careers are more compatible.

The model provides a clear picture of the complexity of the decision making process surrounding a mobility option in a dual career household. How accurate is it, though, in describing the behaviour of real 'dual career' households?

Testing the model: empirical findings
Information used in testing the model was gathered by two methods. First, statistical data were collected by means of a retrospective questionnaire survey of the migration and employment experiences of two cohorts of graduate women from the years 1965 and 1972. The five universities that participated in this study were: Exeter, Hull, Keele, Reading and Oxford (St Hilda's College). This main survey provided valuable information on the relative *scale* of the mobility problems experienced by a representative sample (approximately 200) of educated women (Brzeskwinski, 1984).

The second method involved the use of a written appeal for anecdotal material which was published in a number of journals in the latter part of 1980 (*WRRC Newsletter, Times Educational Supplement, Cosmopolitan, Management Today* and *Personnel Management*). The information gathered in this way provided a detailed insight into the *nature* of locational conflicts in these households.

Migration characteristics of dual career households

By 1980 all of the 1965 cohort (n = 79) and 98 per cent of the 1972 cohort (n = 107) had made at least one geographical move, involving a change in place of residence, since graduating (Figure 10.2). Indeed the modal number of geographical moves for respondents in both groups was three with 78 per cent of 1965 and 59 per cent of 1972 graduates having made at least this number of moves since graduation.

Figure 10.2 Total geographical moves, all respondents

No. of moves per respondent	No.	1965 %	Per cent of cohort making at least x moves	No.	1972 %	Per cent of cohort making at least x moves
0	0	0		2	2	
1	8	10	100	18	17	98
2	9	12	90	24	22	81
3	23	29	78	26	24	59
4	19	24	49	15	14	35
5	6	8	25	15	14	21
6	5	6	17	5	5	7
7	4	5	11	1	1	2
8	5	6	6	1	1	1
	79			107		

Career reasons were overwhelmingly important for the geographical moves for the two cohorts as a whole, whether for respondents' own careers or those of their husbands (Figure 10.3). Indeed, for both cohorts career related moves accounted for over half of all geographical moves made by the respondents.

For married respondents information was also collected on the number of husbands' job moves per household and the specific reasons behind such moves. The data indicated that 61 per cent (n = 43) of married 1965 graduates and 55 per cent (n = 43) of their 1972 colleagues had experienced at least one geographical move made for the sake of a husband's career. The proportions experiencing two or more such moves were 30 per cent (n = 21) and 22 per cent (n = 17) respectively.

The relative importance of different types of husbands' job moves were also investigated. No less than 65 per cent of the career moves of the partners of 1965 respondents were, in fact, voluntary employer changes. In contrast,

Figure 10.3 Reasons for geographical moves, all respondents

Reason	1965 No.	%	1972 No.	%	Total No.	%
Return to home area	18	6	14	4	32	5
Housing	47	16	68	21	115	19
Environmental	8	3	8	3	16	3
Husband's job	81	27	76	24	157	25
Respondent's own career	77	26	92	29	169	27
Marriage	39	13	35	11	74	12
Adventure	16	5	6	2	22	4
Other	11	4	12	4	23	4
Not Stated	1	0	7	2	8	1
Total	298		318		616	

involuntary organisational transfers, the focus of so much of the literature on professional and managerial migration, accounted for just 9 per cent of such moves.

Married women and the determinants of geographical mobility

This model indicates the importance of setting geographical mobility options within a household rather than an individual context. In particular, to what extent are married professional women able to make geographical moves in pursuit of career opportunities when compared with their single counterparts?

In order to investigate this, differentiation was made between moves made by (i) single (i.e. never married) graduate women, (ii) married women *prior to* marriage, and (iii) married women *after* marriage. Among the first group, geographical moves for respondents' own careers were of overriding importance, accounting for 54 per cent of the moves made by the 1965 group and 56 per cent of those made by the 1972 group. The corresponding figures for married graduates *prior to* marriage were 59 and 57 per cent respectively. Yet for women who were married the results clearly indicated that moves due to the demands of a husband's job took precedence and were the single most important cause of household migration, accounting for 45 and 42 per cent of the moves made by the households of the 1965 and 1972 groups respectively. Comparable figures for 'housing reasons' which ranked second in importance among this third group were only 22 and 24 per cent. A further blow to any notions of equality is evidenced by the fact that moves made specifically for respondents' own careers accounted for a mere 5 per cent of the geographical moves made by the households of married 1965 graduates and 4 per cent in the households of their 1972 counterparts. These findings, therefore, lend considerable support to the idea of the contingent nature of much female mobility.

Married women and the consequences of geographical mobility

It has already been noted that among married graduate respondents 'labour migration' is most likely to involve a geographical move for the sake of a husband's career. When asked what they felt had been the overall effect of such 'tied' moves upon their own career development, 38 per cent of 1965 and 36 per cent of 1972 respondents claimed that they had been 'damaging' to a greater or lesser extent compared with 26 and 29 per cent respectively who claimed that these moves had had 'no effect' and 26 and 14 per cent who viewed the overall effect as broadly 'beneficial' to their career development. With regard to this latter group it is worth noting that several respondents were at pains to point out that the 'beneficial' effects of such moves had, in their cases, been entirely fortuitous.

More objective support for the above claims was provided by examining changes in respondents' labour force participation and income contribution in association with household moves for a husband's career. Restricting

Figure 10.4 Moves for husband's careers involving a change of labour market: effects on respondents

(i) LABOUR FORCE PARTICIPATION

Effect	No.	%
No change	80	62
Positive change	7	5
Negative change	28	22
Indeterminate change	14	11
	129	

(ii) INCOME CONTRIBUTION TO HOUSEHOLD

Effect	No.	%
No change	64	50
Positive change	18	14
Negative change	47	36
	129	

analysis to those moves for a husband's career which involved the household in a change of labour market, the pre-move and post-move employment and income characteristics of respondents were compared. A total of 129 husband career moves for the two cohorts were analysed in this way.

As can be seen (Figure 10.4), the majority of husbands' job moves (62%) resulted in no observable changes in a respondent's degree of participation in the labour force. However, slightly more than one in five of such moves were found to result in a negative change – that is, the respondent's labour force participation decreased following the move. Indeed, it can be seen from the table that if a change in participation is experienced following such a move, it is four times more likely to be negative than positive.

Changes in the proportion of overall household income contributed by the respondents were also analysed, and showed that for 36 per cent of wives, their husband's career moves resulted in a significant decrease in their income.

The downward spiral?

A longer term implication of these changes is that, for a significant number of women, moves made for the sake of a husband's job may considerably weaken the influence of their own career in the future household migration decisions. Therefore, as participation rates and income contributions fall, further moves for a husband's job would be likely.

It might be expected, for one of two reasons, that the greater the overall labour force participation of the respondent during marriage, the lower would be the number of moves made for the sake of a husband's career. On the one hand, a record of high labour force attachment for a respondent may be indicative of strong career commitment and in these circumstances a woman is more likely to exercise a brake on household mobility. Alternatively, a record of high labour force attachment on the part of a respondent is also more likely in the absence of many husband-related job moves, simply because a respondent's career is less likely to have been interrupted. Figure 10.5 confirms this hypothesis. Among the group with a low overall record of labour force attachment the numbers making two or more husband related job moves was greater than predicted with expected values of 6.8 for two moves and 4.5 for three or more moves. In contrast, among those working for more than 50 per cent of the time since marriage, the numbers of non-movers and those moving only once for the sake of a partner's job were greater than anticipated when compared with the expected values of 43.6 and 33.7 respectively. The most significant differences between the two groups were found amongst those making three or more husband related job moves.

Figure 10.5 Relationship between respondent's cumulative labour force attachment during marriage and number of household moves made for the sake of a husband's career

Labour force attachment	No. of moves for husband's career				
	0	1	2	3+	
0–50%	17	10	8	9	44
> 50%	45	38	15	6	104
Total	6	48	23	15	148

$x^2 = 8.6$ Significant at .05 level

A similar analysis was undertaken with regard to the relationship between a respondent's level of cumulative contribution to household income and the propensity of the household to have migrated for a husband's career. Once again a statistically significant result was obtained which demonstrated that a clear relationship existed between the contribution level of a wife's income to total household income and the number of husband related career moves undertaken by a household over the survey period.

Locational choices in dual career households

Some of the literature on migration in dual career households has suggested that the influence of a wife's job has an important bearing on *where* a household locates. (Da Vanzo, 1976; Mincer, 1978; Marwell et al., 1979). It has been hypothesised that, other things being equal, dual career couples will tend to concentrate in large labour markets so as to maximise their opportunities of obtaining suitable employment. (Marwell et al., 1979).

Data on the respondents, recording both the size of the labour markets resided in and the labour force participation status for every year since graduation, were compared in order to test this hypothesis. Comparisons were made between the proportion of women in full-time employment and the proportion of those not in the labour force found to reside in any one of the largest fifteen British Standard Metropolitan Labour-market Areas (SMLAs) (i.e. those with populations in excess of 500,000 in 1971) for every year since graduation. The results of the analysis indicate that, for graduate women at least, households where the female partner works are indeed more likely to be located in large labour markets than households with non-working respondents.

If larger labour markets are seen to offer the best hope of suitable employment for these couples, we might also expect the consequences for respondents of husband-related moves to vary with the size of labour market moved to; moves to larger labour markets would prove less damaging in terms of female employment than moves to smaller ones. Using the data on husband related career moves which involved the household in a change of labour market, the moves were subdivided into two categories, using population figures of the origin and destination labour markets as an indication of their sizes. As predicted, moves to smaller labour markets were more likely than expected to result in negative or indeterminate changes of status and less likely than expected to be beneficial, whilst the reverse was true to moves to larger labour markets (Figure 10.6). Similar findings were experienced for changes in income contributions. Clearly then, in the light of

---

Figure 10.6 Effects on respondents' employment of husband's career moves: the influence of labour market size

(i) LABOUR FORCE PARTICIPATION

Absolute figures

Effects	Moves to smaller lab. markets	Moves to larger lab. markets	
No change	44	36	80
Positive change	1	6	7
Negative change	19	9	28
Indeterminate change	10	4	14
	74	55	129

$x^2 = 7.9$ Significant at 0.05 level

(ii) INCOME CONTRIBUTION TO HOUSEHOLD

Absolute figures

Effect	Moves to smaller lab. markets	Moves to larger lab. markets	
No change	38	26	64
Positive change	5	13	18
Negative change	31	16	47
	74	55	129

$x^2 = 7.8$ Significant at .05 level

these findings, the expressed preference of a number of dual career couples for larger labour markets is an entirely rational one.

The influence of family life cycle stages

Whilst the model assumes a childless couple, it is hypothesised that there may be differences in migration behaviour at various life cycle stages and that there may be associated variations in the consequences of household migration for female employment. Five life cycle stages were used for the analysis.

(1)   The first stage corresponded to the 'single' state prior to marriage.
(2)   Stage two commenced with marriage and ended with the arrival of the first dependant.
(3)   Stage three began with the arrival of a pre-school age dependant and lasted until one dependant reached school age.
(4)   Stage four included couples with two or more dependants, where the ages of dependants were 'mixed' (i.e. some pre-school age and some over the age of five).
(5)   The final stage related to couples with all dependants of school age or older.

The major findings of this analysis were that with the arrival of dependants, the influence of respondents' careers on household migration decisions appears to be weakened (Figure 10.7), with accordingly greater chances of a husband's career move resulting in damaging consequences for her career at the five stages of the life cycle.

Figure 10.7   Husband's career moves: consequences for respondent's employment in households with dependants and households without

FEMALE LABOUR FORCE PARTICIPATION

Effect	No dependants	Dependants	Total
No change	51	27	78
Positive change	2	5	7
Negative change	9	19	28
Indeterminate change	9	2	11
Total	71	53	124

$x^2 = 14.4$ Significant at .01 level

Mobility problems in dual career households: a qualitative insight

In addition to the main survey, a large quantity of information was collected in response to a letter published in a number of journals in the latter part of 1980. The letter briefly outlined the research area and requested readers with experience of locational conflict in dual career households to write in. A total of 73 replies was received, many containing a great deal of anecdotal information. A number of themes emerged from this correspondence and these will be examined in turn.

Marital stress in the dual career household

A conflict of career interests was cited by several correspondents as a contributory factor in the breakdown of their own relationships.

> The problems concerned with career changes and leaving an area where I was very happy had a considerable effect on the recent separation.

> Mostly, however, it seems to be the lot of the woman to go whither her man goest – often because of the encumbrance of children. This may well increase the bitterness of career women – with maternal instincts fulfilled and forgotten, and intellectual/vocational resources untapped this can be a delicate period for any marriage. It was certainly one of the causes of our matrimonial breakdown.

One respondent neatly summarised the essence of the dual career dilemma arising as she saw it from . . .

> the desire to satisfy two points, firstly that of living together and secondly that of fulfilling both career ideals. Too often it seems one is the price paid in pursuit of the other.

Locational strategies

A number of respondents commented on the advantages of living in a large city where job opportunities exist in sufficient quantity and variety to suit both partners' requirements.

> We had agreed that I should apply for posts near or in large cities – London, Birmingham and Bristol in that order so that Dave would stand a good chance of finding employment in the same place as me.

Locating centrally so that several possible employment locations were within commuting distance was another solution mentioned. An example of this was given by a research assistant who wrote

> In our present location (Doncaster) the universities of Sheffield, Leeds and York are all feasible for daily travel.

Job search strategies

In other circumstances the career of the wife may simply restrict mobility options, influencing not so much whether geographical moves are made, but rather the timing and direction of the move. How do partners in these situations effectively 'juggle' their careers to ensure that moving results in improved opportunities for both of them, or, at the very least, no actual damage to the career aspirations of either partner?

In a number of cases it seems that the nature of the work of one or other of the partners weighs heavily in the development of a search strategy. A good example of this approach is to be found in the case of one couple where the husband worked as a museum curator while his wife worked in a less specialised field.

> After discussing our relative job prospects, we decided that since museum jobs are much harder to find than jobs in my field we should not move until my husband finds another job, i.e. I should follow him rather than vice versa.

In the case of the respondent below, exactly the same line of reasoning results in the reverse situation.

> I think that all of the possible disasters have been avoided by my husband agreeing to move for me at each turn in events – taking the view that it is more difficult for me to find a suitable job than him – the field of medical statistics being rather specialised and centred in only a few centres in Britain.

Commuting

Where moving proves difficult or undesirable it seems that in some cases the career aspirations of both partners can be fulfilled if either one or both or them are prepared to commute considerable distances to their place of work. For many couples it is the most convenient solution either in the short or long term.

> In general terms, we have found it more practical for at least one partner to commute rather than both move houses or jobs. For the last year we have both had to drive over 500 miles a week but this has been done as it was known that my husband's project would not last more than two years.

The 'dual location' household

Somewhere between the daily grind of extensive commuting and the more extreme and permanent splitting of a household through separation or divorce, lies another solution which, if the experience of this group of dedicated careerists is to be heeded, seems an increasingly common and perhaps inevitable option – that of the 'dual location' household. In this situation members of a dual career household actually reside in two locations (these are usually determined by the respective careers of the partners) and depending on the distance involved, the partners spend time together every weekend/fortnight/month.

> We have only solved the problem by living apart during the week. My husband comes home weekends and, being an academic, has lengthy holidays at home. My career has always been as important as his – in both our views. The constraint now geographically is in taking jobs which allow a continuation of the weekend/holiday domestic routines.

This may in certain cases be seen as merely a temporary solution while one partner undergoes a period of further education or training away from the original place of residence, or waits for a suitable position to become vacant in a new location.

> For three and a half years my husband and I were forced to live apart, meeting only at weekends if we were both to pursue our respective training/careers.

The attitudes of employers

External factors also play a significant part in ameliorating or exacerbating the dilemmas of the dual career family. In this context, the attitudes of both the respondents' employers and those of their partners were frequently highly pertinent to their situations.

For many, encounters with employers over mobility problems had left them extremely frustrated. Underlying the attitudes of many employers, it seems, is the traditional model of the family with the male as dominant breadwinner. Not surprisingly, they find it hard to cope with the shift to the egalitarian ideal in many professional households. This is illustrated in some of the following anecdotes recounted by respondents.

> A point repeatedly stressed during the interview was my responsibility to my husband's career. The interviewers were clearly not happy to accept that a family might follow the wife's career if the husband is a professional man.

> I have also encountered at least one employer – this was the only one to be explicit on the matter – who decided against offering me a research post because my accepting it would have meant living apart from my husband. And my husband has never been refused a job on these grounds.

Others referred to more concrete policies of employers which served to work against them in these situations. Regulations prohibiting the employment of couples in the same school or department still exist. One woman teacher whose husband is headmaster of an isolated village school came up against this.

> There were no posts of responsibility and although the managers wanted me to apply for the Deputy Headship I was banned from applying by a new edict (relating to husband/wife staffing) issued by the Education Committee. There were no special schools in the vicinity. I was stymied all round.

Another woman teacher wrote of the attitude of the Services to problems of locational conflict.

> In my case the simple result was divorce. My husband was in the army, moved every two years usually, at short notice, and never at times coinciding with the school year. I was a school teacher, theoretically

mobile (though not world-wide) but in fact tied by two children, my post of Head of Department and the scarcity of jobs in my subject.

The essence of the problem was, as she saw it, that

The army was never willing to accept that I might want a career.

On a more constructive note, several wives felt that the very least employers could do, when they disrupt a career by moving one partner, was to compensate a spouse for loss of earnings, pension rights, etc. One added, rather apologetically, that she realised this was a somewhat 'Utopian' aim. I doubt however that this is so. In recent years the assistance given by employers to relocated personnel has expanded considerably so that in many cases the schemes have come to reflect more accurately the true costs of moving and now include such things as payments for curtains and carpets, legal expenses, etc. (see Chapter 4). One respondent added with feeling:

My husband's employers would also have paid private school fees of one term if applicable, but to quote their letter to me, '... could take no account of a wife's employment'. Frankly, I have never forgiven anyone for the assumption that I could be moved about the country like any other piece of furniture.

However, there were indications from some quarters that at least a few employers were adopting more positive attitudes to the problem. A personnel officer stated that her firm made a point of asking male applicants about their wife's work and the feasibility of her obtaining employment in the vicinity. A woman, commenting on the attitudes of her husband's employers, maintained that despite their giving little assistance with relocation.

It is their policy nevertheless (verbally) that if an employee refuses a transfer because of marital conflict, this should not affect his future with the company.

Even more encouraging was the response of one leading chain store with a high reputation for good personnel relations, who reserve a number of 'limited' mobility' posts on their Senior Management Training Scheme specifically for those with domestic commitments. Such approaches by employers, although undoubtedly costly in the short-term may well bring important long-term benefits for, as one respondent noted:

When a working mother encounters a sympathetic employer she is loth to move.

Conclusion

In considering geographical mobility, in particular occupationally-induced movement, the effect of marriage on women was considerable. Husbands' careers were seen to assume overriding importance. Once married, a respondent was extremely unlikely to make a geographical move for reasons of her own career but very likely to undertake at least one move for the sake of her husband's. Ultimately, the consequence of this 'tied migration' for the respondent's own career tended to be negative, both in the eyes of the respondents themselves and (when measured objectively) in terms of their labour force participation and income contribution rates.

Nevertheless, the results suggest that some attempts were made to minimise the negative consequences of such relocations by careful choice of destination. Moves to larger labour markets were less likely to be associated with negative consequences for a wife's employment.

The impact of family life cycle stages on migration behaviour caused significant repercussion upon wives' employment. It was found that the arrival of dependants severely weakened the respondent's position concerning household migration decisions. Moves made for the sake of a husband's career at this stage were more likely to have a negative effect upon a wife's career than moves made prior to the arrival of dependants.

The survey findings lend considerable support to the validity of the model outlined at the start of the chapter. Mobility decisions in dual career households are complex and can produce a range of possible outcomes. The model should be developed further to incorporate life cycle stages.

The scope for future research into this aspect of women's geographical mobility is, I believe, fairly broad. The indications are that the numbers of dual career households are likely to continue to rise and may constitute a major pressure group for far reaching and long overdue changes in existing employment practices, especially those relating to geographical mobility. The eventual outcome could well be the demise of the 'mobile' man as an essential element in training and promotion schemes. In addition, the evidence presented in this research on the influence of a wife's work in the locational choices of dual career households may have long-term implications for the siting of industrial and commercial enterprises.

More generally, this chapter has illustrated the centrality of women's place in an area of geographical enquiry where they have hitherto been ignored. It is fitting to end then with a comment from one of the respondents who reminds us that for the present, mobility of labour remains 'a politician's dream and a couple's nightmare'.

References

Brzeskwinski, J. M. (1984) 'The Geographical Mobility of Graduate Women: Some Determinants and Consequences'. Unpublished Ph.D. thesis. University of Lancaster:

Da Vanzo, J. (1976) *Why Families Move: A Model of Geographic Mobility of Married Couples*. Santa Monica: Rand Corporation R-1972-DOL.

Marwell, G., Rosenfeld, R. and Spilerman, S. (1979) 'Geographic Constraints on Women's Careers in Academia'. *Science*. 205: 1225–31.

Mincer, J. (1978) 'Family Migration Decisions'. *Journal of Political Economy*, 86: 749–73.

CHAPTER 11

Migration Behaviour Among the Unemployed and Low-Skilled

Robert Kitching

The immobility of the low-skilled and unemployed

Propensity to migrate has always varied between groups of individuals on the basis of a variety of personal characteristics. Quite often it seems that those workers and their families with most need to move for economic reasons are least likely to do so, despite traditional labour market forces. Hence, as the economy of the UK has improved in the latter half of the 1980s, the distribution of new employment opportunities remains poorly matched with the distribution of the unemployed (Lewis and Townsend, 1989). With the abandonment of a regional policy to influence the location of further growth, much government rhetoric (though less action) has been directed towards encouraging the unemployed to move from one part of the country to another in response to job opportunities (Green *et al.*, 1985). Yet the unemployed and the low-skilled continue to exhibit lower rates of mobility than the population as a whole. The reasons for this form the basis of this chapter.

The chapter begins by presenting some evidence of the relative immobility of this group, and discussing the value of various theoretical approaches to the explanation of why some people do not migrate, despite pressures upon them which would indicate that they should. It goes on to argue that for many people immobility is an entirely rational response to these economic pressures operating in the labour market. The rationale for mobility is then examined, using the results of empirical work carried out in two contrasting local labour and housing markets in the UK. It is argued that whilst labour migration may seem the correct solution for some, immobility is the appropriate strategy for many low-skilled and unemployed households, balancing employment opportunities against a variety of competing factors.

The relationship between occupational status and geographical mobility is well documented. Friedlander and Roshier (1966) compared the social characteristics of migrants and non-migrants in England and Wales among recently married couples, and found that in general manual workers were considerably less mobile than non-manual workers, the differential increasing with distance moved. Likewise, Johnson, Salt and Wood (1975) found that 41 per cent of their sample of labour migrants to four British cities were managerial and professional workers, yet such people only accounted for 17 per cent of the population as a whole. The greater mobility of professional workers was confirmed by the General Household Survey (OPCS, 1977), in which 15 per cent of them had made at least one inter-regional move over the last five years, compared with 4 per cent of unskilled workers. Kennett and Randolph (1978) analysed the differential mobility of socioeconomic groups between 1966 and 1971. The least mobile were manual workers, particularly the unskilled of whom only 31.6 per cent moved during the period, compared with 37 per cent of the total economically active population, and 46 per cent of professional workers.

Unemployment is also related to geographical immobility. Daniel (1940) found that movement was least where unemployment was greatest. More recently, the 1979 Labour Force Survey showed that the unemployed accounted for 10 per cent of the labour force, yet only 4.4 per cent of all recorded inter-regional moves. In contrast, US data suggest that mobility and unemployment have been more positively correlated (Hunter and Reid, 1968; Lansing and Mueller, 1967; Lansing and Morgan, 1967).

Analysis of the 1981 Census for the UK confirms these differences. Although the overall mobility rate of the British population fell over the preceding decade, socio-economic differentials in mobility rates remained distinct, especially over longer distances. A third of all professional and managerial people who moved and went over 20km, compared with only 11 per cent of manual workers, while distances moved by junior non-manuals fell between the two extremes.

Low-skilled and unemployed manual workers in the UK consistently display lower mobility rates than their skilled counterparts, and these differences are more pronounced over longer distances. Yet, despite the conformity of such findings, theoretical approaches to the study of migration often fail to incorporate fully the notion of immobility.

Theoretical approaches to the study of migration

Basic economic and sociological theories

Economic approaches to the study of migration have stressed the role of unemployment and changing labour market structures. This has particular relevance to the UK labour market today, since much of the present Government's philosophy with regard to migration is based on a view of the labour market implicit in neo-classical economics (Green et al., 1985). Simply, the theory suggests that an unemployed worker will be particularly sensitive to employment differentials, and will migrate if unable to find work of a suitable type, or with an adequate wage locally. Thus much recent government attention has focused on freeing the equilibriating mechanisms of the labour market. Failure of unemployed individuals to migrate to other areas which offer better employment opportunities is often viewed as a factor of irrational behaviour, or the inability to overcome a variety of obstacles or conflicting interests. Clark and Whiteman (1983), however, have argued that the parameters defining the economic environment within which individual decisions are made differ. Where uniqueness of skill and wide-ranging information networks are lacking, the labour market process is likely to be more localised. Rather than placing responsibility for labour market disequilibrium on supposed irrational individual behaviour, they suggest that it is precisely those individual rational decisions in the face of varying spatial labour market conditions that preserve inequalities in employment opportunities and local labour market disequilibrium.

Sociological approaches to the study of migration have focused upon social relations, emphasising the importance of social networks and kinship and community ties as determinants of mobility (Taylor, 1969; Jansen, 1969; Pahl, 1980). The general consensus is that low-skilled or working class households will be least mobile, since their kinship and community ties are likely to be stronger, and more spatially constrained.

Much of this theory was developed in the 1950s and 1960s, and it is unclear whether such ties remain as significant a factor in the explanation of working class immobility today, given the extent of population dispersal in such communities over the past few decades. Yet Pahl (1980) argues that such social networks remain important in the operation of informal local economies, which become especially significant to the low-skilled during periods of unemployment. The spatially constrained networks inhabited by working class communities may also be related to the limited range and sources of information available to them on opportunities elsewhere, reliant as many are on contacts with friends and relatives.

Some weaknesses of basic theories

Existing theory has often been developed in a static framework, where a 'snapshot' picture of migration actions at a specific time is examined. Such an approach can easily lead to the study of pattern at the expense of process, failing to locate migration decisions within the context of the evolving household life-cycle. The result is to present a dichotomy of 'movers' and 'stayers' at a given time, where the motivations behind the actions of the former are used to make inferences about the forbearances of the latter. This approach fails to recognise that changes through time for individual households are often more important than differences between households at specific points. A theoretical framework where non-movers or 'stayers' are regarded as a homogeneous group to be contrasted with migrants or 'movers' fails to recognise that many have been migrants in the past, and many may become migrants in the future.

Furthermore, the migrant is often perceived as an individual actor rather than as part of a migrating household. Although information on household size and type is sometimes incorporated into analyses of reasons for movement, there have been few attempts to study the way in which a collection of household members contribute to migration decisions which involve them all.

Finally, examination of migration motivation is often based on single factor analysis, whereby the most important reason behind a particular move is identified in order to classify that action. Details on secondary reasons, in the absence of which the primary reason may not be sufficient to result in a migration, are often overshadowed in attempts to categorise individual migrations by broad types.

Those studies which have explored individual migration decisions in depth, examining the process of decision-making as well as the results, have helped to fill some of the gaps in existing theory. Particularly important is the distinction between willingness and ability to migrate. A survey of attitudes to moving in slum clearance areas of Leeds concluded that the majority of those interviewed showed a strong desire to move (Wilkinson and Merry, 1965). Richardson and West (1964) surveyed attitudes to employment migration amongst unemployed men on Tyneside, and concluded that inability to move was of greater significance than unwillingness; moreover, willingness to move was unaffected by the degree of skill of the interviewee. They concluded that the clearest possible distinction has to be made between psychological unwillingness to move, and physical obstacles to mobility.

More recent surveys of migration attitudes have also yielded some estimates of potential migrants. In the Northern Ireland Mobility Survey (1980) 17 per cent of all employed respondents would have been prepared to move to a suitable job were they to lose their current one. Among the jobless, 9.7 per cent had seriously considered moving, whilst 14.3 per cent were prepared to move if necessary. In a survey of the long-term unemployed in Skelmersdale, 64.5 per cent of respondents claimed they would be prepared to move to another part of the country to obtain work (Riley, 1986).

Answers to glib questions on attitudes to migration which present hypothetical situations vary enormously, and must be treated with caution. However, there are many other indications of unfulfilled potential for migration, or actions which may be regarded as surrogate migrations. Conway and Ramsey (1986) highlighted the housing problems of people moving to London. Many of them, despite finding suitable work, were eventually forced to return to unemployment in their former home area because of the difficulties of finding suitable and affordable accommodation. Furthermore, the gulf in housing costs between the South East and the North leads many unemployed northerners to resort to long-distance weekly commuting. This may involve living in lodgings during the week, returning to home and family only at weekends. One estimate in 1987 was that about 10,000 people were engaged in long-distance weekly commuting, and that this represented rates of up to 4.6 per cent of the male economically active population in some major northern cities (Hogarth and Daniel, 1987; 1988).

These studies raise a number of important questions regarding the place of migration in the balance between work, housing and family. Answering them necessitates analysis at the level of individual households, within local labour and housing market environments (see Chapter 12).

Migration attitudes and migration propensity in Liverpool and Reading

The results reported below are based on structured interviews with members of households in Liverpool and Reading, chosen to reflect extremes on a national continuum of local labour and housing markets (Figure 11.1). Liverpool has had one of the highest rates of unemployment in the UK, with a dearth of new employment opportunities and some of the lowest house prices in the country. Reading, in the heart of the M4 corridor, is its antithesis; with low levels of unemployment, it is characterised by new industries and rapid expansion, resulting in fierce development pressures yielding high land and house prices.

Figure 11.1 Employment and housing profile of survey locations

	Liverpool	Reading
% Population economically active, 1981, (1)	47.1	50.2
% Population 'seeking work', 1981, (1)	8.5	3.3
% Population by social class, 1981, (1)		
IIIm (skilled manual)	25.0	25.5
IV (semi-skilled manual)	15.1	15.8
V (unskilled manual)	7.6	3.7
Housing tenure (% households) (1)		
owner occupied	40.6	60.1
local authority	39.6	20.4
private rented (unfurnished)	10.7	8.1
private rented (furnished)	2.8	7.8
Unemployment rate A (%), 1987 (2)	19.0	6.9
Unemployment rate B (%), 1987 (3)	26.3	7.8

Notes
1 Based on the 1981 Census Small Area Statistics
2 Based on the official Department of Employment count for the parliamentary constituencies (six in Liverpool and two in Reading) which are broadly contiguous with the Census districts.
3 Based on the Unemployment Unit count, using the pre-1979 method of calculation, for parliamentary constituencies as above.

The household sample was drawn using Small Area Statistics from the 1981 Census and a variety of local sources; it concentrates on manual workers and the unemployed, in different housing tenures. One hundred interviews were conducted at each location between September 1986 and October 1987. Figure 11.2 profiles the employment and housing characteristics of the sample. Whilst the sampling frame adopted yielded the same

Figure 11.2 Employment and housing profile of interview sample

	Liverpool	Reading	All
Economic activity			
working	41	59	100
unemployed	28	10	38
retired/inactive	31	31	62
Social class			
I	1	1	2
II	2	9	11
IIIN	13	22	35
IIIM	19	27	46
IV	37	20	57
V	24	14	38
Other/unclassified	4	7	11
Housing tenure			
owner occupied	27	35	52
Local authority	48	39	87
Private rented (unfurnished)	23	6	29
Private rented (furnished)	2	20	22

Source: Household interview survey

number of retired and economically inactive in each location, the relative
balance between the employed and the unemployed, and between different
housing tenures reflected the housing and labour market differences outlined
above. Where social class was identified, 75 per cent were 'manual' (social
classes IIIm, IV and V). It is these which provide the basis for the majority of
the results reported here.

The extreme differences in local context would suggest very different
demands for labour migration, and very different degrees of local attachment. Liverpool represents the declining northern conurbation from which,
traditional labour market theory would suggest, a high demand for out-
migration may be expected. At the same time, it has a strong sense of
identity. Many households can trace back several generations of their family
in the area, and sociological theory would suggest a high level of local community affiliation. Conversely, the expansion of Reading is a relatively recent
phenomenon. Rapid in-migration over the past few decades means that
fewer households living there are from the immediate area, and historic community attachments are less evident. The survey found that although the
differences between the experiences of manual workers and their white-collar
counterparts in each area were more significant than the differences between
the manual workers of each, attitudes to place played an important supporting role.

Migration attitudes

The general issue of prospective migration was clearly a subject of greater significance for the sample population in Liverpool than in Reading: 14 per cent of respondents in Liverpool talked about the subject 'frequently' with family and friends, as opposed to a mere three per cent in Reading. At an informal level, therefore, the local labour market of Liverpool appeared to have produced a more discernible 'climate of mobility' (Rossi, 1955) than that of Reading.

When asked whether they would be prepared to move to another part of the country for employment reasons, just over half of those who answered said yes (55 per cent in Liverpool and 49 per cent in Reading). The difference between the two areas was minimal; however, there were differences between those in work and those out of work: a majority of the former but a minority of the latter were prepared to move. Hence, contrary to the assumptions of neo-classical labour market theory, variations in rates of wages and employment have little impact on willingness to move for work reasons, although they do render the issue more prominent in discussion. Even more surprising, however, is that the unemployed seem less likely to be influenced by such factors than those in employment. However, answers to questions based on hypothetical situations must be treated with caution. For this reason respondents were also asked about their migration behaviour, and about times in the past when the option of migration had been seriously considered, in order to examine the influence of local labour and housing markets on such decisions, and to identify the competing factors which work against potential migration.

Migration behaviour

Information on respondents' past experiences of migration shows that 43.5 per cent of the sample had never lived or worked outside their current county

Figure 11.3 Experience of living and working in other areas

	Liverpool	Reading	All
Never lived or worked outside county	52	35	87
Same home, worked elsewhere in region	1	7	8
Same home, worked elsewhere UK	13	0	13
Same home, worked overseas	12	0	12
Lived only, elsewhere in region, UK or overseas	3	10	13
Lived and worked elsewhere in region	2	16	18
Lived and worked elsewhere in UK	15	23	38
Lived and worked overseas	2	8	10
Other	1	0	1
	100	100	200
Ever lived outside county	22	57	79
Ever worked outside county	45	54	99

Source: Household interview survey

of residence (i.e. Merseyside or Berkshire). This figure is considerably higher in Liverpool (52 per cent) than in Reading (35 per cent) (Figure 11.3). Of those who had worked in other parts of the country, or even overseas in the past, the majority from Liverpool, but none from Reading, had retained the same home base. This fundamental difference between the two areas continues today. Indeed, the very perception of questions related to attitudes to movement emphasised these differences. In Liverpool, when contemplating the question 'would you be prepared to move away for job reasons?', many people immediately interpreted this as meaning working away from home on a short-term basis. The fact that the question related to household migration had to be made quite explicit. In Reading, by contrast, that the meaning was 'permanent' household migration was taken for granted. These differences in the perception of moving away emphasise the different understanding of the relationship between migration and work in the two areas. In Liverpool, the issue of work was more often detached from the home base and viewed as short-term, whereas in Reading the location of work and home were more likely to go hand in hand. Could this be linked to deeper working class attachments to roots and community in Liverpool than in Reading once the availability of work is disregarded? Are these differences in the understanding of work and migration influenced by historical differences in the respective local labour markets?

Whilst many respondents from Liverpool may have worked in other parts of the UK or even abroad in the past, further questioning revealed that they clearly regarded Liverpool as their home throughout the experience. Although some respondents from Reading had experience of working elsewhere in the country from the same home base, none had worked elsewhere in the UK or overseas without also living there (Figure 11.3). Thus 16 per cent of the Reading sample had lived and worked elsewhere in the region (i.e. the South East), and eight per cent had lived and worked overseas, compared with rates of two per cent for each of these categories in Liverpool. At the risk of creating new stereotypes, the interviews revealed a much stronger sense of attachment to Liverpool than to Reading. This attachment is difficult to quantify, but whilst many respondents were prepared to move away from the city as a short term solution to their quest for work, this was usually accompanied by feelings of reluctance at having to do so, and a desire to return at some stage in the future, as and when economic prospects improved. In Reading by contrast, the job was often the prime reason for living in the area, and in some cases the only reason. As one respondent surmised,

> I've lived here all my life, but I feel no particular attachment to the place. In fact if I were to change jobs or something I'd happily leave here tomorrow.

Employment, unemployment and immobility

Although migration is theoretically linked to differentials in employment opportunities, it is clear that many migrants respond not to the opportunities of an area but to the offer of a specific job in that area. For this reason, some recent research has focused on the role of job advertising by employers (Saunders, 1985; and see Chapter 9). Furthermore, skilled and professional employees will move with and at the behest of their employer, as part of their career development (Johnson and Salt, 1980; Salt 1988; and see Chapter 4). For manual workers, however, the opportunity to move with an employer is rare, and notification of vacancies by word of mouth is more frequent (Bradshaw, 1973). Although employers' decisions on how to advertise a particular vacancy clearly influence the geographical spread of information, manual workers are far more likely than their non-manual counterparts to move on speculation (Lansing and Muller, 1967), or in response to inform-ation supplied by friends and relatives in other areas. For this reason, it is important to look at the individual's process of job-search; to identify the influence of the local labour market on that process, and the way in which the consideration of migration may enter this process.

Employment and job-search

Since labour migration is theoretically linked to differentials in wages and employment opportunities, the demand for out-migration among the employed and unemployed in Liverpool should be far higher than that in Reading. Yet this is clearly not the case. Before we can understand the factors which induce consideration of labour migration as an option, therefore, it is important to identify the point at which the process of job-search itself is initiated.

Respondents in both locations were asked why they left their last job, and (if employed), whether they had found a new job before leaving. In Reading, 50 per cent had their present job lined up prior to leaving the former one, compared with 25 per cent in Liverpool. When the various reasons for leaving the last job are amalgamated (Figure 11.4), two key points emerge. First, unemployment between jobs for this group in both areas was common, if not the norm. Second, the likelihood of unemployment between jobs was

Figure 11.4 Reason for leaving previous job

	Liverpool	Reading	All
(a) Redundancy/dismissed	33	14	47
(b) Personal/family	19	13	32
(c) Move to another job	7	24	31
(d) Retirement	10	14	24
(e) End of fixed contract/scheme	12	10	22
(f) Other	16	20	36
No answer/not applicable	3	5	8
	100	100	200

Source: Household interview survey

twice as high in Liverpool. Clearly for the manual worker faced with a situation of unemployment, the option of migration is unlikely to spring to the forefront of the job-search options under consideration if this is regarded as a form of occupational hazard which has been experienced before. It is perhaps the person who becomes unemployed for the first time who is more likely to consider migration.

For those in employment, consideration of wage rates for comparable jobs in other areas appears to have little relevance. Since starting their current job, only three of the 101 repondents to whom the question was appropriate had seriously looked for any alternative. For the vast majority of respondents who were 'satisfied' with the jobs they had, any active job-search was unlikely to occur unless forced through redundancy, dismissal or the like. Moreover, levels of 'satisfaction' with and length of service in particular jobs appeared to be greater in Liverpool, where alternative opportunities were more limited. Clearly notions of career ladders or 'spiralism' (Watson, 1964) have little relevance to the employed population in this survey, the majority of whom merely tried to maintain their current job or level of income. Rather than changing jobs from positions of strength, continually comparing their wages and employment conditions with comparable opportunities locally and in other areas, most were likely to change job only on losing their current one, or when this was perceived to be under threat. Consequently, for the low-skilled, employment migration is generally a response to change, rather than a means of effecting it.

These findings suggest that, for the vast majority of respondents, alternative employment opportunities in the local area – let alone those in other regions – may not be seriously explored until becoming unemployed. Hence, it is particularly important, in explaining immobility, to look in greater detail at those respondents who were unemployed.

Unemployment and job-search

Socio-psychological literature on unemployment suggests a series of stages through which the unemployed job-seeker to passes (Eisenberg and Lazarfeld, 1938; Hopson and Adams, 1976). Harrison (1976) postulates a transitional cycle in which questions relating to the possibilities of work in other areas generally occur toward the end, before the respondent gives up hope altogether. The present results suggest a rather different scenario. Despite hypothetical willingness to move in many cases, most of those seeking manual work do not explore opportunities in other areas at any stage. Those who entertain ideas of migration generally do so very shortly after becoming unemployed. Thereafter, the rapid depletion of personal funds and morale increasingly limits the individual's propensity to consider opportunities in other areas, as well as ability to respond.

Of the unemployed respondents, 33 were genuinely seeking work, yet only three of these had looked for work outside their region at some time since becoming unemployed, and only one was currently exploring opportunities outside the region. The geographical extent of the job-search process of the unemployed was extremely limited, as were the sources of information used. Most had looked for work only within their immediate area, and used local sources of information, like local newspapers, local job centres, and personal contacts; most, in fact, had used all of these at some stage.

The parochialism of the job-search process, however, is not so much the result of the unwillingness to contemplate opportunities in other areas as a reflection of the appropriate search procedure for the type of job sought, almost always manual and requiring few skills (only nine of the 33 unemployed had any 'formal' qualifications). Since these jobs can generally be filled within the local labour market, few employers will choose to advertise them beyond local outlets. This has some important implications for migration, since unemployed job-seekers without access to information on opportunities in other areas are unable to respond to them, even if they are theoretically willing to do so (Saunders, 1985).

Further insights on the job-search process for the unemployed came from group discussions with unemployed job-seekers at local Jobclubs. In all, a total of 20 discussions were conducted, involving a total of 100 unemployed people. These revealed that those who were looking for work in other areas often had to decide first whether to do so, and then where to look. The location decision was freqently based on the availability of suitable contacts in other areas, both as an initial source of information, and as a base from which to search, using appropriate local sources and speculative visits.

The professional or non-manual job-seeker, by contrast, will often be searching for the type of work which is advertised on a regional, national or even international basis. The existence of such sources itself brings an awareness of opportunities in other areas even to those people who have no intention of moving. The process by which a low-skilled job-seeker becomes aware of a suitable vacancy in another area is, therefore, very different from the process by which a more skilled worker becomes aware of such vacancies. In the case of the latter, questions of whether to move, and where to move to, may arise in response to a particular job vacancy, and be inextricably connected to that vacancy. For the less skilled worker, these questions must often be contemplated in a more abstract sense, where information on the availability of work is provided by suitable contacts and personal experience in particular areas.

In explaining the apparent reluctance to take up opportuntities in other areas, therefore, it is important that the 'unemployed' are not perceived as a separate group, but rather as people who were without work at the time of the survey. It became clear from individual employment histories that certain types of work were associated with periodic unemployment (building and construction, farm labouring and dock work being three prime examples). For some people, then, periodic unemployment is an integral part of their employment history. Moreover, employment 'instability' is more likely amongst less skilled and lower status groups of workers (Gordon, 1988). It is, therefore, more instructive to look at their employment histories than at the state of unemployment.

Manual work and career structure

The key to many of the apparent differences in migration propensity between manual and non-manual workers lies in the organisation of work, and the extent of career structure. For many professionals migration is associated with promotion, and the importance of each move in an overriding career structure is understood by both employer and employee. For manual workers, however, employment histories are often chaotic, and are characterised more by diversity and uncertainty. Although their status is often consistent, jobs undertaken may be varied and there is often no logical progression from one to another. Changing jobs is more frequently a response to redundancy and unemployment than a step in the advancement of a particular career.

> My husband works in General Repairs, but he's done lots of other jobs... let me see, he was a chimney sweep, then a bus conductor... he's done steel erecting, pipe fitting... docker and a rigger.

It is the uncertainty of employment which renders migration an inappropriate option in the search for new employment for many households who have much to lose in terms of housing, and local commitments.

> [If I moved] it would have to be where I can guarantee permanent work. Not a situation which is going to be just the same.

Moreover, since promotion is often dependent upon seniority and length of service, redundancies frequently operate on a 'last in, first out' basis, and new jobs are often found through 'word of mouth', many manual workers actually have a vested interest in staying put.

There are exceptions to these socio-economic generalisations, however, which render migration a more viable alternative. For example, for those engaged in temporary, seasonal or short-term contractual work, accommodation is often provided by the employer, but the family is left at home. In such cases, the maintenance of a secure housing base in the home area provides a vital 'fallback' option.

> Well in my job I get shifted around. The first move after Christmas will be High Wycombe. That's alright because I get lodging allowance.... If I jacked the job in I'd go back to Wales [the family home].

Housing and immobility

General considerations

Thus far the causes of immobility have been viewed principally in labour market terms, but housing plays a major role too, not only as a barrier to movement, but also as an alternative set of processes which may generate immobility.

The influence of housing upon labour mobility has been well documented. (Cullingworth, 1969; Johnson, Salt and Wood, 1975; Conway and Ramsay,

1986; Minford, Peel and Ashton, 1987). Housing-based studies of migration have traditionally focused on tenure-based models of residential mobility, and have attempted to explain working class immobility in relation to the operation of the local authority housing sector in which the low-skilled are disproportionately concentrated (Hughes and McCormick, 1981, 1985; National Consumer Council, 1984). Present government policies with regard to local authority rented housing seem likely to exacerbate the current process of socio-tenurial polarisation, whereby the most disadvantaged groups become increasingly residualised in this contracting sector (Hamnett, 1984; Bentham, 1986). As the owner occupied sector becomes relatively more important within the UK housing market, and as home-ownership is extended to sections of the population who have traditionally been excluded, differences within this sector may become more important than differences between it and other tenures. (Forrest, 1987; Forrest and Murie, 1987b).

This section does not attempt to review again the relationship between mobility and housing, but instead focuses on the dual issues of opportunity and constraint for the low-skilled. It is argued that individual migration decisions will seek to balance opportunities in the housing market with those in the labour market, within a given set of financial and other constraints. Since the framework of opportunities and constraints within which a low skilled or unemployed household must formulate its decisions is very different from that in which its better off counterparts will operate, then the balance between housing and employment may also be very different.

Within the owner occupied housing sector, the frictional effect of house price differentials on migration has been well publicised over the past few years. Although current regional house price differentials render movement from depressed to prosperous areas difficult for households of all socio-economic groups, the option may just not be available to many low-skilled home owners, concentrated as they are at the cheaper end of the market. For example, house values among owner occupiers in the Liverpool sample ranged from £12,000 to £30,000, whilst those in Reading ranged from £40,000 to £80,000. Thus the most expensive house in Liverpool was valued at £10,000 less than the cheapest house in Reading.

The household interviews indicate that access to home ownership in Liverpool extends further down the social scale than it does in Reading. Thus whilst many middle class professionals would be forced to lower their housing standards significantly in order to move from the former area to the latter, many of those in manual occupations would have to exit from the sector completely in order to effect such a move. But, since areas of high house values also tend to be characterised by the most acute shortages of private-rented accommodation, and local authority housing allocation usually demands a minimum period of residence in the local area, the ability to respond to better employment opportunities in other areas is seriously limited by the need to maintain adequate housing.

Extreme regional house price differentials also inhibit movement in both directions, because migrating households usually view the move as one step in a sequence, taking a very long-term view of the costs and benefits involved.

Thus some households are fearful of losing equity by leaving a buoyant housing market for an area where prices are lower. This problem is encountered to some degree at all levels of the owner occupied housing market, but is disproportionately felt by those in lower socio-economic groups for a number of reasons. First, they are likely to be concentrated at the lower end of the housing market, and are more at risk from exclusion at times of rapid price increase. Second, they are more likely to be faced with fragile or uncertain employment opportunities in other areas, which may not entail any promotion or wage increase. Third, as they are less likely to be moving at the behest of an employer, they will rarely have access to the financial assistance which this often provides.

Since cost will exclude many low-skilled households from owner occupation, the opportunities and constraints imposed by the operation of the public housing sector are arguably of greater significance to their mobility. The influence of local authority allocation procedures has been well documented, but little attention has been paid in the literature to the responses of individual households to them. The importance of this is demonstrated below, by looking first at the constraints on choice, and then at how individual households respond in order to maximise their opportunities within those constraints.

Housing choice

When questioned on the reasons for choosing to live in their current house, a large number of respondents claimed that they had no choice. Indeed their perception of the question was often more instructive than the answers recorded, since it emphasised the different ranges of options available to different socio-economic groups. Moreover, the perception of these opportunities is often historically determined, being dependent upon former housing experiences, including those as children. For example, the response

Figure 11.5 Reasons for choosing current housing

	Liverpool	Reading	All
(a) Allocated by local authority	24	26	50
(b) Housing factors	14	28	42
(c) Locational factors	9	20	29
(d) Compulsory purchase of former home	25	2	27
(e) Family/friends already here	6	13	19
(f) Other family reasons	12	3	15
(g) Other	7	7	14
No answer/not applicable	3	2	5
	100	100	200
Household decision-making (b + c + e + f)	41	64	105
External decision making (a + d)	49	28	77

Source: Household interview survey

'we had no choice' was far more evident in Liverpool than in Reading. There is some evidence that this is related to the experience of compulsory purchase of former homes: one in four households in Liverpool had moved into their present home through some form of compulsory relocation, compared with one in fifty in Reading (Figure 11.5).

For those households which feel they have little choice in housing, perceived opportunities of accommodation elsewhere will be very limited. Although apparent lack of choice was not confined to the local authority sector, it was most pronounced there. When moves are continually determined by outside institutions (in this case the local authority), sometimes forcibly, then one important part of the decision-making process is removed, in part, from the arena of the household. It is externally and bureaucratically controlled by management institutions, whose policies vary from place to place, depending on political priorities, set within a framework of central government control. The range of options available to a particular household in a particular locale will, therefore, reflect first the historical inheritance of housing, second the policies of central government, and third, the priorities of local government within these parameters.

Despite this seeming rejection of the notion of choice by many households in local authority accommodation, the tracing of their employment and housing histories illustrates that they are not necessarily mere passive agents within a bureaucratic system. Although choice was often reduced to the ability to accept or reject a specific offer of housing, many households interviewed were acutely aware of their relative position within the local authority sector, and of the means by which they would be able to improve this position. When attempting to enter the sector initially, households were generally prepared to accept the first offer of accommodation in order to get onto the lowest rung of the ladder. Thereafter, if the local authority wished to move them again, they could afford to be much more selective about the offers they accepted.

Local authorities in the UK generally allocate housing through a points system based on social needs, household size, and length of residence in the local area. For this reason many households are unwilling to relinquish the position they have established within the local hierarchy for the prospect of better employment opportunities in other areas, since despite schemes which facilitate the movement of local authority tenants between areas (most notably the National Mobility Scheme), it is often difficult for them to realise the true value of their accumulation, especially in areas where competition for local authority housing is more intense. Even where some form of transfer into comparable accommodation is possible, those local authority tenants who have achieved a secure position within a local market are often reluctant to close the door behind them by moving, since it is unlikely that they would be able to re-enter the system again at the same level, should they wish to return at some stage in the future.

This problem is compounded by the fact that the best opportunities in a local authority housing market are likely to be found in areas with the worst employment prospects. Interviews in Liverpool yielded numerous examples of households which preferred to maintain their housing strengths, even though local employment prospects were poor. Conversely, interviews with households in Reading which were trying to enter the local authority housing market yielded examples of households who were contemplating movement to areas where they would be more likely to receive an offer of local authority accommodation, even where this meant moving to an area where employment prospects were more limited.

It is clear that for many low-skilled households which have little strength in the labour market, and where employment histories are characterised by uncertainty, strength and security in a local housing market provides important stability. In this way, strength in the labour market is balanced against strength in the housing market. The assumptions of labour market theory suggest that housing is one of a series of obstacles to be overcome by households attempting to respond to differentials in wages and employment prospects. Whilst this may be true for the majority of the population, this survey suggests that many low-skilled households, whose employment opportunities are relatively limited in any labour market area, are more inclined to regard the lack of employment as an obstacle to be overcome in their attempts to respond to better housing opportunities.

The rationale for immobility

The picture which emerges from this discussion of the immobility of the low-skilled and unemployed is a system of migration actions and decisions in stark contrast to that associated with middle class 'careerists', progressing in tandem up local and national employment and housing ladders.

For most households in the survey, aspirations were satisfied within local labour and housing markets. Employment histories revealed an absence of any order whereby one job is linked to another in a logical career progression. Rather, such histories were characterised by diversity and uncertainty, with enforced periods of idleness between jobs. In general, promotion was achieved through seniority and on-the-job experience, favouring the absence of movement. The search for an alternative job was rarely undertaken whilst the respondent was still employed in a reasonably secure position. Job search procedures were highly localised and were dependent upon a variety of local information sources and informal contacts. Where migration was considered, job-search was still focused on very localised areas in alternative labour markets, often dictated by the location of existing contacts or past experience.

Set against the uncertainty of many low-skilled jobs, the chance of secure housing provides a reassuring cushion. For this reason local authority accommodation is often preferred to buying or renting from a private landlord. Ladders in the owner occupied sector rarely extended beyond the first rung. Ladders in local authority housing were more evident, though the patterns of household development which are likely to ensure rapid progression up these ladders provide a contrast to those associated with better off home owners. Strength in the local authority market is achieved through long periods of residence in the local area, overcrowding or rapid family growth, and (sometimes) low pay and unemployment. Moreover, the factors which enable progression through the local authority system are precisely those factors which mediate against geographic mobility.

Once a particular household has achieved a strong position in the local housing market, it is often reluctant to relinquish this for the uncertain prospects of better employment opportunities elsewhere. In consequence, strength in the housing market is often balanced against weakness in or even exclusion from the local labour market.

Generally, the households interviewed were best able to balance their housing needs and preferences with the employment needs of their constituent members by not moving, or by doing so only locally. Of the households which did try to migrate at some stage, there were many which were unable to realise these aspirations. Among those who were able to move sucessfully, local housing processes were often of paramount importance, and employment opportunities merely needed to be in accordance. For most low-skilled and unemployed households, however, it is clear that the housing, employment and household considerations which they must balance are likely to entail strategies which involve movement only within a local employment and housing market. Hence the rationale for mobility cannot be fully understood without insight into this parallel rationale for immobility.

References

Bentham, G. (1986) 'Socio-tenurial polarisation in the United Kingdom'. *Urban Studies*, 2: 157–62.

Bradshaw, T. F. (1973) 'Jobseeking methods used by unemployed workers'. *Monthly Labour Review*, 96: 35–40.

Clark, G. L. and Whiteman, J. (1983) 'Why poor people do not move: job search behavior and disequilibrium amongst local labor markets'. *Environment and Planning A*, 15: 85–104.

Conway, J. and Ramsay, E. (1986) *A Job to Move*, London: SHAC.

Cullingworth, J. B. (1969) *Housing and labour Mobility*, Paris: OECD.

Daniel, G. H. (1940) 'Some factors affecting the movement of labour'. *Oxford Economic Papers*, 3: 144–79.

Eisenberg, P. and Lazarfeld, P. F. (1938) 'The Psychological Effects of Unemployment'. *Psychological Bulletin*, XXXV: 358–90.

Flowerdew, R. (1982) 'Institutional effects on internal migration' in Manion, T. and Flowerdew, R. T. N. (eds) *Institutions and Geographical Patterns*, pp. 209–227, London: Croom Helm.

Forrest, R. S. (1987) 'Spatial Mobility, Tenure Mobility and Emerging Social Divisions in the UK Housing Market'. *Environment and Planning A*, 19: 1611–30.

Forrest, R. S. and Murie, A. S. (1987a) 'The affluent home owner: labour market position and the shaping of housing histories' in Thrift, N. and

Williams, P. (eds) *Class and Space*, pp. 370–403. London: Routledge and Kegan Paul.

Forrest, R. S. and Murie, A. S. (1987b) 'The housing histories of home-owners'. *Sociological Review*, **35**: 370–403.

Friedlander, D. and Roshier, R. J. (1966) 'A study of internal migration in England and Wales, part 2'. *Population Studies*, **20**, 1: 45–59.

G.B. Department of Employment (1979) *Labour Force Survey*. London: HMSO.

Gordon, I. R. (1988) 'Unstable jobs, unstable people and unstable places: the case of resort labour markets'. Paper presented to the RSA/IBG IAADSG conference on the Geography of Labour Markets, London.

Green, A. E., Owen, D. W., Champion, A. G., Goddard, J. B. and Coombes, M. G. (1985) 'What contribution can labour migration make to reducing unemployment?'. CURDS Discussion Paper 73, presented to the Joint Studies in Public Policy conference on Unemployment at the Policy Studies Institute, London (November).

Hamnett, C. (1984) 'Housing and the two nations: socio-tenurial polarisation in England and Wales, 1961–81'. *Urban Studies*, **43**: 389–405.

Harrison, R. (1976) 'The demoralising experience of prolonged unemployment'. *Department of Employment Gazette* (April).

Hogarth, T. and Daniel, W. W. (1987) 'The long-distance commuters'. *New Society*, 29 May: 11–13.

Hogarth, T. and Daniel, W. W. (1988) *Britain's New Industrial Gypsies*. London: Policy Studies Institute.

Hopson, B. and Adams, J. (1976) 'Towards an understanding of transition: defining some boundaries of transition dynamics' in Adams, J., Hayes, J. and Hopson, B. *Transition*. London: Martin Robertson.

Hughes G. and McCormick, B. (1981) 'Do council housing policies reduce migration between regions?' *Economic Journal*, **91**: 919–37.

Hughes, G. and McCormick, B. (1985) 'Migration intentions in the UK'. *Economic Journal* (supplement), **95**: 113–23.

Hunter, L. C. and Reid, G. L. (1968) *Urban Worker Mobility*, Paris: OECD.

Jansen, C. J. (1969) 'Some sociological aspects of migration' in Jackson, J. A. (ed) *Migration*. Cambridge: Cambridge University Press.

Johnson, J. H. and Salt, J. (1980) 'Labour migration within organisations: an introductory study'. *Tijdschrift voor Economische en Sociale Geografie*, **71**: 227–84.

Johnson, J. H., Salt, J. and Wood, P. A. (1975) 'Housing and the geographical mobility of labour in England and Wales: some theoretical considerations'. in Kosinski, L. A. and Prothero, R. M. (eds) *People on the Move*, pp. 91–101, London: Methuen.

Kennett, S. and Randolph, W. (1978) 'The differential migration of socio-economic groups 1966–71'. Discussion Paper 66, Graduate School of Geography, London School of Economics and Political Science.

Lansing, J. B. and Morgan, J. N. (1967) 'The effect of geographical mobility on income'. *Journal of Human Resources*, **2**: 449–60.

Lansing, J. B. and Muller, E. (1967) *The Geographic Mobility of Labour*. Michigan: Institute for Social Research, University of Michigan.

Lewis, J. and Townsend, A. (eds) (1989) *The North South Divide*. London: Paul Chapman.

Minford, P., Peel, M. and Ashton, P. (1987) *The Housing Morass*. London: The Institute of Economic Affairs.

National Consumer Council (1984) *Moving Home: Why is it Difficult for Council Tenants?* London: NCC.

Northern Ireland Mobility Survey (1980) *Summary of Findings*. St Albans: Economic and Spatial Planning Ltd.

Office of Population Censuses and Surveys (1977) *General Household Survey*. London: HMSO.

Office of Population Censuses and Surveys (1981) *Census of Population*. London: HMSO.

Pahl, R. E. (1980) 'Employment, work, and the domestic division of labour'. *International Journal of Urban and Regional Research*, 4: 1–19.

Richardson, H. W. and West, E. G. (1964) 'Must we always take work to the workers?' *Lloyds Bank Review*, 71: 35–48.

Riley, F. (1986) *People in Need of a Future: A Survey of the Long-Term Unemployed in Skelmersdale*. Skelmersdale: Workbase.

Rossi, P. H. (1955) *Why Families Move: A Study in the Social Psychology of Urban Residential Mobility*. New York: The Free Press.

Salt, J. (1988) 'Highly skilled international migrants, careers and internal labour markets'. *Geoforum*, 19: 387–399.

Saunders, M. N. K. (1985) 'The influence of job vacancy advertising upon migration: some empirical evidence'. *Environment and Planning A*, 17: 1581–9.

Taylor, R. C. (1969) 'Migration and motivation: a study of determinants and types' in Jackson, J. A. (ed) *Migration*, pp. 99–133, Cambridge: Cambridge University Press.

Watson, W. (1964) 'Social mobility and social class in industrial communities' in Gluckman, M. (ed) *Closed Minds and Open Systems*, pp. 129–57. Edinburgh: Oliver and Boyd.

Wilkinson, R. and Merry, D. M. (1965) 'A statistical analysis of attitudes to moving, *Urban Studies*. 2, 1: 1–14.

CHAPTER 12

Moving Strategies among Home Owners

Ray Forrest and Alan Murie

Introduction

Studies of residential mobility and migration have been somewhat out of fashion in recent years. Certainly in mainstream housing research the shift in focus from preference and choice models to perspectives which emphasised institutional constraints and deeper structural processes, pushed the household and household decision making to the periphery of analyses of the housing market. The critical questions were about subsidy structures, state regulation, patterns of ownership and control, and the production and consumption of housing as a commodity. The relationships between particular housing tenures and the capitalist economy involved a crude assumption that home ownership was politically, ideologically and economically supportive of capitalist social relations, whereas council housing was oppositional and hindered the market economy. And in that context, concerns about labour and residential mobility were heavily focused on the bureaucratic constraints of state housing.

The recognition that human agency, the household and individual life paths remain a legitimate and important object of study has coincided with the realisation that the expansion of home ownership in a period of significant social and spatial change throws up a whole new series of issues and relationships. Three issues can be seen to be of particular significance.

- First, as home ownership encompasses a more diverse group of people and properties, it becomes more difficult to generalise about the dominant characteristics of the tenure. In other words, home owners are becoming increasingly stratified and the assumed features of indi-

191

vidual home ownership (e.g. relative affluence, easy mobility) are seen to be contingent rather than necessary.

● Second, the historical development of home ownership has reached a point where there are a large number of outright owners who will be passing on properties of varying value to subsequent generations. This relates in turn to a concern with the ways in which housing histories are shaped and influenced by investment factors and the incidence or otherwise of inherited property wealth.

● Third, the increasing dominance of home ownership combined with inter- and intra-regional price differentials and the lack of alternative forms of housing provision has created new difficulties in relation to labour mobility. The housing market now more closely mirrors the broader pattern of economic prosperity or decline. Home ownership may now inhibit inter-regional mobility. Thus, the assumed compatability between the capitalist economy and a housing market dominated by individual home ownership is seen to be problematic (for a general discussion see Allen and Hamnett, 1989).

These and other factors have both direct and indirect implications for patterns of internal migration. A highly stratified home ownership tenure may be reflected in highly differentiated and particular patterns of mobility and immobility. The transfer of the ownership of dwellings from councils to private owner occupiers is likely to affect household movement decisions and the ability of households to make such decisions. The increasing numbers of retiring home owners may generate a higher level of mobility in later life. These movements may have strong regional dimensions depending on relative property values.

Alternatively, it may be that social scientists have over-emphasised the importance of housing tenure on people's lives and movement strategies. The overwhelming impression from the mobility studies which have been undertaken over the past decades is that patterns of migration are highly differentiated by class. Longer distance migrants are overwhelmingly drawn from those in higher status employment (for an interesting discussion of this issue see Cote, 1983). Despite the major shifts in housing tenure and housing provision which have occurred in the post war period, migration patterns display a high degree of stability and continuity. This is not to say that apparently similar outcomes as regards mobility and immobility may be the product of quite different processes and circumstances. For example, working class areas with extreme differences in housing tenure patterns (i.e. high levels of council housing as opposed to high levels of home ownership) may have similarly localised and limited patterns of residential mobility. Both the circumstances under which people move, exercise choice and their patterns of association may be very different and only become apparent under detailed scrutiny at the local level.

Mobility and migration studies have tended to involve the manipulation of large data sets. Of necessity, individual details become lost in the analysis of aggregated data. Case histories can therefore provide a useful complement to such larger scale quantitative studies and may generate ideas and issues which can ultimately be explored more systematically through conventional social surveys. In this chapter we draw our evidence from in-depth interviews carried out in two areas of Bristol. The research was designed to explore aspects of stratification and mobility in the owner occupied sector (Forrest and Murie, 1985). It should be stressed that the four case studies presented in this paper are not claimed to be representative and only make sense when set against a background of other evidence about residential mobility and migration which is available elsewhere in this volume. They have been selected to illustrate different aspects of mobility and immobility and the different circumstances of entry to and movement within the owner occupied sector.

But the cases are real cases and do not suffer from the problems of the averages of aggregated situations where such averages may not reflect the actual situation of any one case. Used in conjunction with other evidence, illustrative cases and in-depth interviews allow a different kind of account of processes, and may both raise questions and focus attention on different issues than those which arise through other research which may be more heavily structured by the preconceptions of the researcher (see also Mitchell, 1985; Bertaux, 1982). The research referred to here grew out of a concern with changes and differences in the housing market. In particular it was concerned with how people had arrived at different housing destinations. Had people arriving in similar housing destinations also had similar housing origins? If so, what processes determined a similar housing history — the way the housing market works, similar jobs and employment careers, or similar patterns of family building and change? And if there were not similar housing origins, which of these factors explains why households arrived at similar housing destinations?

In the research referred to here, some of the moves, and especially those by company executives, were long distance moves with company assistance. The longest case study referred to below is an illustration of such a move. As the literature suggests, shorter distance moves were less likely to be associated with job changes. However, in longer distance job-related moves, housing considerations are involved. There is a need to build an understanding of housing processes and how they relate to job moves into discussion of migration. At least for high paid company executives, housing elements are taken into account by employers and the executives themselves. The way this works is illustrated by the contrast between the housing histories of households in different jobs with different migration histories.

Underlying these considerations are issues about housing preferences, choices and constraints and how individuals and families make choices relating to housing and employment. Decisions to move or not to move, the distance and direction of move and the package of housing tenure, costs, size, type, location and other factors are complex decisions which relate to work, home and family. The way these factors interact is outlined by a range of survey data. This chapter seeks to illustrate the diversity of considerations and outcomes which is apparent from such data by reference to four different

194

experiences. Before doing this some reference to the context and to the research study involved is provided.

Context

The context for current studies of household movement and migration includes uneven patterns of economic development, changes in employment, unemployment and the labour market, and restructuring of housing tenure. In relation to the last of these the growth and change of home ownership has been a key feature. Home ownership is now the dominant tenure in Britain and in 1988 involved some 65 per cent of all households. In many areas the formerly easy-access private rented sector is so small or of such poor quality or so expensive as to offer little, even as a stop-gap while moving. Households in employment, and especially those moving beyond the area in which they currently live, are most likely to be contemplating home ownership — and indeed to be moving within that tenure. But home ownership is far from a uniform tenure. Diversity has become more apparent with its growth, its incorporation of a wider range of properties (including older and ill-maintained properties), the transfer of households from private and council renting, and its widening social base, especially among skilled manual and white collar workers. At the same time, households contemplating moving in a largely owner occupied market, and certainly those seeking home ownership, face a different set of institutional and financial engagements and transactions than in the past. Transaction costs are high and processes of bidding, borrowing and buying are very different from the processes in other tenures — or from those familiar to the tramping artisan or the mobile worker of previous generations. And the calculations involved for households are more complex. They are no longer just about obtaining shelter or about distance from work, the time and financial costs of getting to work, and the trade-offs between these costs and housing costs. Nor are they just about liking the area, the status of the area or access to other facilities such as shops and schools. Critically they are increasingly about investment and about the accumulation of wealth. Gains to be made out of the appreciation of the asset value of owner occupied housing could considerably exceed those made out of employment. Making the wrong housing choice could reduce the returns made. These considerations complicate movement decisions. But what leverage they have on decisions is not easy to assess. For example, some speculations about the significance of the returns which could be made through housing suggest that they would dominate the process of household decision making and could be more important than job considerations. Thus Farmer and Barrell (1981) suggest that house price inflation and the opportunities for accumulation through home ownership have meant that 'entrepreneurial ability has been sucked into the home owning sector'. They provide no direct evidence to support their speculation. Similarly, Saunders and Harris (1988), drawing on household interviews, conclude that:

... not only do home owners make real gains out of their housing, but most of them are aware of this and many develop strategies designed to maximise it. (pp. 32-3)

On closer examination Saunders and Harris's view is not based on direct evidence but is based on an argument that:

... the fact that owner occupiers now move so frequently and yet across such small distances would support the view that many of them are following a deliberate and coherent investment strategy through the housing market. (p. 32)

In fact Saunders and Harris's data do little more than reinforce the view, established by other data, that investment considerations are one factor but not the dominant factor in housing moves. The assertion about many home owners developing strategies to maximise investment is open to question. However the view that housing investment is likely to be a conscious consideration in most movement decisions by home owners is difficult to dispute.

These contributions raise wider debate about choice and constraint, the considerations influencing all household movement, whether long or short distance, and the basis of decisions about the choice of particular dwellings. Contributions to this debate over recent years have cast doubt on approaches which emphasise choice and neglect constraints related to access and institutional arrangements as well as income and knowledge; which imply that moves which coincide with different stages of the family life cycle are all caused by such changes; which imply that moves which involve tenure change or change in other housing characteristics are designed to achieve such changes rather than being changes consequent upon a range of considerations (of which they may be part); and that housing moves involve maximising particular dimensions (such as investment) rather than satisficing across a wider range of dimensions (Murie, 1974; Murie *et al.*, 1976; Payne and Payne, 1974; Rossi, 1980; Rossi and Shlay, 1982). In spite of this there is room, especially using different research methods, to reconsider these elements among home owners and to consider how far investment and other considerations have affected housing histories of home owners and how the housing elements are taken into account in different types of movement decision.

Home owners in two neighbourhoods

This chapter draws on a study which has been described in detail elsewhere (Forrest and Murie, 1985; 1987; 1989). It involved interviews with 35 households in two contrasting small areas of Bristol in 1985. The two localities chosen were strikingly different physically and visually and in terms of market position. One area was consciously chosen to include the top of the owner occupied market within the city boundary, while the other was an older (Victorian rather than inter-war), long established, stable, working-class area. The detached suburban houses in the former area were much larger with substantial gardens and occupied the space of ten or more of the terraced houses in the working-class area. Full descriptions of the interviews carried out for this study are available in the references cited above.

In brief, the households living in the working-class area were mainly locals. Most of those interviewed had strong family links with the area, had lived there for long periods and left it only for short intervals during the war or for employment. Most were in semi-skilled or service employment and some had moved out of skilled employment (had been deskilled). This income and employment pattern was only broken by a small number of younger, white collar workers in the area. Again in both housing and employment terms these households had limited access to more expensive parts of the housing market.

In striking contrast, few of those in the up-market district were locals. Few had been born in the neighbourhood or indeed in Bristol and few had lived in working-class terraced dwellings similar to those in the other locality at any stage in their lives. The two groups of households had been selected from two contrasting destination areas. And the processes of arriving at those destinations had largely been conducted in separate worlds.

One couple (referred to below) in the working class area had always been owner occupiers, and their parents had in both cases been homeowners. But this was unusual. Typically in this area, parents had been in rented or tied accommodation and only three couples had bought houses at marriage. Older persons in the area had experienced a marked improvement in their housing conditions during their lives. Their most common tenure experience in childhood and as adults (prior to ownership) was of privately rented or tied accommodation. For most of the couples interviewed in this area their current house was the only one they had owned and only two couples had ever owned more than one other dwelling. None had had second homes or 'investment' properties. The majority of those who had married had lived in only two or fewer dwellings since marriage.

In contrast, for those in the affluent areas it was relatively common for a parental home to have been owner occupied. There was also, however, a considerable experience of tied housing and private renting. No one in this area moved into their home as a home owner prior to marriage. And not all became owner occupiers on marriage. Indeed, an early start in owner occupation was not a common feature of this group. Nor was it the case that these households had been involved in a whole series of moves 'climbing the housing ladder'. For one household their present dwelling was the only one ever owned and for six others only two dwellings had ever been bought. However, there were some households with a long experience of buying and selling and of a significant escalation in the value of their homes. The greater rate of movement in this area since marriage and as home owners was a major difference between households in this area and those in the working-class area. A significant element in this difference was job history. In the wealthy area all of the households had embarked upon executive careers or had family businesses. The history of their housing moves was largely a history of job changes which required movement between cities.

What was evident about the contrasting housing histories of the two groups was the importance of employment factors in the shaping of their housing experiences. Factors such as parental tenure, age of marriage, when children were born, and early or late entry to owner occupation did not emerge as key differentiating factors. The major contrast was between those owners whose housing histories had been shaped by the distinctive nature of employment as business executive, salaried professionals and officers in the armed forces, in contrast to those whose skills were less specific and more easily obtained in other areas.

And there was a wide range of attitudes towards home ownership. Few people had coherent images of the range of tenures on offer. People offered views of housing tenure reflecting their own experience as adults and children. For some this was exclusively an experience of home ownership. For others the reference point for attitudes to tenure was tied accommodation or private renting. Very few 'affluent' owners had experiences of council housing. And for some renting was associated with higher costs of tied housing with very regular disruptive movement. In this sense, attitudes towards, and the meanings attached to, home ownership can only be made sense of in the light of past experience and cannot be assumed to reflect some commonly held values and aspirations or strategies towards investment or trading up.

It is in this context that the following illustrative cases are presented. The first two are drawn from interviews in the working class area and the second two from the affluent area. They refer to households with very different housing, employment, family and migration histories. Such histories connect with categories which emerge from larger data sets and help to make sense of the real situation lying behind the analysis of such data.

No moving strategy

The extreme case of non-moving home owners was a husband and wife aged 67 and 71 respectively at the time of interview. The wife had lived the whole of her life in the same house in the working class area. She had been born there. Her parents had rented it for 12–15 years before purchasing it as sitting tenants for £187 shortly after the First World War. Her husband had moved into that house at marriage in 1940. Prior to that he had only lived in one house and that was 'four turnings down on the left'. He had been born and raised there and his parents owned it. The husband had been called up for military service shortly after their marriage in 1940 and by the time of his de-mobilisation in 1946 his father-in-law had died. He and his wife lived upstairs with his wife's mother downstairs. In 1950 they bought the house (from the wife's mother) for £1,250 with an £800 mortgage involving repayments of £5 per month. Subsequently they once took out an additional mortgage to rebuild the rear extension (at a cost of £1,000 with a £600 increased mortgage).

Apart from wartime service the husband spent his life working (for 40 years) in the same job in the transport industry ending up in a supervisory position. His wife had been evacuated and directed to wartime work but otherwise had mainly worked as a hairdresser and latterly had worked part-time as a shop assistant.

This couple inevitably had strong local links. Both their son and daughter lived nearby and both owned their houses – both had been helped in this by their parents. They were conscious of a change in the area:

> ... a lot of the younger ones come into these houses because they are cheaper to run when you're first married and then after a while they do the house up and they sell it. Before, people tended to stay where they were.

For the discussion in this chapter the most interesting questions relate to the 'failure' of this couple to adopt a trading up or investment strategy or indeed to move at all. Strong local links, continuity of work and involvement in leisure activities were important aspects of this. While they had helped their children with housing they themselves had never received any financial or other help with housing from family or employers. They had never owned a second home or any other property. For them the advantages of owning were not investment: 'The first thing is you can do what you like with it.' Disadvantages related to the lack of a garage and garden but proximity to shops and public transport were a convenience. When asked about the initial decision to buy their house the response was that 'at that time it was convenient for us' and the widowed mother needed looking after. They had considered moving or trading-up but 'we never really had the wages' and a contemplated move shortly before retirement had fallen through and been complicated by deteriorating health. 'In the end it proved a blessing that we never left here.' They had not been tempted to move when their family was younger because nearby schools were acceptable and increased costs were not worth contemplating and whatever they would have sold their house for would not have been sufficient to enable them to obtain anything very different 'certainly not 30 years ago'.

When asked their view of the proposition 'some people look on housing simply as an investment – have you ever seen it in that way?' the response was a very firm 'No, it's a place to live'. Again they responded with a firm negative to a question about whether they had ever regarded it as important to maximise their mortgage. Considerations about having a property to leave to the children were, however, important.

This household had a foot on the home ownership ladder at a very early stage and had no experience of any other tenure. They did not pursue a housing investment or trading up strategy. This partly reflected a view of the market at that time but also reflected the advantages of low housing costs and low levels of borrowing, attachment to locality, the nature of employment (and absence of any need to move for job reasons) and the impact of this strategy on the availability of money for other expenditure. Rather than present this as a non-rational housing strategy and regard it as 'cultural', 'class' or 'generational', it appears that rational non-investment and non-moving strategies are real and should be recognised in debates about housing and employment decisions.

Tying up housing and employment

In contrast to the previous couple, this couple, interviewed in the same area, had much greater experience of geographical mobility and of housing movement. They were a younger couple (aged 36 and 42 at the time of the interview). Both had moved to Bristol from rural areas. The wife was the daughter of a farmer and had lived in the same farm house in Southern Ireland until moving to London when she was 18. She had chosen London because of family connections – she lived in a room in her sister's house. After five years she moved to Bristol and lived in her brother's house. In both of these moves the aim had been 'to see somewhere new' and the location was determined by family links (and nursing skills which could be used anywhere) rather than by job or housing. After two years in Bristol she married. Her husband's father had been a highly skilled agricultural worker who had regularly moved with his job. He chose to move regularly and had skills which made it easy. As a result the interviewee had been to 15 different schools between the age of five and 15. This involved more than one move a year in a variety of locations in the South and South West of England. The family had lived mainly in tied accommodation but with short periods living with grandparents and renting from private and council landlords. His dominant impression of renting was of tied accommodation (often of low standard) and of the constant disruption of moving house. His own early work experience after leaving school was of factory and farmwork alongside his father and still moving house regularly – five times between leaving school and when he left his parental home – aged 22. It was at that stage that he moved to Bristol – because he 'wanted the job' involved. Although the job was what he had wanted to do since childhood it was not well paid. A short period in the YMCA was followed by four different addresses, graduating from sharing a room in lodgings to renting a small self-contained flat.

At this point – seeking somewhere to live following marriage but with limited income – an opportunity to obtain tied accommodation arose. The information about this came through the husband's work. This involved the couple in acting as 'domestic servants and chauffeur' in exchange for free accommodation in an elderly couple's house near to the husband's place of work. In spite of his aversion to tied housing they entered into this arrangement. It worked successfully for seven years until the death of the elderly couple. With the tied employment terminated the accommodation was sold and the couple were forced to look for somewhere else to live for themselves and their son. They moved out of the area of Bristol they had been living in – and the area where the husband was working – to buy their present house. The house needed a lot of modernisation: 'it didn't have a bathroom'. It was difficult to buy at the time with a lot of gazumping and they were affected by this. In the end they did not pick the house:

> We were let down by the other house and didn't really like this. We had to get out by a certain date, the other one fell through and this one was offered me by someone at work. We took this house on the basis that it gave us somewhere to live to start with. It was pretty rough to start with. In a bad state, but when we found we'd been here for a while and

started to decorate it, it wasn't as bad as it looked. It was a lot sounder than we thought. It's quite a warm house and is close to schools and shops.

Prior to moving they:

> ... knew nothing about this area and were not keen on it – people said it was rather a ropey district compared with where we had been living.

Having lived in an 'elderly' area with few children around their son's age they 'wanted to be in an area where he could find friends ... and it worked out fine'.

An immediate problem arose with unsafe wiring. This and other expenditure on an unmodernised house put too much pressure on their income.

> The basic fact was that after we moved to here on the money I was making I couldn't pay the mortgage so we had to decide whether we gave up the house or the job. So I gave up the job.

There followed a period of 18 months doing various unskilled jobs and some periods without work before obtaining a better paid secure job within walking distance using his skills and experience. He has remained in this job ever since (10 years).

While this couple now felt the area was a friendly close-knit community, their own relatives, with one exception, were not in the Bristol area and most of their close friends were work associates. Their attitudes to tenure again reflected their own housing experience. Owning for them was about self-containment, stability and privacy in contrast especially to their immediately previous experience of tied accommodation – and to a longer history of sharing accommodation and constant movement. So, 'the main advantages of owning your own home' were:

> Freedom and being able to shut your door and go into your own little world if you feel like it; in someone else's house you haven't that choice ... it was a tie, it really was a tie because we had to almost explain where we were going towards the end because they relied on us so much ... and you felt somewhat indebted ... living in the same house. Even if you didn't feel too good you had to pull yourself together and help out.

The disadvantages similarly related to their own experience: 'money, it's a great struggle to start with' and:

> ... you can't always afford maybe where you would like to live. We'd have liked to have lived in a different type of house with a nice garden and that but you have to live where you can afford to live comfortably. We would rather live here and have some money to enjoy life rather than live in a more expensive house and have nothing left.

This concern to have money to do other things – going to the theatre and shows and 'enjoying life' – was evident. Decorating and improving the house had been hard work.

They had thought of moving but had decided not to do so as they would have had to pay a lot more and not gain very much. They preferred to maintain their financial flexibility and to wait until their son had finished his education. They had looked 'more or less in the same area, for a house with a garden'.

> The original feeling I had about this house when we moved here, being brought up in the country the thing I didn't like about it was that I couldn't walk around it. That upset me for a long time. We were also used to bigger rooms.... We've now adapted to it and adapted the house to ourselves.

In five years time they expected that they would have moved probably locally or a bit further out towards the country.

When asked if they were conscious of the value of their house they replied that they were but that this was 'not something that really concerns us'. When asked specifically about investment considerations they replied:

> Not really, it's what we can afford comfortably, somewhere nice, that you're happy to come into. We're not ones that want great wealth really . . . as long as we've got enough, a bit in the pocket to go and do a few things we want to do and what the boy wants to do.

As stated at the outset this illustration is of a very different mobility, housing and job experience. The house and home was not a familiar or even chosen haven and knowledge and contacts in the locality were limited. Home ownership was achieved later in the family cycle and housing and employment aspirations did not match. The strategies which emerge in adjusting housing and then job involved difficult choices. They were not investment strategies. Indeed if anything they involved attempting to limit housing expenditure in order to achieve other objectives related to family, leisure and consumption.

The international company executive

Households in the affluent area had very different work experiences from either of the two presented above. They were all professionals, company executives or managers or involved in substantial family businesses. The household discussed in this section again consisted of a husband and wife aged 53 and 50 respectively at the time of interview. Their four children were all still in full-time education or waiting to go to university. The husband had been born in Yorkshire. After living in two rented houses in the same area the family moved when he was seven to another rented house in Leicestershire after the father was promoted in his job. The family moved to join the father in a newly built semi-detached house which they bought. After staying there for seven years his parents bought a large (five bedroom) Victorian terraced house in the same area. When he was 18 he left school and went into the Air Force for two years. On leaving the Air Force he joined a large multi-national and lived in a company hostel for two years undergoing training. Following that training, working for the same company involved a move to the Middle East and then South America. After three years 'I came back and decided that if I was going to be an accountant I was going to be a proper accountant and had to qualify so I took articles'. This involved living in lodgings, two bed-sitters in succession, and back into lodgings. Following that period and towards the end of his studies he moved to a bed-sit in Oxford. At that stage – nearing the point of qualifying as an accountant – he married.

His wife had been born in Derbyshire. Her father's business had failed in the depression and he obtained engineering work which involved his moving all over the country. While they bought a house in Bexley Heath 'at some stage before the war' the family moved with the father's work to a variety of places including Kent and the county of Stirling. During the war the father worked on military stations and continued to move around. The family settled in Leicestershire after going to stay with grandparents and finding the next door property available to rent. She stayed there for 11 years until she was 15 when the whole family moved with the father's job. After a period of work she went to university. She then worked in Leicestershire (first of all living in a flat and then in a bed-sitter) before moving to Oxford and marriage.

The early experience as a married couple was of uncertainty at work and moving house. The husband's first job after qualifying fell through and he again joined a large company and the couple rented a cottage for six months in the Midlands. A successful job application meant moving to a new company and to the West Midlands where they bought an inter-war house. After five years there they moved because of his job – to Swindon. The move involved paying significantly more for a house. They had had trouble selling the previous house but wanted to move quickly and to keep the family together. After only two years in Swindon the husband moved to his company's European Headquarters in Belgium.

At this point his household dropped out of home ownership and lived for four years in two successive rented properties.

> From a tax point of view if you were a temporary resident you got a 50 per cent reduction in your income tax which was worth having. At that stage nobody knew what being temporary meant but there was a general feeling that being temporary meant that you didn't own your own house and so we rented as everybody else did. The kids were at at the . . . school, the company was paying. We were saving money. The overall tax rate was low. It makes a big difference . . .

Until these leases had run out it was difficult to move except with the same company – otherwise it would have been too expensive to give up the lease. However after four years (and the termination of the leases) he got a new job in a senior executive post with a large multinational company. This was a different company and involved a move to Bristol where they spent a temporary period in a 'semi-furnished', rented, detached house which they heard of through work. They lived there for one year in all, including 7 or 8 months while work was carried out on the house they had bought. The choice of Bristol was because 'that was where the job was. We didn't know Bristol at all, neither of us did, and we had never come here when we had lived in Swindon'.

They bought the Bristol house for £34,000 – 'We were horrified'. House prices inceased enormously in the period since they had sold their house in Swindon for £8,000 four years earlier. When asked if they had consciously invested the cash from the previous sale in anticipation of getting back into the housing market or if they had a strategy in relation to this the response was:

> No, I don't know how you'd do it. We didn't know house prices would shoot up. We knew we were off the housing ladder. There's no way in which you can plan for that because we didn't know how long we were going to be and we didn't know if we would have dared to buy a house in Belgium. We had looked on two or three occasions at things that we might buy but then when you looked at the comparison between the mortgage conditions and the up-front taxes that you paid we decided it was going to be a very expensive long-term thing.

There were 'lots of horror stories' of people who bought (or kept) a house in Britain and let it out so they did not do that. Also the wife's family experience influenced them. The house the wife's family had owned in Bexley Heath had been let (to prevent its being taken over by the local authority in the war) and subsequently they could not get the tenants out or make an income from letting. If they had kept their house in Swindon:

> ... we didn't know how many people would want to rent a house in Swindon, we wouldn't have gone back there very often to have a look at it and see how it was and the people we knew from there seemed all to be moving at the same time so we didn't have anybody to keep an eye on it.... Mind you if we had known how much house prices were going to go up we might have ...

The company had not had a scheme for this. It was a US company and 'generally speaking it was much easier to let a house in the US'.

When they moved in to the Bristol house it had required a lot of work and the experience of this 'was enough to put you off moving again' and they had not yet given any serious thought to moving – partly because of their children's ages. Asked about the immediate neighbourhood:

> You have to ask the question whether it's a community at all. Everybody goes to different schools. There's no community spirit at all.... It's a dead end and people go up and down in their cars. People never walk down. We don't know them personally and don't visit ...

The couple had never owned a second home or housing other than that they lived in. When asked what they considered the main advantages of owning their own home their initial comments were references to previous landlords and the experience of renting but:

> I think the big advantage is the capital gain. That's the best reason. It's one of the very few things that keeps up with or ahead of inflation.

Disadvantages related to maintenance and rates and the (large) size of the garden.

In looking for the house in Bristol, having lived nearby for some time in the rented house:

> We decided two things. It could be a beast to travel in from outside . . . and then we looked at schooling and came to the conclusion that the system which was ruling then had a creaming effect and that the only sensible thing was to put the kids into private education, a thought which would never have struck me 10 years ago or 15 years ago. The good comprehensives would have meant moving too far out and raise all the problems of coming in. The effect of the private education system here, the creaming effect means that what's left in the state system isn't as clever as it should be.

They subsequently found that the local primary school was very good and did send their younger children to the state school.

> One of the reasons for coming back to England was to try to get the kids doing more . . . there was very little for them to do.

Asked about expectations of where they would be living in five years the response was 'I don't know, I don't think I ever try to plan that far'.

They were conscious of the effect of immediate circumstances on the value of the house: 'If another insurance company came to Bristol I would be disappointed not to get a hundred' (thousand). Asked if they saw housing as an investment and if they had sought to maximise their mortgage the response was:

> Certainly when we bought this house one of my objectives was to maximise the mortgage. At that point what we could get was a 75 per cent mortgage and a £25,000 limit so I wanted to be paying somewhere in the region of £32,000 . . . . It's a good principle to put as much money as you can into a house because it's going to keep its value.

But there were other considerations. The houses they had lived in in Belgium had been large and 'we'd have both felt a bit put down if we had gone back to a house that was the sort of house we'd left in Swindon. We didn't find too many houses that we liked'.

In their various moves the couple had benefited from help with housing from an employer on more than one occasion.

> Bridging loans are an essential part of employing people after a certain standard – you have to give them a bridging loan and help with curtains and carpets.

> If a company wants you to go and live in a particular area it will give you a bridging loan. This applies if you changed company or within company.

> With the Bristol move the company also paid rent for about six months – the period they would otherwise have put you up in a hotel.

This evidence of the importance of company policies and company assistance also emerged from other interviews with professionals and executives. Some of these other interviews are reported in publications cited above. Company assistance was also a significant feature of the next and last example.

This third example contrasts strongly with the previous two in terms of destination, the link between job and housing moves and the availability of employment-related assistance with mobility. More than either of the other households, and as with others in a similar income and employment situation, maximising a mortgage was important. It may be argued that given their income situation this did not involve choices about trimming other expenditures comparable with those of the lower income household referred to in the last example. Indeed accumulation through non-housing processes was important in overall calculations. The decision to buy up-market was partly related to investment considerations. But it was not the only consideration. Size of house, distance from work and proximity to schools were important. If this household is represented as having a housing strategy it is clear that the term strategy should not be assumed to involve clear forward planning of housing moves. All housing moves after their marriage were employment led (the husband's employment) when the moves occurred and what town was involved was determined by job factors and not family or housing. What house was bought was influenced by investment as well as other factors.

A case of social and spatial mobility

As was stressed earlier in the paper, the two groups of households in the affluent and working class areas were differentiated as much by their housing origins as by their current housing positions. In other words, those now living in the upper middle class residential area were generally from upper middle class backgrounds. An exception to this rule, however, was a middle aged couple (aged 49 and 47) from Coventry with working class origins who had been brought up in a residential environment very similar to the working class area of Bristol referred to earlier. Both their parents had rented small Victorian terraces from private landlords. They had both lived in the same dwelling throughout their childhood and in the wife's case her mother still lived at the same address. Their roots remained very much in Coventry where their surviving parents and relatives lived in relatively close knit communities.

> We are very different from them (other family members). You will appreciate we come from a working class background and we are unique in the family environment. None of the others would have moved. To move 10 miles would have been a colossal adventure, whereas we've moved so many times it isn't true – and the sort of socio-economic fences we have jumped . . . the process can be a problem sometimes for people.

They had met at the local youth club prior to his departure for Bristol University where he read engineering. She attended a commercial college in Coventry. On marriage, they both finally left home and from then on their housing history was one of marked social and spatial mobility. Excluding short periods in hotels or lodgings they had moved 10 times in less than 30 years five times as home owners between 1961 and 1978. In 1961 they had paid £2,300 for a small bungalow which they sold two years later for £2,800. There followed a series of moves through the 1960s and 1970s culminating in the purchase of their current dwelling for £55,000 in 1978. At the time of the interview, this property had just been sold for £146,000. He was taking early retirement and they were moving to a new waterfront development in Bristol.

On the surface their housing history had all the characteristics of a success-ful middle class strategy. After a few years in the private rented sector saving for their own house (a period in Norwich and Kings Lynn), they then moved in the owner occupied sector from Kings Lynn to Bristol, to Nottingham, to Surrey, to Birmingham and back to Bristol. Having bought a house in Surrey in 1968 they benefited from the extraordinary house price inflation of the next few years and had realised £24,000 when they moved again in 1972.

> The prices changed £1,000 a week! And that's not exaggerating, that's absolutely true. A guy came over from another company, from Japan and bought it. And I've still got the letter I think. He wrote to me and said you'll be sorry to know I'm moving on again and he didn't even move into it. He sold it and covered all his legal costs, including the move, and that was just in a few weeks.

Behind this rapid acceleration up the owner occupied housing ladder was the need for frequent moves to sustain the husband's career advancement. He had worked for the same multi-national since leaving university and, apart from their planned move into early retirement, only one other residential move had been for 'voluntary' housing reasons. Promotion necessitated the willingness to move on when the company required you to do so.

> I mean, if you want to arrive, if you wanted promotion, you just have to go. It's not all bad – well, it's a culture and you either understand it and live with it or it'll kill you. So life became terribly flexible.

Their housing history was therefore fundamentally structured by the nature of the internal labour market of his company. And it had certain distinct features. Periods when the family were split up were not uncommon. He would move on immediately and live in hotels in the next destination until a new house was found and the previous one was sold. Sometimes delays in being reunited were due to aspects of the children's schooling – examinations to sit or the need to finish the school year. Company assistance with moves related to legal costs, fixtures and fittings and bridging loans and was ex-tensive. The ability to sell quickly and easily was a prominent consideration in every purchase. Compared to other households in the area, whose housing moves were company-led, they were unusual in investing energy and resources in their various purchases. In general the mobile executives interviewed favoured newly built developments which minimised the disruption and promised a residential culture where everyone was new to the area. This household, however, had bought dwellings which required considerable input of their own energies. The first house they bought had been built for them by a friend who was in the building profession. They had bought a plot of land for £400 and involved themselves in the design of the dwelling which cost £1,900. Each subsequent purchase had involved considerable time and money on refurbishment and repair. Their current dwelling (which they had just sold) had cost them £55,000 but they had spent an additional £3,000 on major structural alterations and repairs.

> It was in a terrible state. It was dreadful. I bought it for less than I sold my previous house for.... The roof was about the one thing that was alright.

This housing move had also reflected a planned shift in his employment strategy. From his already senior position in the company, a further promotion would have meant an inevitable move to London. His final company move to Bristol was a change of location but not of status.

> I've always said I'm going to retire at 50 so I knew I wouldn't move again. If they wanted me to move I would say 'No thank you', or words to that effect!.... I mean this was a sideways move because we didn't want to go back to London.... Surrey was impossible, it was an hour and half each way. If I got home for the 9 o'clock news that was good.

The pattern and timing of their housing needs was shaped essentially by *his* employment strategy. Indeed, a general feature of the housing histories of households in the more affluent area was their dominance by features of the male's occupation. This household's pattern of residential mobility was certainly not housing led. However, there was a strong sense of the investment potential of owner occupied housing.

> For working class people you know it's the only way of acquiring capital. There isn't any other way that I'm aware of anyway.

In response to a question about the advantages of home ownership they saw the benefits contingent upon the economic gains:

> I'd like to talk about peace of mind and all that rubbish but capital appreciation is what it's all about, which does bring peace of mind.

Conclusions

The illustrative cases referred to here and elsewhere do not support a retreat into an 'every case is different' model. There are even similar themes and expressions between what are four different cases in terms of age, class and mobility. The initial conclusions relate to the question of investment strategies outlined at the start of this paper. None of the home owners referred to here or in the study as a whole conform to an investment maximising model – with regular moves designed to maximise mortgage or housing investment. However, all households knew, at least roughly, what their property was worth. Two propositions about housing investment strategies are plausible. The first is to regard them as part of a broader housing strategy referred to below and not to seek to over-emphasise investment in discussion of how decisions are made. The second is to regard them as the preserve of the affluent. Certainly it is reasonable to argue that the experience of housing and employment is different for affluent groups. Incremental salary scales, high incomes, fringe benefits and mobility packages put these groups in a different position. However, there should be some caution over representing these as unconstrained positions. The reality is often one of making the best of migration decisions, especially those triggered off by employment change. The constraints are very different from those experienced by lower income home owners or those unable to buy. But they do exist. In particular, company strategies and personnel officers' decisions relating to recruitment, training or promotion create the framework within which household decisions are made. If the nature of employment and employment opportunities interact with housing decisions (and vice versa) it is also evident that family and community links, stage in the family cycle, schooling and a variety of related considerations all affect decisions. One-dimensional, mono-causal representations of decisions relating to job and housing moves are rarely if ever likely to be accurate. In these cases even the assumptions about home ownership prove flawed. The real world calculations mean that, in particular circumstances, tenure is only one consideration and is not insisted upon by those who can buy.

If this cautions against assumptions about housing strategies and their relationship to employment and other moves it does not necessarily mean rejecting any notion of strategy. Decisions make sense in terms of previous experience and frames of reference, family circumstances and needs. They make sense if they are seen to involve a range of considerations and attempts to satisfy a number of wants – about shelter, size of dwelling, security, location, on-going costs, longer term value and so on. This means that they may result in decisions not to move – indeed they produce this result much more often than a trading-up strategy. It also means that some caution should be exercised about notions of strategy which imply master plans and long-term goals. Households are not sure how things will turn out and many of the variety of factors which form part of decisions do change. Strategies are much more likely to be shorter term, coping strategies, although there will be continuities and consistent elements especially related to past experience, to general aspirations and preferences, to employment and bargaining power in the labour and housing markets and to the ability deriving from this to deal with the framework of constraints affecting individual and household decisions.

References

Allen, J. and Hamnett, C. (1989) *Housing Markets and Labour Markets*. London: Hutchinson.

Bertaux, D. (ed) (1982) *Biography and society: the life history approach in the social sciences*. Beverley Hills: Sage.

Cote, G. L. (1983) *Moving On: Area, migration and socio-economic attainment in sociological perspective*. D. Phil thesis, Department of Sociology, Oxford University.

Farmer, M. K. and Barrell, R. (1981) 'Entrepreneurship and government policy: the case of the housing market'. *Journal of Public Policy*, 1, August: 307–32.

Forrest, R. and Murie, A. (1985) *Housing Origins and Destinations*. End of award Report, Grant No. DUU23/2033, available from the Economic and Social Research Council.

Forrest, R. and Murie, A. (1987) 'The affluent homeowner: labour market position and the shaping of housing histories'. *Sociological Review*, 35, 2: 370–403.

Forrest, R. and Murie, A. (1988) 'The Social Division of Housing Subsidies'. *Critical social policy*, Issue 23, Autumn: 83–93.

Forrest, R. and Murie, A. (1989) 'Housing Markets, Labour Markets and Housing Histories' in Allen, J. and Hamnett, C. *Housing Markets and Labour Markets*. London: Hutchinson.

Forrest, R., Murie, A. and Williams, P. (1989 forthcoming) *Home Ownership in Transition*. London: Unwin Hyman.

Green, F., Hadjimatheou, G. and Smail, R. (1984) *Unequal Fringes*. London: Bedford Square Press.

Mitchell, J. Clyde (1985) 'Case and situation analysis'. *Sociological Review*, 31, 2: 187–207.

Murie, A. (1974) *Household movement and housing choice*. Occasional Paper No 28. University of Birmingham: Centre for Urban and Regional Studies.

Murie, A. *et al.* (1976) 'New Building and Housing Needs'. *Progress in Planning*, 6, 2. Pergamon.

Murie, A., Niner, P. and Watson, C. (1976) *Housing policy and the housing system*. London: George Allen and Unwin.

Payne, J. and Payne, G. (1974) 'Housing pathways and social stratification: a study of life chances in the housing market'. *Journal of Social Policy*, 6, 2: 125–56.

Rossi, P. (1980) *Why Families Move*. 2nd edition, Beverley Hills: Sage.

Rossi, P. and Shlay, A. (1982) 'Residential Mobility and Public Policy Issues: "Why Families Move" revisited'. *Journal of Social Issues*, 3: 21–34.

Saunders, P. and Harris, C. (1988) *Home ownership and capital gains*. Working Paper No 64, Urban and Regional Studies. University of Sussex.

Author Index

Numbers in **bold** type indicate authorship of a chapter

Abegglen, J. C. 33, 35, 49
Adams J. 181, 189
Akerlof, G. A. 122, 133
Allen, J. 192, 209
Amrhein, C. G. 138, 152
Anon., 48, 49
Appleyard, R. T. 55, 68
Armstrong, H. 121, 134
Armstrong, M. 148, 152
Arrow, K. J. 121, 134
Ashton, P. 184, 190
Assistant Masters and Mistresses
  Association (AMMA), 97, 98
Atkinson, J. 55, 56, 67, 68
Aubrey, B. 107, 110

Bains, M. A. 144, 152
Baker, D. de, 84
Barrell, R. 194, 209
Baumol. W. J. 120, 134
Beardesworth, A. 153
Belcher, J. C. 150, 152
Benhabib, J. 128, 134
Bentham, G. 184, 188
Beret, P. 101, 110
Berg, I. 21, 29
Berger, M. 99, 110
Bertaux, D. 193, 209
Beumer, R. J. 72, 84
Blinder, A. S. 120, 134
Bonnar, D. S. 137, 152
Boudol, J. 99, 101, 110
Bowman, L. A. 86, 98
Bradshaw, T. F. 138, 144, 152, 153, 180, 188
Braithwaite, R. 139, 142, 144, 148, 152
Brett, J. M. 21, 27, 29
British Rate and Data, 144, 148, 152
Brown, L. A. 132, 134, 150, 152
Bryman, E. 153
Brzeskwinski, J. 151, 152, 155, 160, 171
Buitendijk, D. 72, 84
Bull, C. 128, 134
Business Week, 19

Carlson, J. A. 129, 130, 134
Cebula, R. J. 121, 134
Cézard, M. 101, 110
Champion, A. G. 13, 172, 189
Chauvire, Y. 100, 111
Checkland, P. 139, 152

Clark G. L. 139, 152, 174, 188
Clark W. A. V. 115, 136, 142, 153
Cole, R. E. 34, 50
Collie, H. C. 27, 29
CBI, 57, 65, 66, 68
Conlisk, J. 122, 134
Conway, J. 175, 183, 188
Coombes, M. G. 13, 172, 173, 189
Corbel, P. 105, 110
Cote, G. L. 192, 209
Courgeau, D. 101, 110
Craig, A. M. 36, 37, 50
Crosby, M. 27, 29
Cullingworth, J. B. 183, 188
Curtis, G. L. 36, 50

Dalton, D. R. 21, 29
Daniel, G. H. 173, 188
Daniel, W. W. 175, 189
Dannefer, D. 19, 35
Dasgupta, M. 142, 153
Davanzo, J. 22, 29, 164, 171
David, P. A. 115, 134
De Jong, G. F. 115, 134
Devis, T. 139, 142, 153
Dicken P. 59, 68
Doeringer, P. B. 7, 12, 60, 68
Doorn, P. vii, **70–84**
Dore, R. P. 36, 50
Duggan, E. P. 88, 91, 98
Dunnell, K. 153

Economisch Technologisch Instituut. 74, 84
Edstrom, A. 22, 29
Eisenberg, P. 181, 188
Employee Relocation Council, 19, 27, 29
Engelsdorp-Gastelaars, R. van, 71, 84

Farmer, M. K. 194, 209
Faur, J-P. 99, 101, 110
Fawcett, J. T. 115, 134
Fielding, A. 99, 111
Flinn, C. J. 128, 134
Flowerdew, R., ix, 5, 6, 12, 38, 48, 49, 50,
  61, 155, 133, 137, 139, 153, 188
Ford, J. 153
Ford, K. 23, 29
Forrest, R. S. vii, 184, 188–189, **191–209**
Fowler, A. 144, 153
Freijsen, G. 71, 84

210

Frey, W. H. 24, 31
Friedlander, D. 173, 189

Galbraith, J. R. 22, 29
Gehert, J. 23, 29
Gerking, S. 118, 136
Glazer, H. 37, 50
Gleave, D. 138, 139, 142, 150, 153
Goddard, J. B. 13, 172, 173, 189
Goldstein, S. 24, 31
Goodman, J. L. 124, 134
Gordon, I. R. 182, 189
Gould, P. 143, 153
Granovetter, M. S. 138, 142, 153
G.B. Dept. Employment, 189
Green, A. E. 2, 13, 172, 173, 189
Green, F. 209
Greenberg, D. 88, 91, 98
Greenbury, L. 67, 68
Greenwood, M. J. 115, 133, 134
Gregory, J. 27, 29
Guergoat, J-C. 105, 110
Gustavus, S. D. 132, 134
Guttridge, M. 153

Hackett, P. 148, 152
Hadjimatheou, G. 209
Hägerstrand, T. 37, 50
Hall, J. R. 127, 134
Hall, W. R. 26, 30
Hamnett, C. 184, 189, 192
Hanami, T. 33, 50
Hanemaayer, D. E. 70, 84
Hansen, K. A. 30
Harris, C. 194–5, 209
Harrison, R. 181, 189
Hartnet, B. 18, 30
Harts, J. J. 72, 84
Head, E. 153
Heckman, J. J. 128, 134
Heelsbergen, K. M. van, 70, 71, 84
Hilsum, S. 86, 88, 98
Hodson, R. 21, 30
Hogarth, R. M. 121, 134
Hogarth, T. 175, 189
Honda, S. 48, 50
Hopson, D. 181, 189
Huff, J. O. 115, 136
Hughes, G. 184, 189
Hugo, G. J. 132, 134
Hunter, L. C. 173, 189

Ickes, B. W. 21, 30
Inagami, T. 33, 34, 35, 50
Incomes Data Services, 65, 68
Isserman, A. 118, 136

Jansen, C. J. 174, 189
Jay, L. T. 88, 98
Jayet, H. 101, 111
Jenkins, G. M. 139, 153

Jennings, E. E. 59, 68
Johnson, C. 36, 39, 50
Johnson, J. H. vii, 1–13, 32, 50, 54, 68, 137, 138, 153, 173, 180, 183, 189
Jones, H. R. 150, 153

Kallenberg, A. L. 21, 30
Kanter, R. M. 21, 30
Kasteleijn, F. C. H. 70, 84
Kau, J. B. 115, 135
Kaufman, R. L. 21, 30
Keil, E. T. 153
Kennett, S. 173, 189
Kitching, R. vii, **172–190**
Koike, K. 33, 50
Kokudochō Keikaku Chōseikyoku 32, 50
Kontuly, T. 99, 111
Kreps, J. M. 120, 135
Kubota, A. 39, 50
Kuwahara, Y. 49, 50
Kuyper, N. 71, 84.

Ladinsky, J. 139, 153
Landsberger, M. 128, 135
Lane, K. E. 20, 28, 31
Lansing, J. B. 137, 138, 153, 173, 180, 189
Laulhé, M-C. 105, 110
Lazarfeld, P. F. 181, 188
Levine, S. B. 33, 50
Levy, M. B. 115, 135
Lewis, J. 172, 190
Lippman, S. A. 124, 126, 127, 128, 135
Lomas, E. 152, 153
Long, L. H. 17, 18, 30, 151, 153
Long, S. O. 37, 50
Loth, Betty, M. 28, 30

Mass-Droogleever Fortuijn, J. C. 71, 84
McAfee, R. P. 129, 130, 134
McCall, J. J. 88, 91, 98, 124, 126, 127, 134, 135
McCormick, B. 184, 189
McKay, J. 22, 30, 38, 46, 50, 54, 68, 137, 138, 154
MacKinnon, R. D. 115, 135, 138, 142, 152
McKinsey & Company, 73, 84
Maier, G. vii, **115–136**, 138, 153
Mann, M. 21, 30
Mannari, H. 47, 51
Margolis, D. R. 21, 30
Marwell, G. 164, 171
Mazie, S. M. 153
Merrill Lynch, 20, 27, 28, 30, 56, 65, 66, 67, 69
Merry, D. M. 175, 190
Miller, E. A. 150, 154
Mincer, J. 164, 171
Minford, P. 184, 190
Miron, J. R. 115, 135
Mitchell, J. C. 193, 209
Morgan, J. N. 173, 189

212

Morgan, P. B. 128, 131, 135
Morgenstern, O. 122, 123, 126, 136
Morrison, P. 22, 29, 133, 135
Mueller, E. 137, 138, 153, 173, 180, 189
Murie, A. S. vii, 184, 188-9, **191-209**, 193, 195, 209

Nam, C. B. 23, 30
National Consumer Council, 184, 190
Neumann, J. v. 122, 123, 126, 136
Noda, K. 36, 51
Noguchi, P. H. 37, 51
Noin, D. 100, 111
Northern Ireland Mobility Survey, 175, 190
Nozeman, E. F. 70, 73, 74, 75, 83, 84

OPCS, 154, 173, 190
Ogden, P. E. 99, 105, 110, 111
Ojimi, Y. 36, 51
Ono T. 34, 51
Ottens, H. F. L. 72, 84
Owen, D. W. 2, 13, 172, 173, 189

Packard, V. 8, 13, 30
Pahl, R. W. 174, 190
Palm, R. 139, 154
Palmer, D. 138, 139, 142, 150, 153
Payne, G. 195, 209
Payne, J. 195, 209
Pederson, K. G. 88, 98
Peel, M. 184, 190
Peled, D. 128, 135
Perlman, R. 120, 135
Perreaux, P. 101, 111
Personnel Administrator, 19
PHH Homequity, Ltd. 56, 66, 69
Pickles, A. 138, 154
Piore, M. J. 7, 12, 60
Plath, D. W. 37, 51
Power, M. G. 23, 30
Pred, A. R. 59, 69
Pumain, D. 101, 110

Ramsay, E. 175, 183, 188
Randolph, W. 173, 189
Rault D, 101, 110
Reder, M. W. 121, 134
Reid, G. L. 173, 189
Reinganum, J. F. 129, 135
Richardson, H. W. 121, 135, 175, 190
Rietbergen, A. v. vii, **70-84**
Riley, F. 175, 190
Rima, A. 71, 84
Roberts, B. 19, 24, 30
Rōdōshō. 42, 48, 51
Rogerson, P. 115, 135, 138, 142
Rohlen, T. P. 35, 39, 51
Rōmu Gyōsei Kenkyūjo, 48, 51
Rosenbaum J. E. 22, 30
Rosenfeld, R. 164, 171
Rosenfield, D. 130, 131, 135

Roshier, R. J. 173, 189
Rossi, P. H. 149, 154, 178, 190, 195
Rothschild, M. 129, 131, 136
Roy, D. 130, 131, 135

Salt, J. vii, **1-13**, 32, 50, **53-69**, 137, 138, 153, 154, 173, 180, 183, 189, 190
Samuels, R. J. 36, 39, 51
Samuelson, L. 21, 30
Sargent, J. 34, 39, 51
Saunders, M. N. K. vii, 133, **137-154**, 180, 182, 190
Saunders, P. 194-5, 209
Schofield, B. vii, **85-98**
Schubert, U. 118, 136
Schwarzkopf, E. A. 150, 154
Sell, R. R. vii, **17-31**
Shapiro, B. 130, 131, 135
Shapiro, P. 115, 136
Shimada, H. 35, 51
Shlay, A. 195, 209
Silvers, A. 138, 154
Simon, H. 121, 136
Sirman, C. F. 115, 135
Sjaastad, L. A. 115, 136
Skinner, K. A. 36, 37, 38, 51
Smail, R. 209
Smidt, M. de, 70, 84
Smith, T. R. 115, 136
Snaith, J. viii, **155-171**
Somers, G. G. 120, 135
Sorenson, A. B, 21, 30
Speare, A. 24, 31
Spilerman, S. 164, 171
Stalk, G., Jr. 33, 35, 49
Start, K. B. 86, 88, 98
Stewart, W. A. C. 88, 91, 98
Stigler, G. J. 124, 136
Straten, E. v. 71, 84
Suzuki, N. 34, 35, 38, 52

Taal, F. 71, 84
Taylor, C. 118, 136
Taylor J. 121, 134
Taylor R. C. 174, 190
Todor, W. D. 21, 29
Togura, N. 47, 52
Townsend, A. 172, 190
Tsuji, K. 34, 36, 52
Turnbull, P. 90, 98

Vanderkamp, J. 115, 136
Veiga, J. F. 21, 22, 23, 31
Vining, D. 99, 111

Wadycki, W. J. 115, 135
Walen, B. J. 73, 74, 75, 83, 84
Watson, W. 181, 190
Weiss, P. 121, 135
West, E. G. 175, 190
White, H. C. 22, 31, 37, 43, 48, 52

White, P. viii, **99–111**
White,R. 143, 153
Whitelaw, J. S. 22, 30, 38, 46, 51, 54, 68, 137, 138, 154
Whiteman, J. 174, 188
Whyte, W. H. 59, 69
Williams, G. 90, 98
Wilkinson, R. 175, 190
Wilson, A. G. 139, 154
Wiltshire, R. viii, **32–52**
Winchester, H. P. M. 99, 105, 110, 111

Wissen, L. G. J. v. 71, 84
Wood, P. A. W., 1, 9, 13, 54, 68, 138, 153, 173, 183, 189
Woolwich Building Society, 65, 69
Wrigley, N. 150, 154

Yamaguchi, K. 34, 36, 39, 46, 52
Yellen, J. L. 122, 133

Zabalza, A. 90, 93, 98
Zipp, J. F. 20, 28, 31

Geographical and Subject Index

American Housing Survey (AHS)
Annual, 18–21, 23
Amsterdam, 72
Australia, 22, 30, 51, 54, 55, 68, 137
Auvergne, 103

Behavioural approaches. *See* Decision making; Job search.
Belgium, 202, 204
Berkshire, 179
Bexley Heath, 202–3
Birmingham, 167, 206
Black Horse Relocation, 66
Bristol, 167, 193, 195–207.
Britain, 2, 3, 17, 53–69, 137, 168, 194. *See also* United Kingdom
British Telecom, 58–9
Brittany, 102, 108–9
Burgundy, 103
Burnham Committee, 86, 97

Career mobility, 34–7, 40–6
International 201–5
manual workers, 183
teachers, 95–6
Census
France. 101–2
Great Britain, 2
United States, 18, 23
Centre (France), 102, 108
Champagne, 103, 108–9
Clwyd, 146, 148
Confederation of British Industry, 64–5
Corporate transfers, 18–29
frequency, 19–20
structure, 20–1, 46–7
Corsica, 101
Counter-urbanisation, 3, 99–111
Coventry, 205–6

Decision-making, 5, 6, 9–12, 17, 18, 57, 115–6, 120–33, 159–60, 163, 175, 186, 194, 208
Derbyshire, 202
Dual-career households. *See* Households

Employee Relocation Council (ERC), 19–20, 27, 64
Employers *See* Institutions
Employment Security Section (ESS), 40–5
England, ix, 2, 85, 86, 96, 143, 173, 204
East Anglia, 65, 90
North, 89, 175
Northwest, 89
Southeast, 89, 90, 97, 175, 179
Southwest, 90, 91
West Midlands, 89, 202
Yorkshire and Humberside, 89
Essex, 97
Europe, 48
Exeter University, 160

Financial packages, 8, 26–7, 48, 53, 64–5
housing, 204–6
taxation, 67
teaching allowances, 90
Florida,
Boca Raton, 28
France, 6, 7, 17, 54, 99–111. *See also* individual departments
Franche-Comté. 103, 109

General Electric Corporation, 19, 24
Greater London, 91

Haarlemmermeer, 72
Hague, 72–3, 83
Harlow, 57
High Wycombe, 183

214

Hiroshima, 41-2
Home-owners, 24-5, 191-209
  investment property, 196, 198
  non-moving, 197-8
  owner-occupiers, 65, 187
Households, 6, 75, 175, 191
  dual-career, 8, 10, 27, 67, 155-171
    models of, 156-60
  dual-earner, 27, 28, 63, 76, 80-1, 179
  dual location, 34-5, **168-169**, 175
  relocated, 26, 54, 92-5
  single-person, 2, 10, 76
Housing, 9, 55, 183-7
  council, 48, 184-7, 194, 197
  costs, 26, 29, 91, 150, 175, 185-186, 193
Housing market, 9, 84, 91, 185, 193
  and home owners, 192
  local, 3, 25, 172, 178, 187-8
  role of institution in, 6, 25, 65-6
Housing tenure, 176-7. *See also* Home-
  ownership; Housing
Houten, 72
Humberside, 89, 90

Île-de-France, 102, 105, 108-9
Immobility, 172-3, 183-8, 197-8
Information, 3, 5, 6, 8, 11-12, 62, 174, 180
  economics of, 115, 122-9, 137-154
Institut National de la Statistique et des
  Études Économiques, 102
Institutions
  agencies, 6
    relocation, 66
    job centres, 182
  employers,
    France, 101-2
    Japan, 32-52
  local governments, 143-50, 185-6
  relocation of site, 7, 20, 57, 70-84
  United Kingdom, 53-69
  United States, 17-31
  influence on migration process, 6-9, 133,
    137-43, 150-151
Isère, 105

Japan, 6, 7, 32-52, 54, 206
  Ministry of Labour, 39-49
  Ministry of Construction, 46
Job-search, 5, 6, 8, 11-12, 124-133, 137-54,
  167, 180-2, 187
Journey-to-work, 3, 4, 70-84, 116-20, 168
  long-distance commuting, 3-4, 35, 47, 49,
    110

Keele University, 160
Kent, 202
  Tonbridge and Malling Borough, 146,
    148-9, 150
Kings Lynn, 206

Labour-force Sample of the Netherlands,
  73, 75
Labour Force Survey, 2, 54, 55
Labour market, 3, 9, 10, 84, 133, 163-4, 165
  (SMLAs)
  external (ELM), 28, 54, 59
  free, 4
  internal (ILM), 7, 32, 37, 40, 48, 53-68,
    71, 101, 105, 144
  local, 3, 4, 12, 172-4, 178, 187-188
  model, 129
  submarkets, 3, 84
  role of institutions in, 6
  theory, 187
    neoclassical, 116, 120-2, 178
  urban, 10, 84
lancaster, 146, 148, 150
Leeds, 175
  university, 167
Leicestershire, 201, 202
Leidschendam, 83
Life-time employment system, 32-9, 49
Limousin, 102, 108
Liverpool, 176-81, 184-7
Local Education Authorities (LEAs), 87, 88
Loire, 102, 109
London, 3, 86, 90, 187, 199, 207
  See also Greater London

Merseyside, 179
Middle East, 201
Migration of labour
  attitudes, 176-9
  definition, 1-3
  inter-regional, 102-3
  theories, 57-9, 116-22, 173-6
Miyoshi, 41-2

Nagoya, 32
National Land Agency (Japan), 32-3, 38
Netherlands, 6, 70-84
New towns, 2-3
New York (Long Island), 28
Nieuwegein, 72-83
Nippon Steel Corporation, 39
Non-Metropolitan District Councils
  (NMDCs), 143-52
Normandy (Lower), 103, 108
Norwich, 206
Nottingham, 206

Occupation,
  change of, 3, 5, 21, 24
  status differential, 25-6, 28, 35-7, 41-5
  training for, 5, 7, 34, 35, 57, 63, 144, 208
  types, 3-5, 19, 21, 23, 28, 33, 75, 104-6,
    109, 146, 173
  low-skilled, 8, 11, 22, 56, 68, 172-90
  managerial, 28, 33, 36-8, 41-5, 56, 60,
    62-3, 66, 104, 109, 137

manual, 138, 143–4, 146, 148, 173, 177,
    181–3
non-manual, 138, 144, 146, 173
professional, 5, 6, 56, 85–98 (teachers),
    137, 144, 146, 173, 180
skilled, 5, 6, 11, 56, 76, 101–2, 104–5,
    110, 137
unskilled, 5, 11, 101–2, 104–105, 110, 137
Organisation man. 32–9, 49, 59
Ōsaka, 32, 42, 43, 44
Oxford, 202
Oxfordshire,
    Vale of the White Horse, 146, 148
Oxford University,
    St, Hilda's College, 160

Paris, 105
Paris Basin, 100, 102
Picardy, 103
Poitou-Charentes, 103, 109
Population distribution, 22, 71, 75–6
Professional Executive Register (PER), 144
Professional organisations, 4, 8
Provence, 102–3, 108
Prussia, 20
Public Employment Security Office (PESO),
    40–9

Randstad, 72
Reading, 176, 184–7
    universty, 160
Recruitment, 11, 38, 54, 63, 139, 143, 146,
    150–1, 208,
    agencies, 8
    policy, 7, 152
Relocation,
    agencies, 8, 66
    corporate, 18–29
        frequency, 19–20
        structure, 20–1, 37–9, 61–3
    hospital, 73–5
    policy, 26–8
    problems 66–7
Residential mobility, 78–81
Retired workers. 107, 144

Rhone, 103
Rhone-Alpes, 108
Rijswijk, 83
Rotterdam, 72

San Diego, 91
School of Exceptional Difficulty Allowance,
    90
Seine, 103
Sheffield University, 167
Skelmersdale, 175
South America, 201
Southern Ireland, 199
Stirling, 202
Surrey, 206, 207
Swindon, 202–4

Tōkyo, 32, 40, 42, 43, 44, 46, 49
Tonbridge, 146, 148, 150
Trade Unions,
    National Association of Local
        Government Officers (NALGO),
        148–9
    national Union of Public Employees
        (NUPE), 148–9
Tyneside, 175

United Kingdom, 2, 6, 7, 47, 53–69, 172–3,
    179, 184
United States of America, 6, 7, 8, 17–31, 47,
    48, 54, 86, 88, 96, 97, 137, 173, 203
    census bureau, 18
Utrecht, 72, 78–81, 83
    city of, 73, 74, 75
    province of, 74

Voorburg, 83

Wales, ix, 2, 86, 143, 173, 183
Wassenaar, 83

Yorkshire, 201
York University, 167

Zoetermeer, 72, 73, 75, 76, 80, 82–3